PERSONAL IDENTITY, NATIONAL IDENTITY AND INTERNATIONAL RELATIONS

Cambridge Studies in International Relations is a joint initiative of Cambridge University Press and the British International Studies Association (BISA). The series will include a wide range of material, from undergraduate textbooks and surveys to research-based monographs and collaborative volumes. The aim of the series is to publish the best new scholarship in International Studies from Europe, North America and the rest of the world.

CAMBRIDGE STUDIES IN INTERNATIONAL RELATIONS

PERSONAL IDENTITY, NATIONAL IDENTITY AND INTERNATIONAL RELATIONS

WILLIAM BLOOM

*Occasional Lecturer, Department of International Relations,
London School of Economics*

CAMBRIDGE
UNIVERSITY PRESS

Published by the Press Syndicate of the University of Cambridge
The Pitt Building, Trumpington Street, Cambridge CB2 1RP
40 West 20th Street, New York, NY 10011–4211, USA
10 Stamford Road, Oakleigh, Victoria 3166, Australia

First published 1990
First paperback edition 1993

Printed in Great Britain at the University Press, Cambridge

British Library cataloguing in publication data

Bloom, William
  Personal identity, national identity and
  international relations – (Cambridge
  studies in international relations: 9)
  1. Foreign relations. Psychological aspects
  I. Title
  327.1'01'9

Library of Congress cataloguing in publication data

Bloom, William, 1948–
  Personal identity, national identity and international relations
  / William Bloom.
  p.   cm. – (Cambridge studies in international relations, 9)
  Bibliography: p.
  ISBN 0 521 37316 6
  1. International relations. 2. Nationalism. I. Title
  II. Series.
  JX1395.B568   1990
  327.1'01–dc20   89–7150   CIP

ISBN 0 521 37316 6 hardback
ISBN 0 521 44784 4 paperback

For the Master Rakoczy

CONTENTS

PREFACE

Social and political theory presents an ongoing problem of conceptualisation. In the attempt to bring intellectual order and comprehension to the grand kaleidoscope of human behaviour, it is essential either to categorise or to abstract. By the very nature, however, of the processes of categorisation and abstraction, there is an unavoidable tendency to move, by degrees, away from the existential flesh and blood reality of humans in action towards concepts about their action. Of necessity these concepts are theoretical and ideological. They are intellectual modes of comprehension. Frequently, they are lenses through which behaviour is examined, rather than the behaviour itself perceived in new forms. As the concepts concerning behaviour become more abstract, or borrow by analogy from other fields of 'scientific' research, so the actions under study become less the flesh and blood humans and increasingly the reified ideas of the researchers themselves. This intellectual procedure is elegant, exciting and often insightful – but, by its very nature, it risks distance from human reality.

The natural, intellectual dynamic of removal away from existential reality is compounded by the scarcity of generally agreed psychological and social–psychological theories which can facilitate – by way of being clear methodological tools – the researchers in remaining in contact with their living, breathing subjects.

This tendency of abstraction away from the dynamic realities of human action exists in International Relations as much as in any other academy of the social sciences. There is, however, a certain explicit drama in world politics – its archetypal actors are the gods *War* and *Peace* – which can make any such abstraction appear insensitive scholasticism. Yet, intellectual rigour demands that we be able to categorise and to abstract the crucial issues of international political behaviour.

The research presented here is concerned with certain fundamental problems in political and social theory. These problems can be stated quite crudely. Why do individuals and mass national populations give their loyalty to the nation-state? Why are they prepared to die for it? What are the structure and dynamics of their psychological attachment? How is it evoked? How does it affect government decisions and international politics?

This work, then, is precisely an attempt to understand this one particular aspect of international political and social theory in a theoretically insightful and methodologically rigorous way without at any time losing sight of the essential human actor. To do this, it employs a psychological theory which acts as the methodological bridge between individual action and theoretical interpretation. The first chapter provides a general background to the use of psychological theory in political research and the second chapter explicates the actual theory – identification theory – which is used as the methodological tool of this research. The reader who is in a hurry may, if she or he wishes, read only the opening and closing pages of both those chapters and skip the detailed expositions. The reader, however, seeking a secure anchor in the psychological theory employed, will need to follow the psychological thread all the way through before it is applied to the actual stuff of politics.

A brief word about rigour. Because this research is concerned with mass action, and with the structure and dynamics of the nation in relation to the state, its mode of approach is necessarily one of macro-theory. The historical and empirical evidence presented to illustrate the theory is, therefore, of a macro and of a general nature. The canvas is unavoidably large and, as such, the brush strokes are also large. This necessary tendency towards generalisation is offset, I trust, by the strict rigour with which the theoretical thread is pursued. My argument stands or falls on the strict coherence of its internal logic as identification theory is applied first to the individual, then to the mass national group and then to its effect on international political behaviour.

My research also indicates that identification as a dynamic behavioural imperative has not previously been made explicit. As such, it has not previously been applied to social theory generally or to international relations theory in particular. I feel myself lucky to have been able – via an exegesis of Freud, Mead, Erikson, Parsons and Habermas – to make explicit the dynamic character of identification, the imperative to identify and then to enhance or defend identification. I apply it in this book to the problematics of national political integration and of mass national mobilisation as it affects international relations, but am certain that a dynamic identification theory can be the basis for substantial further research in other areas. It solves the problem, in many situations, of finding a coherent methodological link between individual and group or mass behaviour.

My concern with holding a clear theoretical focus on the human dynamic is based partly in the fact that during the years 1969–72 I was lucky enough to undergo psychoanalysis with one of the founders of the psychoanalytic school in Britain, Edward Glover. He was in his eighties by the time that I lay on his couch (in fact, a very comfortable armchair) and I was, in fact, his last analysand. My analysis did not keep to the strict psychoanalytic rules as we often entered into discourse and I was deeply impressed by his clear, rigorous and insightful mind. Eight years and a career-change later, as a 'mature' student studying for my first degree – in International Relations at the London School of Economics – I found myself reading his books *War, Sadism and Pacifism* and his wonderfully titled *The Dangers of Being Human*.[1] I owe him a great debt of gratitude.

At the London School of Economics I had the good fortune to be taken under the wing of Professor F.S. Northedge. His major interest, as a student and then as a teacher of International Relations, had been in a psychological approach. In fact, his first completed manuscript had been precisely an attempt to integrate twentieth-century psychological theory with International Relations theory. This had been unsuccessful, he explained to me, because it lacked an integrating skeleton. He nevertheless had the generosity of spirit to lend me his thirty-year-old manuscript as an example of 'how not to do it'. Later, as we discussed my own ideas, he aggressively warned me not to write anything that was obvious. His was a strenuous but enjoyable encouragement for which I am grateful. I admired his rigour, his good humour and his Christian socialism.

I am also grateful to the whole Department of International Relations at the London School of Economics, students and staff, for their stimulation and companionship.

For detailed and extremely helpful comments on an early manuscript, my thanks to James Mayall. Professor Percy Cohen was kind enough to read and then be encouraging about an early version of chapter 2. Michael Nicholson was also generous in his analysis and his encouragement, helping me to clarify certain important points.

This book was originally written as a piece of doctoral research at the London School of Economics. Michael Banks was an admirable supervisor, leaving me alone when I wished to be left alone and rigorous in his analysis when necessary.

I need also to acknowledge the Montagu Burton scholarship which helped fund me for two years of my research.

I am grateful to Rachel Neaman of the Cambridge University Press for her careful and astute editing.

And thanks to my family: Freddy Bloom looked at an early manuscript and put forward many helpful suggestions. James Bloom was impressed by my working on this project and his consistent and sympathetic enthusiasm genuinely encouraged me.

1 THE PROBLEM STATED AND A REVIEW OF POLITICALLY APPLIED PSYCHOLOGICAL THEORY

INTRODUCTION

The major popular image of world politics is that it consists of the relationships and interactions of nation-states. There may indeed be other major actors – class, multinational corporations or transnational bodies – but on the stage of world political action, the roles of these actors appear complementary, subservient, out of the limelight. It may indeed, for example, be class forces in the form of covert centre–periphery relations which determine a developing state's internal economic policy and external foreign policy – but the form in which these effects and decisions appear is that of the nation-state.

Implicit in this image of nation-states being the major international actors is a further more subtle image. This more subtle image is based in the political norm – and if not the norm, then certainly the assumption – that state power rests in a popularly legitimised authority. There may be no formal or recognisable form of democratic participation, but nevertheless the state, it is thought, should be one with the people who are its nation. International politics, then, is not simply the relations between state structures, but is also the relations between the *nations*. In international politics, people, government and state fuse into one image.

Thus one popularly says, 'Zimbabwe's attitude to South Africa . . . France declared war on England . . . The relations between Indonesia and Saudi Arabia . . .' The implication of these statements is that total peoples have a joint attitude. Certainly such statements can be made, but their academic integrity and intellectual credibility are severely strained. This is not due to differing political notions concerning the nature of 'legitimate' popular or democratic participation. This strain is due to the lack of theory which in a methodologically coherent way explicates the relationship between a mass national population and its state. In much political analysis this is not a crucial issue, as the focus is

1

upon political competition and the resolution of that competition within the domestic framework. It is, however, crucial in terms of political integration and nation-building. It is also crucial in terms of international relations – inter-nation relations as opposed to inter-state relations – as without such a methodology the mass national population lacks any coherent theoretical status in terms of its state's foreign policy decision-making. This echoes, of course, the profound issue in political and social philosophy concerning the relationship of citizens to state.

The specific purpose of this research, then, is to examine the possibility of a psychological theory – identification theory – giving the mass national population of a state just such a theoretically coherent status.

This recognition that the mass national population lacks any theoretical status – that the Emperor of the nation-state wears no clothes – became apparent in International Relations theory only as recently as the 1960s when the behavioural or 'scientific' upheaval took place.[1] This upheaval, which saw the introduction of a more rigorous methodology derived from the physical as well as the social sciences, involved an attack on the epistemological bases of the classical, or historically based, school in International Relations. Although this school appeared to repel the attack,[2] its students nevertheless took on board the need for the appearance, at least, of a certain intellectual rigour resonant with a respect for the methodology of modern social theory; historical analysis had not only to be scrupulous in its selection of facts, but had also to be more self-aware of the explanatory modes it utilised. The behavioural approach had, in fact, enjoyed a relative victory and in the new atmosphere much of the careless conceptual language of the historical approach disappeared.

In particular, the language of anthropomorphism in which nation-states as apparently coherent personalities acted and reacted on the international stage – 'Nicaragua decided . . . Japan declared . . .' along with notions such as 'national honour', 'national prestige' and 'national character' – was shown up as having little if any explanatory power and certainly no methodologically coherent internal logic. This lack of logic can be made clear if one posits four crucial questions that require satisfactory answers before it is possible to give the mass national citizenry a methodologically coherent status. These questions are:

1 Is it possible to know the attitudes of individual citizens?
2 Even if one does know these attitudes, is it possible to predicate that these attitudes will dictate action?
3 Is it possible to aggregate or generalise from an individual

citizen's attitude in a way that explicates the attitude of the total citizenry? Can there be an explicit theoretical link between individual attitudes and mass national attitudes?

4 Is there a method for explicating the relationship between these mass attitudes and actual foreign policy decisions?

Although the first question, concerning individual attitudes, could be answered and, in fact, received much empirical attention in the United States, particularly under the study of public opinion, the other three questions were, and remain, unresolved.[3]

Thus, one of the results of the introduction of a more scientific approach to the study of International Relations was that the mass of a state's people – the *nation* indeed – became disengaged from any analysis of inter-state behaviour, as the discipline became self-aware of the fact that it did not have the theoretical tools to handle the issue. The movements, communications and transactions of the national population were, in fact, excluded from mainstream power political analysis.[4] A certain irony can be perceived here, for in an 'era of the masses' – or, at least, professed popular democracy (and is there any state which, in its public statements, eschews this?) – an analysis of inter-state behaviour that does not include the mass national population as a major variable is obviously lacking holistic perspective. The problem which this book addresses, then, is how to find a theoretically coherent method for understanding the mass national population and its relationship to the state, state foreign policy and international relations.

At the same time that the International Relations academy was disengaging the mass population from its theories, another field of the social sciences was involved in an attempt to do precisely the opposite. The post-war, post-colonial independence of so many African and Asian states produced a new problematic for students of comparative politics. This problematic was concerned with the difficulties that these states were confronting in terms of *modernisation*, both economically and politically.[5] Politically, the major structural problem was that of building or creating political integration, that of evoking the mass of the new citizens' loyalty towards the new state, of nation-building.[6] This was particularly a problem due to tribal, ethnic or religious cleavages – or to the vast difference in life-style between metropolitan elites and rural masses.

The academic study of modernisation floundered in several ways, but mainly due to a eurocentric attitude which projected the historical western process of progress as a universal to be applied to all developing states.[7] Moreover, nation-building as a particular area of study was

3

beset by its own lack of a consistent theory which could explain the mass citizenry's transfer of sentiment and loyalty to the new state. This lack of consistent theory reflected the parallel problem in International Relations of being unable to give clear theoretical status to the mass national people in relation to international politics; namely, how is one to understand the way in which the mass citizenry is linked together and linked to the state? Is it possible to explain how these millions of individuals are joined together to act as one force?

In practical terms, this lack of an organising methodology for the mass citizenry is not simply a 'nice' theoretical problem, but is concerned with quite crucial political realities. It is concerned with those essential factors which, at one end of the spectrum, evoke and create social harmony and political integration; and which at the other end of the spectrum promote revolution, secession, civil war and international war. It is the masses of people who are the citizens to be integrated and built into the nation; it is these same masses who in waves of hundreds of thousands are prepared to die in physical conflict. Further, without a coherent theory which explicates the links between the mass citizenry and their polity, there is no possibility of clarity in the analysis of, or prescription of, policies that seek political integration or mass public involvement in foreign policy.

It is the purpose of this research to approach this problematic from the perspective of social psychology. This seems wholly appropriate as the core of the problem is concerned with human sentiment, human attitude and human loyalty. This is not to deny or to marginalise socio-economic or political factors. It is only to recognise that *whatever* the configuration of socio-economic and political realities, and no matter how powerful and determining they may appear, there always remains the psychological dimension of the nature of the relationship between the citizen and the state. I suggest that it is this lack of clarity concerning the nature of this *psychological* relationship between citizens *en masse* – the nation – and the state which is the precise source of the lack of any coherent theoretical status for the mass national population. Identification theory, which is concerned precisely with the deep psychological relationship between an individual and his/her social environment – the internalisation of 'social attitudes' – provides the possibility of an analytical tool which clarifies the attitude and the motivation of both the individual and the mass citizenry in relation to their state and their state's international relations.

This chapter now proceeds with a survey of the application thus far of psychological theory to political analysis. It also discusses sociologi-

4

cal theory which possesses inherent psychological assumptions. From a political theorist's perspective, this survey may be too detailed; from a social psychologist's perspective, it may be too restricted and cavalier. Some survey, however, is required for it gives the background and 'launch pad' from which identification theory, the backbone of this research, can be applied.

HUMAN NATURE AND POLITICAL THEORY

In a certain sense, it can be said that all political theory is to a degree unavoidably informed by an attitude or idea about human nature and human psychology. Any political theory, whether purely analytical or part of a policy science, is necessarily coloured by the view that its author takes of human nature and of human psychology; for example, at a most basic level, does the author think that human nature is essentially nice – or nasty? A particular idea of human nature obviously works towards defining the way in which human behaviour in general, and political behaviour in particular, will be perceived and understood. This is particularly so in classical political theory in which the political analysis is only a part of a far greater endeavour to uncover the whole nature and purpose of the individual-in-society and to prescribe for the 'good life'. In fact, as Gabriel Almond noted, 'Classical political theory is more a political sociology and psychology and a normative political theory than it is a theory of the political process.'[8]

There are several essays and texts which rehearse the various assumptions about human nature made by the classical political theorists.[9] It is difficult, however, to produce a coherent taxonomy into which these assumptions can be sensibly and economically bundled. The most frequent mode of division in this literature is that between those theorists whose view of human nature is cynical or realistic (nasty), and those whose view is more benign (nice). Thus, for example, men act aggressively *en masse* because they are essentially aggressive and are cooperating simply for self-preservation; or humans integrate peacefully because they are essentially cooperative. Hobbes and Machiavelli, for example, are obvious members of the group which views human nature as nasty and brutish.[10] Equally obvious, Marx or Rousseau belong to that group in which human nature is understood as being essentially good, but misled and thwarted by social constraints. Bridging the two groups, perhaps, are those, such as Plato or Hegel, who take a more metaphysical view of human psychology and purpose. These kinds of division, of course, blur substantially as philosophers adopt different attitudes and approaches to different issues.

In his essay 'Towards a Theory of Human Nature', John Chapman proposes a three-fold arrangement of the different assumptions about human nature:[11] (1) behaviourism or plasticity; (2) instinctivism; and (3) developmentalism. The behaviourist understands human beings to be essentially plastic and passive recipients of cultural and social conditions, and into this group Chapman provisionally places Aristotle, Hobbes, Hume and James Mill – also Hegel and Marx. In the second group, the instinctivists or nativists – those who believe the human creature has certain innate instinctive drives – Chapman places Plato and Nietzsche. And into the third group, the developmentalists who understand humans to be bundles of potentialities thwarted or fostered by their institutions and beliefs, he places Rousseau, Aristotle and Plato. Again, of course, the divisions are self-evidently extremely fluid and Chapman safely concludes that each theory of human nature has 'formulated some aspect of the truth about nature and our dynamics' and that 'there is no necessary mutual antagonism between the theories'.[12]

The major problem, of course, with all blanket assumptions about human nature and political behaviour is that the assumptions can only be applied to appropriate situations. That man is naturally brutish is only relevant to situations in which he is behaving brutishly, but not to those in which he is behaving cooperatively. Equally, he is only, for instance, plastic and subject to political systems when he is not behaving deviantly. Explanations of political behaviour that rely on general assumptions concerning human nature are based only on evidence that fits the bill. They are, therefore, methodologically flawed by being purely tautological. There is a great difference between the statement, 'Men behave aggressively because human nature is aggressive', and the statement, 'Men behave aggressively because there is an aspect of human nature which tends towards aggression.' The first statement ducks the necessity for a clear analysis of human nature and of the external determining factors; the latter is open to intellectual enquiry.

To a degree, there has been no necessity for classical political theorists – or contemporary ones – to be too bothered with an exact analysis of mass loyalty and mass mobilisation. What is certain is that people do display mass loyalty and mass mobilisation. The main question asked has been, 'Why should I obey the state?' Brian Redhead, amusingly but insightfully, summarised the answers put forward by political philosophers:

> Why should I obey the state?
> 'Because if I don't they will cut my head off.' [Pragmatic]
> 'Because it is God's will.' [Theological]
> 'Because the state and I have done a deal.' [Contractual]
> 'Because the state is the actuality of the ethical idea.' [Metaphysical][13]

The research of this book is not concerned with those types of answer at those levels of analysis, but seeks an answer at a distinct psychological level of analysis. Indeed, until the twentieth century there was no clearly defined psychological level of analysis with discrete methods. To pursue this investigation using the methodology of modern psychology is not to be casual about the profound discussions that have taken place in philosophical political discourse concerning these issues. It is merely to travel using an alternate mode of enquiry.

MODERN PSYCHOLOGY

The turn of the century saw the introduction of a more carefully theoretical and observed approach to psychology with the emergence of the two major schools, the psychoanalytic and the behaviourist.[14] In political theory itself, this emerging scientific psychology was reflected in Graham Wallas's influential book, *Human Nature in Politics*,[15] which called on political theorists to overcome 'the tendency to exaggerate the intellectuality of mankind' and to seek to understand the different 'impulses and instincts'[16] which governed man's behaviour, particularly, of course, his political behaviour.

In fact, the two major schools of psychology, the psychoanalytic and the behaviourist, led, as William Stone has pointed out, to two general approaches to political analysis.[17] The psychoanalytic mode has been used in an attempt to explain political *action* and the behaviourist in an attempt to explain *attitude*.

The psychoanalytic approach

Freud himself took the lead in attempting to use psychoanalysis as a tool for political explanation in his works, 'Thoughts for the Time on War and Death', *Civilisation and its Discontents*, and 'Why War?'[18] In fact, the most substantial portion of the psychological investigation into international conflict has been undertaken by psychoanalytical writers discussing the motivation that leads individuals and masses into war.[19] The psychoanalytic approach is

7

two-fold, one level concerned with inherent instinct and the other level concerned with the psychic mechanism of displacement. First, it proposes that there is an inherent instinct in human beings that is destructive and moves towards self-destruction. Freud described this instinct as the opposite to the principle of Eros and called it Thanos and the Death Wish;[20] it is illustrated, for example, in the pleasure that a child gains from knocking down a construction. Second, it is proposed that individuals displace emotions, frustrations and aggressions which are essentially part of their private emotional lives away from their personal relationships and project them into political life. Projection is 'an attempt to convert an inner (psychic) stimulus into an outer (reality) stimulus, an inner enemy into an outer enemy'.[21] Alix Strachey gives a graphic and entertaining illustration of this psychoanalytic approach to international political life, which is worth quoting in length:

> the state . . . enables its members to gratify many of their more specific instincts and attitudes – usually infantile ones – which have been repressed and inhibited in private life . . . Mr Briggs, in insisting on his country's holding on to its colonies, is no doubt obtaining a (psychologically, if not socially) sublimated gratification of his early anal-retentive instincts; Signor Cappello, in egging his country on to territorial conquests, is obeying the dictates of his own displaced instinct of acquisition; and Frau Schultz, in so strongly resenting any insult offered to her country, is perhaps seeking to combat her sense of inferiority due to her castration complex; and so on. The secret agent who spies for his country when he would not spy for himself is gratifying his ancient *voyeurism* in a legitimate way and without offence to his super-ego; and the politician who tells lies and spreads false propaganda to bolster up his own country, or undermine another, is not only prolonging his past belief in his and his parents' greatness, but is at the same time exercising and enjoying his first-found ability to take them in. Even the ruin which such behaviour sometimes brings upon a nation may not merely gratify concealed masochistic trends in many of its people once it has happened; it may in some measure have been brought about by those very trends.[22]

The explanation, then, of mass mobilisation for international aggression is that it is essentially mass pathological behaviour, the international scene being merely the opportunity to express it. It says nothing, however, about the triggers or circumstances, about leadership, or about the many times that humans do not react aggressively. Moreover, it does nothing to explain the sustained aggression of war which may endure, sometimes for decades. It is also unhelpful with regard to political integration and the mass cooperation needed for organised mobilisation. In fact, with regard to mass mobilisation behind an aggressive foreign policy, it suggests an immense coincidence of psychoanalytic conditions in which all the participants desire to displace on to an external enemy their internal infantile conflicts – but there is no methodologically coherent explanation of how this coincidence might occur or is triggered. Freud did, however, offer a more coherent preliminary explanation of group integration in an analysis which suggests that psychologically integrated groups share a common symbolic parental figure; this is an aspect of identification theory which is analysed in full in the next chapter.

The psychoanalytic method has also been used as a useful theoretical tool for analysing leadership behaviour and motivation, both generally and specifically in the form of psycho-biographies of political leaders. The most well-known proponent of the psychological analysis of leadership is Harold Lasswell[23] and its most well-known victim, Woodrow Wilson – although one might add that any analysis of Hitler which does not include some form of psychoanalytic approach is obviously severely lacking.[24] These approaches were not, however, generalised to apply to mass attitudes or action.

The behaviourist approach

The early behaviourist movement had an approach to national mass political behaviour which was based in an anthropomorphisation of the nation-state. A national people was understood as being a single psychic being demonstrating all the psychological attitudes and traits of a coherent individual.[25] This early behaviourism had as its theoretical base a crude neo-Darwinism which understood nations as being the repository of a pool of genes which gave rise to particular national characteristics. Although this approach has been thoroughly discredited as being self-evidently illogical – an infant displays the culture of wherever it is brought up whatever the infant's origin – it is a notion which still pervades popular and tabloid consciousness. This notion once had academic credibility; it is worth quoting in length from a study which was published by Princeton University Press in the 1920s and is the father still to certain more general and misguided notions.

> The Nordics are . . . rulers, organisers and aristocrats . . . individualistic, self-reliant and jealous of their personal freedom . . . As a result they are usually Protestant . . . The Alpine race is always and everywhere a race of peasants . . . The Alpine is the perfect slave, the

9

ideal serf . . . The unstable temperament and the lack of coordinating and reasoning power so often found among the Irish . . . We have no separate intelligence distributions for the Jews . . . Our army sample of immigrants from Russia is at least one half Jewish . . . Our figures, then, would rather tend to disprove the popular belief that the Jew is intelligent . . . He has the head, form, stature and colour of his Slavic neighbours. He is an Alpine slave.[26]

This unpleasant mixture of a behaviourist approach to intelligence measurement, a Darwinian approach to racial genetics and a Hegelian approach to the nation, although methodologically ruled out of court on all counts,[27] is nevertheless interesting for what it has to say about the mass national people and international relations theory. It is interesting because it does at least provide a coherent psychological theory of international politics, providing one accepts that nations can be understood as anthropomorphic beings. Psychologically, the individual and the nation-state are linked – either genetically or mystically. Nation-states, therefore, are coherent individualistic personalities which react to and act towards each other as individualistic personalities. This notion solves all the theoretical problems of integration and mobilisation. The psychological link between individual and nation-state is absolute, being based either in genes or in spiritual diktat. Anyway, given the lack of any other theories of international politics that can be popularly understood, it is not surprising that this kind of simplistic theory retains its appeal as a popular explanatory tool, especially in times of international crisis.

In mainstream social and political theory, however, the behaviourist approach – apart from that crude anthropomorphism – set a standard of scientific observation and method for the analysis of human behaviour. This was observation and analysis which was not to be obscured either by general assumptions about human nature or by attempts to generalise from the distinctly unscientific psychoanalysis; the work was purely to observe and then analyse with methodological coherence *patterns of behaviour* – hence the term 'behaviouralism'.[28] According to Richard Jensen, its major exponents had by 'September 1924 revolutionised political science by converting virtually every leader of the profession (in the United States) to the behavioural persuasion'.[29] However, despite this wide acceptance of the behavioural method, the behavioural approach has by no means enjoyed the operational success that it originally promised. It has not provided clear political analysis. The reason for this can be exemplified by the most well-known political work of the school, B.F. Skinner's

Walden Two, which was an explicit model for moulding psychologically plastic individuals into a peaceful well-ordered society.[30]

Based in the core of behaviourist theory – that all human behaviour is the result of prior conditioning and can be encouraged or blocked by either beneficent or negative stimuli – the proposition of *Walden Two* is that people can be politically and socially conditioned *en masse* into the 'good life'. Unfortunately, this basic premise, in terms of practical politics, implicitly suggests and recommends a totalitarian culture which has little room for political deviance or creative political initiatives. Its terms of reference do not include an analysis of *motivation* for either individual or mass action and action is surely the essential stuff of politics. The human being is seen as being primarily a plastic creature. It is little wonder, therefore, that it has found little sympathy amongst political theorists who are concerned more with choice and action than with social engineering.

Studies of public opinion, however, more purely concerned with attitude formation, were bound to be and were, in fact, more fruitful, beginning with Graham Wallas's star student Walter Lipmann with his *Public Opinion* through to V.O. Key's *Public Opinion and American Democracy*. These studies, however, put forward no methodologically coherent theory concerning the links between attitude and political behaviour.[31]

THEORIES OF COLLECTIVE BEHAVIOUR

Another psychological approach that has a bearing on this discussion is the study of crowd or collective behaviour. This may seem a crude suggestion, implying as it does a similarity between the integration and mobilisation of a state and the integration and mobilisation of a mob. As Perry and Pugh pointed out, 'The stereotypes of collective behaviour as completely spontaneous, unplanned and totally unorganised have tended to isolate the field from general theoretical developments in the social sciences and create a gap between the fields of collective behaviour and general sociology, which has traditionally made a sharp distinction between purposive, goal-oriented behaviour and seemingly irrational conduct.'[32] However, regardless of apparent political coherence or rationality, both fields do display the same basic feature: large groups of humans acting together for a common purpose.

There is no shortage of sociological theories for explaining collective behaviour.[33] Psychological theories which specifically address them-

11

selves to analysing collective behaviour are, however, more rare. The publication of Gustav Le Bon's *The Crowd* in 1895 marks the beginning of this field of research.[34] Le Bon was deeply suspicious of crowd behaviour which he interpreted as destructive, atavistic behaviour in which the individual, no matter how civilised or apparently cultured, surrendered to an unconscious collective mind which was racially derived. This led to an enhanced sense of power, a sense of anonymity and therefore a lack of personal responsibility; this in turn led to stupid and impulsive behaviour which was highly sensitive to any form of suggestion. The style of Le Bon's writing was more journalistic than analytic, which was in keeping with his political, rather than theoretical, goals; his concept, therefore, lacked any methodological coherence particularly in terms of explaining the notion of the savage racial mind.

In *Instincts of the Herd in Peace and War*, published originally in 1916, Wilfred Trotter made no recourse to a metaphysical idea such as the collective mind, but firmly grounded human collective behaviour in her/his biological origins, describing humans as being both naturally gregarious and capable of herd panic.[35] This, however, provided no explanation of the careful, thoughtful and organised way in which disciplined groups, for instance states and their mass national publics, integrate and mobilise.

Following Mead, Herbert Blumer presented the major interactionist approach (1939) in which people, anxious or frustrated, mill together and, referring only to perceptions of each other, create imitative behaviour spirals through a process of 'circular reaction', which lead to extreme modes of action.[36] Again, implicit in this approach is a form of atavism, for the actual motivation toward the extreme action is the reward-in-itself of the euphoria of crowd contagion; however, it again provides no explanation of the thoughtful and disciplined approach to war. A further interactionist model is the emergent norm perspective in which a crowd creates its own norms outside the usual constraints and referents of the greater social system.[37] This, it is proposed, happens in times of extremity or change; in these extreme situations an individual refers to and internalises the emergent norms – even if the emergent norm (riot, lynching) is contrary to the usual mores of her/his society. Here, no motivation other than sociological determinants is explicated.

Talcott Parsons, particularly in his co-authored *Towards A General Theory of Action*,[38] attempted a particularly ambitious analysis of social action which combined psychological, cultural and sociological factors in one scheme. This, however, was criticised almost universally for being a static model incapable of explaining change, precisely because it explicated no theory of human motivation within the social system. As this particular issue is a major concern of the next chapter, I shall not take it up now. Following Parsons, Smelser also published an important analysis in this field.[39] This also gave no explicit theory of human motivation, although in general it posited a view that there was a pursuit of interests rather than the fulfilment of an instinct. It was also bound by Smelser's own injunction, quoted below, that there was no satisfactory methodology linking the individual with the collective. The notion, however, that humans are simply pursuing their interests is explicitly employed by Richard Berk's theory that crowds make a rational calculation of what will achieve their ends and act accordingly.[40] The logic of the argument, however, is boldly counter-intuitive to the apparent reality of crowd behaviour and self-sacrifice in conflict.

IMPASSE

There appear to be two major difficulties in applying psychological theory to political analysis, particularly to political integration and mobilisation. The first is, as Lipset has noted, that 'psychology itself has come to no agreement about how to characterise personality, or how to resolve differences concerning competing models'.[41] The second, as Smelser pointed out in his important paper, is that 'we do not at present have the methodological capacity to argue causally from a mixture of aggregated states of individual members of a system to a global characteristic of the system'.[42] Fred J. Greenstein put precisely the same point in his equation (where $\neq$ means *does not equal*):

Personality structures $\neq$ political belief $\neq$ individual political action $\neq$ aggregate political structures and processes.[43]

Echoing both Smelser and Greenstein, and working on his approach developed in his *Opinions and Personality*, M. Brewster Smith produced a conceptual map of all the variables that might be involved in a social–psychological analysis of political behaviour and suggested that the first feature which the map points out is that 'we cannot take for granted just which of a person's attitudes will become engaged as a codeterminant of his behaviour in a political situation'.[44] He also points out that to take the map seriously is 'to regard the old quarrel between psychologists and sociologists about the relative importance of personal dispositions versus situations as silly and outmoded: the two classes of determinants are jointly indispensable'.[45] It was precisely this division between personal and situational variables which Talcott Parsons attempted to bridge and integrate.

13

SOCIALISATION

In his attempt to integrate the psychological and sociological, Parsons, however, was not working from a base in psychological theory that had been created purely by the great psychological theorists such as Freud, Mead, Erikson and Piaget. He was working also from a crucial psychological insight which had been put forward by Emile Durkheim and which is implicit in all general twentieth-century social theory. This insight was that the stability of any social system and the authority of its government were not based purely in structural constraints and balances, but were based in social norms which had somehow been taken into the characters of that society's members and which created what Durkheim called a 'collective conscience'. It was this collective conscience which created the organic solidarity of the functional interdependence of dissimilar individuals. Durkheim wrote for example in *The Division of Labour in Society*:

> The totality of beliefs and sentiments common to the average citizens of the same society forms a determinant system which has its own life; one may call it collective or common conscience . . . It is, by definition, diffuse in every reach of society . . . It is, in effect, independent of the particular conditions in which individuals are placed; they pass on and it remains . . . Moreover, it does not change with each generation, but on the contrary, it connects successive generations with one another.[46]

and

> In the first place, whenever we find ourselves in the presence of a governmental system endowed with great authority, we must seek the reason for it, not in the particular situation of the governing, but in the nature of the societies they govern. We must observe the common beliefs, the common sentiments which, by incarnating themselves in a person or in a family, communicate each power to it. As for the personal superiority of the chief, it plays only a secondary role in this process. It explains why the collective force is concentrated in his hands, rather than in some others, but does not explain its intensity.[47]

Durkheim was making explicit the psychological attachment which exists in a stable social system. He did not, however, provide a psychological theory which methodically explained exactly how the 'common sentiments' actually 'incarnated themselves' in individuals or groups. Nevertheless his insight was taken fully on board by twentieth-century social science in the concept of socialisation. In the broadest sense, socialisation can be defined as that 'whole process by

which an individual, born with behavioural potentialities of enormously wide range, is led to develop actual behaviour which is
confined within a more narrow range – the range of what is customary
and acceptable for him according to the standards of his group'.[48] The
actual structure and internal dynamics of this social–psychological
glue are, of course, crucial for a clarifying analysis of political integration and mobilisation.

Theoretically, of course, socialisation is the precise point at which
the individual meets society, at which psychology meets sociology.
The study of socialisation, however, has tended to be more sociological
and concerned with how society determines individual attitude.
Psychological analysis in relation to socialisation has, therefore, been
almost purely behaviourist and cognitive with very little attention
addressed to the issue of motivation or psychological process. As
Danziger wrote, about this tendency to define socialisation in terms of
its *effects*, 'the best that can be hoped for in that direction is a little more
light on some vexing social problems. No advance in our understanding of the fundamentals of human behaviour is likely to follow,
because no fundamental questions are being asked.'[49] Psychological
approaches to the process and motivation involved in socialisation
have been limited almost purely to the mechanistic stimulus–response
model of social reinforcement.[50] Even when working at a level of
analysis which is concerned purely with the individual and the subjective mechanism of internalising the external norms, the tendency has
been to explain this in terms of social imposition.[51]

The one writer who followed Brewster Smith's ideal of an investigation in which personal dispositions complement situational
determinants, was Erik Erikson whose model of successive human
stages placed the individual human being in balance with social
constraints.[52] Erikson's approach is discussed in detail in the next
chapter. Generally, however, with regard to theoretical psychological
approaches to the process and mechanism of socialisation, there is, as
Child notes, 'no hard core of well-established and interrelated
principles around which the study of socialisation is focussed'.[53]

POLITICAL SOCIALISATION

The general study of socialisation provided the background to
the more specific study of *political socialisation* which 'in the broadest
sense, refers to the way society transmits its political culture from
generation to generation'.[54] The issue, of course, is not new, for the
political education and politicisation of youth have been major con-

15

cerns of all practical political theorists beginning at least with Plato. Since the late 1950s, starting with Herbert H. Hyman's *Political Socialisation*,[55] however, it has been a particular focus of attention in political study.[56]

As with socialisation generally, any psychological approach to political socialisation has been one of external determinants (e.g. family, school, polity, society) acting upon the individual with a subsidiary focus upon the various personality attributes which act as variables. In general, the research goals have been either to explain socialising agents or to examine the personality and socialising variables which lead to different modes of political attitude and behaviour; the latter has had a particular focus on the possible links between childhood environments and adult modes of political behaviour, for example on the democratic to authoritative/submissive spectrum. More recently, however, there has been a move towards a study of political socialisation which is more concerned with the dynamics of the individual. As the Schwartzes stated, 'We argue, then, for a greater recognition of the role played by the individual in political socialisation. His needs and attitudes are an integral element of the interaction, and attention to them will assist us in developing a more dynamic conceptualisation and a more precise explanation of the process of political socialisation.'[57] This, of course, is precisely what is required if one is to move towards any meaningful theory in which political socialisation is understood as a dialectic relationship between the individual and her/his political environment.

Working from a base in Maslow's hierarchy of needs theory, Stanley Allen Renshon has come closest to supplying such a theory.[58] Maslow's theory states that there is a hierarchy of human needs, each level of which requires fulfilling before the next becomes relevant. This hierarchy, in order of ascendance, is (1) physiological needs, (2) safety needs, (3) love needs, (4) self-esteem needs, and (5) self-actualisation needs. The second set of needs, the safety needs, divide into two categories: (a) bodily safety, referring to absence of physical threat; and (b) psychological security, referring to a predictable world.[59] Renshon uses Maslow's theory as the lynchpin in his basic suppositions about political socialisation:

> 1) that the child acquires basic beliefs about the nature of the world at an early age, 2) that these basic beliefs are acquired in the attempt to satisfy certain basic human needs, and 3) that this process of basic belief acquisition has crucial implications for the political socialisation process.[60]

In a key passage, Renshon points out the crucial link between a need for safety and for a predictable world, and the need to have control over the relevant aspects of one's physical and social life-space, and then continues to propose an ontological origin for the need for personal control.[61] Referring to 'one of the few cultural universals that anthropologists have been able to find', Renshon derives the need's motivation from the prolonged dependency of the human infant.[62]

> The child arrives in the world with hunger and thirst needs, but no knowledge of how to satisfy them. At a minimum, unsatisfied hunger and thirst needs create physiological discomfort; and the child has few ways to communicate these needs. Typically, the child begins to thrust and cry, until an alert parent (traditionally the mother) interprets the cries correctly and feeds the child. From the child's point of view, there is no connection between his crying and the arrival of food. This means that the child is experiencing *two*, not one, unpleasant experiences. The first is the discomfort of the unmet needs, and the second is the fear (anxiety) that these needs might not be met again in the future. Out of these twin discomforts, the need for personal control is born.[63]

Renshon goes on to argue:

> In the complex interchange between the child's biological needs, their frequency and the nature of their satisfaction, basic beliefs about the nature of the world are being developed. These basic beliefs are not in themselves political, but I would argue that they have important political implications.
>
> What the child is beginning to learn is a basic belief in controllability of the world in general and his ability to control it in particular. This has the most profound implications for political life.[64]

Renshon's awareness, however, of the human *needs* involved in internalising political culture is crucial. It is crucial because it suggests that the human infant has an active need to internalise social mores in order to make sense of, and achieve security in, the complex human social environment. This is in stark contrast to the more sociological approach which sees social mores being imposed on the infant by the need for stability in the social system. The sociological approach's terms of reference do not allow for an analysis of human motivation and, therefore, action. A human needs approach, however, suggests the possibility of just such an analysis.

Renshon indeed makes out a trenchant case for the crucial importance of childhood socialisation and goes some way towards explaining an individual's motivation for socialisation, but an explanation of the psychological dynamics is not attempted; nor is an attempt made to generalise any theory of collective political action.

NATIONAL CHARACTER

Of particular relevance to the study of international politics is that the concept of political socialisation, when applied to a specific geographical region, provides a methodologically coherent base for the idea of *national character*. Within the framework of political socialisation, national character is explained as that particular set of cultural mores and political norms which, through socialisation, are passed down from generation to generation within a particular ethnos.[65] Thus, culture by culture, there will be different sets of general ideas and behavioural norms concerned with political methods and structures. Joseph Frankel in particular suggested that foreign policy decisions were guided by core values distinct to particular nation-states; and Nathan Leites, in his description of the Soviet Politburo's operational code, suggested that a particular ideological and cultural frame determined decision outcomes.[66] It might appear, then, that some academic basis has now been provided to the popular notion that distinctive types of national character lead to distinctive types of foreign policy behaviour; that nation-states have particular aggregated psychological tendencies which directly influence and motivate their foreign policy decisions.

Academic research has not, however, been able to uncover any coherent links between national character, mass mobilisation and foreign policy decisions. As Otto Klineberg noted, 'The realignment of political powers has had little relationship to national stereotypes or prejudice or hostilities or individual attitudes of any kind. The national stereotypes and attitudes have followed rather than preceded the realignment . . . individual tensions seem to follow rather than to precede changes in intergroup relations'.[67] In chapter 4 on foreign policy I return to this subject in greater detail.

PSYCHOLOGICAL THEORY AND INTERNATIONAL RELATIONS THEORY

Within the academic realm of International Relations itself, there have been relatively few attempts to incorporate psychological theory.[68] The most well-known, of course, have been the psychoanalytic approaches to war which were discussed above. At a more general level, Otto Klineberg provided a very useful overview of the various psychological factors which are relevant to international relations, pointing out the potential for, and the actuality, of human irrationality at various levels of analysis.[69] He did not, however, attempt to extrapolate any form of specific or general theory concerning mass national loyalty or mass national behaviour.

This more general approach has also been demonstrated in the work of Herbert C. Kelman, Jerome D. Frank, Ralph K. White and Joseph de Rivera, Oppenheim's more recent survey and Mitchell's very useful outline of the general psychological features that make for inter-group conflict.[70] Kelman, however, did grasp the nettle of the crucial issue of the psychological link between the individual and the nation-state, recognising its pivotal place in any attempt to work towards a psychological theory of international relations. In two essays in particular, Kelman presented a framework which distinguished different patterns of involvement in the national political system and then traced how these different patterns would affect foreign policy orientation.[71] In his own words, he distinguished 'two types of motive that lead the individual to cathect the system'. These were the 'sentimental' and the 'instrumental'. He then distinguished three components of the national social system via which members might be bound into it: 'Ideological', 'Role Participant' and 'Normative'. These two sets of variables led to different forms of involvement.[72]

These, in turn, had varying implications for foreign policy orientation. One of the more interesting insights was, for example (following Galtung), that since 'there is generally a lag in communication of basic foreign policy orientations from the centre to the periphery, the normatively oriented individual (who typically resides at the periphery) may finally adopt a conception of the "proper" foreign policy stance that the elite was propagating earlier just when the elite has abandoned this conception in favour of a new approach'.[73]

This insightful and useful proto-classification of the types of involvement in the national system did not, however, analyse the circumstances or the motivation that led to the types of cathexis and involvement, nor did it progress to any attempt to generalise from the classification to any theory of international politics or foreign policy decision-making. In practical terms it is also a problematical classification as individuals move between various classifications according to the particular situation. For example, an industrialist at the metropolitan centre may have a purely functional attitude to foreign policy with regard to tourism or economics, but have an extremely sentimental attitude if the nation is threatened by international aggression.

The writer who has dealt with this issue with the greatest analytical precision, albeit briefly, is Daniel Katz in his essay 'Nationalism and International Conflict Resolution'.[74] Katz distinguished four types of latent forces in the individual which can be aroused so that the individual assumes his/her role as a national. These four are:

1 Emotional and behavioural conditioning to national symbols: those aspects of the political and general socialisation process in which the child is 'trained' to a sentimental attachment to symbols of the nation, such as the flag, national anthem and head of state.

2 The sense of personal identity as a national: those general aspects of socialisation by which an individual comes to perceive her/himself as being of a particular nationality. This is associated with education concerning a common history, fate and culture, and is established in contradistinction to out-groups which display different histories, fates and cultures.

3 Compensatory and defensive identification with militant nationalism: that 'type of national identification that is based not so much on the individual's attraction by the advantages of group belongingness as on his attempts to solve his own internal conflicts and insecurities'. This involves the mechanisms of displacement and projection which were discussed above.

4 Instrumental involvement in the national structure: this can best be highlighted by appreciating the results of rejection of the national structure which would 'vary from imprisonment and exile to virtual ostracism'.

Katz points out, of course, that 'a number of these motive patterns reinforce each other'. His useful analysis, however, is not carried through with any methodical linking to actual foreign policy decision-making or international posturing, although the nature of the psychological attachment becomes clearer. But, once more, the crucial explication of the dynamics of the interaction between the individuals and the political system which could lead to any operationalisable political theory is missing.

One further attempt to deal with the problematic which requires mentioning is J. David Singer's essay 'Man and World Politics: The Psycho-Cultural Interface'.[75] This remarkably ambitious and cavalier approach attempted to provide a useful taxonomy within which a range of theories about the interface could be developed. Having first delineated certain attributes of the international system, Singer proposed the three psychological variables of: (a) personality, (b) attitude and (c) opinion which interact with the system. He then grasped the individual–aggregate problematic by the horns stating that, 'Even though no social group can be properly thought of as having a personality, an attitude or an opinion, we may nevertheless attribute certain properties to a group on the basis of the distribution and configuration of these psychological properties. In other words I would hold that the aggregation of individual *psychological* properties provides a quite sufficient base for describing the *cultural* properties of the larger social entity which is comprised of those individuals.'[76] He repeated further on that, 'The position taken here is that the cultural properties of any subnational, national or extranational system may be described in a strictly aggregative fashion, by observing the distribution and configuration of individual psychological properties.'[77] He also argued that any epistemological or methodological problem with this assumption is only caused by trying to explain too much and that the assumptions work providing that one adheres strictly to a clear level of analysis. I am unhappy with the construction of his argument as he appears to be having recourse to the tautological assumptions of systems theory, assumptions which he does not make explicit; this is a particular theoretical issue to which we shall return in chapter 5. He also fails to operationalise any part of his proto-theory or taxonomy. At his level of analysis, however, I think his observation is correct. He is simply stating: this is the way it is; let's accept it. My hope is that identification theory and the argument presented in this book will go some way to explaining *why* it is that way and *how* it functions.

This lack of progress in this particular field of a psychological approach to politics has not, however, been reflected in other areas of psychological research, particularly those dealing with perception and small group decision-making. Although they are not directly relevant to the argument of this thesis, it is worth briefly discussing them to fill in the complete canvas of the current state of the relationship between psychological theory and international political theory. It also demonstrates that a very fruitful concord between the two fields is indeed possible.

Following on from Snyder *et al.*'s work on decision-making,[78] which placed a clear analytical focus on the individual decision-makers involved in world politics, two threads of psychological research have proved particularly fruitful. The first concerns perception and misperception, and the second is concerned with the behaviour of decision-makers in small groups, particularly in times of crisis.

21

The seminal work on perception in world politics is Robert Jervis's *Perception and Misperception in International Politics*.[79] The basic thrust of this theory is that a human being is capable of processing only a limited amount of incoming information and that the incoming information is perceived in a mode that is resonant with already set patterns of comprehension, expectation and perception. This, in turn, leads to direct misperception of external realities; Jervis supplies a depressingly long list of such misperceptions in international politics. The usefulness of misperception as a tool for analysis is such as to have spawned a large literature and the words 'perceive', 'misperceive', and 'perception' have all become part of the ordinary rhetoric of everyday political discussion. There is also, of course, a crucial issue in the matter of what information is made available to a mass national public – what it is that is projected at them to perceive.[80]

The analysis of the behaviour of the decision-makers themselves made explicit the fact that their motivations and decision-making processes were not necessarily rational. This was due not simply to their misperception of external realities, but had other sources. Allison's analysis of decision-making during the Cuban missile crisis, for example, put forward a bureaucratic model of political process in which leading proponents represented their bureaucratic interests rather than a rational national interest.[81] It was also noted that decision-makers' irrationality was increased in small group situations and in times of crisis.[82] K.J. Holsti also produced an interesting taxonomy of the various role orientations which inform the expectations of legislators and decision-makers.[83]

What is clear from the whole of the preceding review is that there is no psychological theory which precisely explains how to argue coherently from the individual to aggregate group or mass behaviour, which explains political integration and mobilisation. From the sociological perspective, it has been enough – following Durkheim – simply to accept that there is a psychological mechanism by which social mores 'incarnate themselves' in the mass of individuals who make up a society, thereby providing the social glue and 'collective conscience'. How this works at an individual and motivational level has not been crucial as sociology has generally kept to the methodological injunction that sociological phenomena are to be explained by sociological, and *not* psychological, factors. Talcott Parsons, of course, sought a general explanation which included psychological theory and his ideas are discussed in detail in the next chapter. Political psychologists such as Kelman and Greenstein have, however, been acutely aware of the need for a coherent psychological theory which could be applied so as to aggregate from the individual out to the group.

IDENTIFICATION THEORY

Identification theory is a psychological theory which holds out the possibility of providing a psychological key to this problematic of integration and mobilisation. It holds out this possibility because it states that:

> In order to achieve psychological security, every individual possesses an inherent drive to internalise – to identify with – the behaviour, mores and attitudes of significant figures in her/his social environment; i.e. people actively seek identity.
>
> Moreover, every human being has an inherent drive to enhance and to protect the identifications he or she has made; i.e. people actively seek to enhance and protect identity.

What is crucial for my argument, then, is that *given the same environmental circumstances* there will be a tendency for a group of individuals to make the same identification, to internalise the same identity.

Similarly, again *given the same environmental circumstances*, there will also be a tendency for a group of individuals to act together to protect and to enhance their shared identity.

Thus, there is the possibility of: (1) delineating the factors and circumstances which work towards evoking a shared national identity; (2) delineating the factors and circumstances in which people who share the same national identity may act towards enhancing or defending it; (3) explicating the relationship between this mass psychological dynamic – one might call it the 'national identity dynamic' – and the political environment.

The next chapter, then, is concerned with a clear exposition of identification theory. It presents the theory mainly by way of an exegesis of the relevant work of Sigmund Freud, George Herbert Mead, Erik Erikson, Talcott Parsons and Jurgen Habermas; it also explicates how the identification dynamic works in group form.

Chapter 3, *Nation-building*, is then concerned with describing how a general national identification is evoked. It suggests that mediaeval England and France can be used as paradigms for this process, and lays out the factors involved in the early evocation of English and French national identity. It suggests that these structural factors, working at a psychological level of analysis, can be applied to the nation-building

23

process of other states regardless of particular political or socio-economic circumstances.

Chapter 4 is concerned with a state's foreign policy and discusses how the dynamic of national identity influences, or is manipulated and appropriated by, decision-making. It puts forward a general model for this interaction and then illustrates it with historical examples.

Chapter 5 proceeds to discuss what all this has to contribute to international political theory generally, particularly in terms of enlightening or resolving the major theoretical arguments within the discipline.

It can be seen, then, that the general logic of the ensuing four chapters is to work out from the individual to more general propositions. The final chapter is concerned first with a self-reflective criticism of the theory and second with an attempt to derive tentative prescriptions from it which are relevant to nation-building, foreign policy and world politics.

2 IDENTIFICATION THEORY – ITS STRUCTURE, DYNAMICS AND APPLICATION

INTRODUCTION

The purpose of this chapter is twofold:

1 To explain identification theory.
2 To demonstrate how it provides a solution to the problem of not having, in Smelser's words (quoted above), 'the methodological capacity to argue causally from a mixture of aggregated states of individual members of a system to a global characteristic of the system'.

The theory itself is presented through an exegesis of the identification theories of Sigmund Freud, George Herbert Mead, Erik Erikson, Talcott Parsons and Jurgen Habermas. The general flow of the chapter is to focus first on the psychology of the individual and then to work outwards, through the psychology of small social groupings, to the psychology of mass national society.

That both Freud and Mead can be understood as adopting the same theoretical stance towards identification provides the crucial epistemological basis for this chapter. This is so because Freud and Mead are respectively the theoretical patrons of the two major contemporary and contending schools of psychology: the introspective or analytical, and the behaviourist. Although the two men and the two schools differ substantially in most other theoretical areas, they find common ground in their understanding of identification.

Erik Erikson is centrally important, for it was his writings which demonstrated the crucial nature of satisfactory identifications for personality integration and stability. He made clear the fundamental importance of identity in the health of the individual and demonstrated its dynamic adaptive quality from infancy through to old age. It was Erikson who was chiefly responsible for making the concepts of identity and identity-crisis key issues for contemporary social theory.

Insomuch as every identification is made with an external social actor, identification is, of course, a social act as much as a private psychological one. It is, therefore, a concept as crucial to sociologists and social theorists as it is to psychologists. Since Durkheim at least, a central concept in sociology has been that the solidarity, the 'glue', of any social system is to some degree based in the fact that individuals internalise their society's values, norms and accepted patterns of behaviour. Identification is a core issue, then, in the work of the two most prominent social theorists of the last half-century, Talcott Parsons and Jurgen Habermas.[1] Their major concern, then, is with individuals as they make up society. Both writers have made substantial attempts at constructing a general theory for comprehending human social action and the nature of identification has been a crucial element in their analyses. In making explicit their approaches to identification, and in drawing out their implicit propositions that identification is a dynamic human imperative, some progress is also made in clarifying their own general stances and in rebutting critiques of their work which perceive an apparently static quality in their models.

The methodological capacity to argue from the individual through to the aggregate is provided in the proposition that:

> Through a shared identification, individuals are linked within the same psychological syndrome and will act together to preserve, defend and enhance their common identity.

Thus a people who share a common national identity will, within a certain configuration of circumstances, tend to act as one unit and mobilise as a coherent mass movement. Identification theory not only explicates the structure and dynamics of this common psychological bond, it also suggests the pattern of social and political circumstances which may create this bond and which may trigger the syndrome of defence and enhancement associated with it.

The chapter ends with a summary which explains the basic model by which identification theory can begin to be operationalised for political analysis.

Freud

There is ongoing debate and controversy – some of it extremely vehement – concerning much Freudian and psychoanalytic theory. This controversy exists not only between psychoanalytic theorists and non-psychoanalytic behaviourist theorists, but also within the psychoanalytic school itself. Freud's followers have fragmented into many schools with different theoretical approaches, the most well-known perhaps being those of Jung, Adler and Klein. Despite these divisions, however, there exist certain fundamental insights which Freud pioneered and which are certainly accepted by all psychoanalytic thinkers and, to a degree, by behaviourists. One of the most basic of these insights, for example, is the notion of an unconscious which motivates and affects conscious thought and behaviour; this is hardly contentious. Another area of Freudian thought held by all branches of the psychoanalytic school and accepted, albeit in a modified theoretical form, by behaviourists, concerns identification.

Freud's approach to identification did not rise out of any interest in creating a model of how social identity *per se* was formed. It arose out of an analytic curiosity about the psychodynamics of the mechanism which satisfactorily dampened down the megalomania and self-love of an infant in the face of family and social realities. 'Satisfactorily' was the key word, for this was posited in opposition to the possibility of the infant becoming, for example, pathologically depressive or paranoiac in the face of social constraint, and of being thwarted in his/her demands. How was it that the megalomaniac, all-demanding infant could tolerate being thwarted? Working at the time on the concept of repression – the mechanism whereby instinctive demands and impera- tives which would create unbearable tension if expressed openly were kept in check – Freud was aware that parental or societal ideals (e.g. where and when one defecates or feeds) became part of the infant's own personality structure. He wrote at the time:

> We have learnt that libidinal instinctual impulses undergo the vicissi- tude of pathogenic repression if they come into conflict with the subject's cultural and ethical ideas. By this we never mean that the individual in question has a merely intellectual knowledge of the existence of such ideas; we always mean that he recognises them as a standard for himself and submits to the claims they make on him. Repression . . . proceeds from the ego; we might say with greater precision that it proceeds from the self-respect of the ego . . . For the ego the formation of an ideal would be the conditioning factor of repression.[2]

The crucial question, however, concerned where this self-respect originated in the infant's own personality. How did the megalomaniac infant take on this ideal? And why? In the same paper, Freud went on to suggest:

> It would not surprise us if we were to find a special psychical agency which performs the task of seeing that narcissistic satisfaction from the ego ideal is ensured and which, with this end in view, constantly watches the actual ego and measures it by that idea. If such an agency

does exist, we cannot possibly come upon it as a *discovery* – we can only *recognise* it; for we may reflect that what we call our 'conscience' has the required characteristics . . .

What prompted the subject to form an ego ideal, on whose behalf his conscience acts as watchman, arose from the critical influence of his parents (conveyed to him by the medium of the voice), to whom were added, as time went on, those who trained and taught him and the innumerable and indefinable host of all the other people in his environment – his fellow-men – and public opinion . . .

The institution of conscience was at bottom an embodiment first of parental criticisms, and subsequently that of society . . .[3]

It was a year before he continued this theme in *Mourning and Melancholia* (1915),[4] and it was in this paper that the term 'identification' was used for the first time. Freud's focus of attention now was the critical agency for the particular pathological state of melancholia, and it was only later that he regarded its mention of identification as significant. In this paper 'the identification' replaces an object in which the individual has invested libidinal energy (*cathexis*). Identification is suggested as a preliminary stage of object-choice in a process in which the ego seeks to 'devour' an object cathexis.

It was then six years later, in *Group Psychology and the Analysis of the Ego* (1921), that identification was given extended treatment, and in this paper Freud concluded:

> First, identification is the original form of emotional tie with an object; secondly, in a regressive way it becomes a substitute for a libidinal object-tie, as it were by means of introjection of the object into the ego; and thirdly, it may arise with any new perception of a common quality shared with some other person who is not an object of the sexual instinct. The more important this common quality is, the more successful may this partial identification become, and it may thus represent the beginning of a new tie.[5]

His conclusion went on tentatively to apply this insight to social groupings:

> We already begin to divine that the mutual tie between members of a group is in the nature of an identification of this kind, based upon an important emotional common quality; and we may suspect that this common quality lies in the nature of the tie with the leader.[6]

The dynamics of the mechanism were hypothesised by Freud as being of two types: defensive and emulative. The defensive model was based in the experiences of the infant boy, whilst the emulative, or anaclytic, model was based in those of the infant girl.

Within the conceptual frame of the Oedipus complex, Freud posited that the infant son finds himself in competition with the father for mother's affection. The father is an inherently hostile image and, by virtue of size and precedence, father dominates. Self-defensively, in order to avoid a suicidal confrontation, the son takes on the attributes of father. By internalising father's attributes and by, in a sense, becoming father, not only does the son neutralise the threat but the son may also now share in the father's exclusive relationship with mother; thus is Oedipal strife resolved.

The daughter, on the other hand, does not have these grand problems. She is not threatened by father and the originating dynamic of identification in her case is based in an affectionate bond with mother, partly emulative and partly the replacement of an object cathexis.

Freud recognised the patness of this binary scheme and suggested that, in fact, the two motivations merged and that identification was partly emulative and partly defensive. These two models have provided the base paradigms for subsequent theories of identification within psychoanalytic theory.[7] Writing several years later, and explicating his model of id, ego and super-ego, Freud repeated that he was dissatisfied with his ideas on identification, 'but it will be enough if you can grant me that the installation of the super-ego can be described as a successful instance of identification with the parental agency'.[8] And in the same essay he suggests that a psychological group is one in which the individuals have 'introduced the same person into their super-ego'.[9] There are two threads to be drawn out here.

The first is that whether the motivation for identification is based on the defensive or the emulative model, its purpose is survival. The mythical nature of the Oedipus complex may distract from the underlying and very real drama. This drama is that, for the immensely vulnerable infant, the parents are the only means of survival – warmth, nourishment and protection – and that when a parent threatens the infant with not gratifying primary needs, the threat to the infant organism is ultimately one of death. The defensive adaptation to the parental ideal, the successful resolution of the Oedipus complex, is thus not only the source of other more complex and subtle psychological dynamics, but is also a *real* source of survival in the infant's threatening environment. Equally, the emulative, 'female' identification has the same crucial motivation. What is being emulated and internalised is the being who supplies food and warmth. It is not hyperbole to observe that to become like that being is to gain control over the source of life itself. To be ostracised for not internalising parental models is, for the infant, not a social sanction but fatal.

Second, at a more general sociological level, Freud was aware not only of the socialising effect of identification, but also of the potential insights it held for understanding the psychology of group cohesion in terms of a generally shared identification. This was to say that the super-ego – that part of the psychological topology responsible for holding the parental, and then wider societal, ideals – though unique to each individual in certain respects, also shared common identifications with the super-ego of other individuals. This was not, however, an issue which he pursued to a point of clarity. Although in his essay on 'psychological groups' he stated that the basis of its members' common identification was that they had a common leader,[10] in his discussion of what prompted a subject to form an ego-ideal in common with others, he suggested that the initial impetus came from the parents but was later subsumed by 'all the other people in his environment – his fellow-men – and public opinion'.[11] Identification, then, was made not only with specific individuals, but also with more diffuse groupings.

It is worth being clear, risking over-simplification, about what Freud suggests. He suggests: (1) the infant human absorbs into her/his own psyche attitudes of important external figures, primarily parents; (2) these internalised attitudes act as inner watchers (super-ego) censoring behaviour; (3) adults also internalise significant figures and the nature of a group is that it shares a common identification – it shares a common inner censor of behaviour.

Mead

Although the original focus of Mead's postgraduate work was in physiological psychology, his thinking was concerned very early on with the problematic of finding 'such a place for mind in nature that nature could appear in experience',[12] and his realisation that a purely physiological approach was inadequate. From his colleague, Charles Horton Cooley, Mead had also absorbed the concept that there is 'a social process going on, within which the self and others arise'.[13] This notion was put forward by Mead in opposition to the strict behaviourism of John Watson. Mead was sympathetic to this strict behaviourism in terms of its general thrust in avoiding an introspective and solipsistic psychology, but he faulted it for taking this avoidance so far that it denied both individual initiative and individual consciousness. As a psychological functionalist, Mead thought that mind, or consciousness, emerging as it did at a late stage of biological evolution, performed a distinctive function in the life of the organism.

Mead's crucial point here was that the *human nervous system* had evolved to a stage where it was capable of reacting *in itself* to the symbols and gestures which it communicated to others. There was thus in the human creature an obvious distinction between body and self, between physique and consciousness. 'The self has the characteristic that it is an object to itself, and that characteristic distinguishes it from other objects.' The self, then, was 'both subject and object'.[14] The central question which then followed was how the self, as a psychological construct, arose. Mead was meticulous in locating the genesis of self in a behavioural process:

> The individual experiences himself as such, not directly, but only indirectly, from the particular standpoints of other individual members of the same social group, or from the generalized standpoint of the social group as a whole to which he belongs. For he enters his own experience as a self or individual, not directly or immediately, not by becoming a subject to himself, but only in so far as he first becomes an object to himself just as other individuals are objects to him or in his experience; and he becomes an object to himself only by taking the attitudes of other individuals toward himself within a social environment or context of experience and behavior in which both he and they are involved.[15]

The process of personality formation, then, was one of the infant, and then the adult, taking into her/himself the social roles of significant others. This was not to describe an ephemeral or shallow process of imitation, but was to delineate the basic mechanism in the creation of the self. Nor, for Mead, was this to rule out individuality, for this was inherent in the uniqueness of every individual's biological make-up, history and present. It was, however, to say that the personality is a purely social construct. Mead differentiated two stages by which this process takes place. The first of these was specific, in terms of a one-to-one relationship. The second was more diffuse in terms of the general patterns of interlinking behaviour in all the individuals of a particular society. To illustrate his point he used the example of a child playing baseball.[16] For the game to make sense in a sufficiently coherent way for the child to participate harmoniously, the child must be able at any given time to understand the game from the perspective and experience of each of the other players. Without this general understanding of each player's role, the game would be incomprehensible; the child would be outside the game or, as this is a metaphor for social life, the child would be outside social life and asocial.

I have pointed out, then, that there are two general stages in the full development of the self. At the first of these stages, the individual's self is constituted simply by an organisation of the particular attitudes of other individuals toward himself and toward one another in the specific social acts in which he participates with them. But at the second in the full development of the individual's self that self is constituted not only by an organisation of these particular individual attitudes, but also by an organisation of the social attitudes of the generalised other or the social group as a whole to which he belongs . . . So the self reaches its full development by organising these individual attitudes of others into the organised social or group attitudes, and by this becoming an individual reflection of the general systematic patterns of social or group behaviour in which it and others are all involved – a pattern which enters as a whole into the individual's experience in terms of these organised group attitudes which, through the mechanism of his central nervous system, he takes toward himself, just as he takes the individual attitudes of others.[17]

The dynamics of this process were, for Mead, to be found in the exchange of significant gestures, concerning which each transmitter may be self-conscious. The source of this, in turn, was found in a Darwinian understanding of the evolution of the human nervous system which had successfully adapted to environmental challenges.

Freud and Mead

At a level of analysis that is concerned with the *mechanics* of this agency of internalisation, Freud and Mead are opposed to each other. Mead saw the mechanics of this agency working through the individual's ability to be self-reflective about significant gestures. Freud, more concerned as a physician working with distressed human beings, understood the mechanics to be based in an infant's need successfully to sublimate its anxious demands in the face of family/social reality.

Yet there are two other levels of analysis at which the two psychologists are apparently in concord: one level is concerned with the social determinism of personality, and the other level is to do with the source of the mechanism's dynamic.

For both Freud and Mead, personality was a social construct and the result of social interaction. (They disagreed, of course, about the unconscious mechanisms and drives that affected personality *behaviour*.) They both recognised the difference between the unique biological individual and the social individual. This is reflected in their topologies of the human psyche. In the classic psychoanalytic model, the ego as an organising principle mediates between the biologically based drives/instincts of the id and the requirements/sanctions of the super-ego. Although containing only two basic features, as opposed to Freud's three of id, ego and super-ego, Mead's topology is similar. The self is differentiated into an 'I' and a 'me'. The 'me' is that self which, in interaction, is the social self. The 'I' is that self's unique history and present, which, situation by situation, allows for unique reaction and creation. Although Mead judged the psychology of the Freudians as 'fantastic',[18] he explicitly recognised the similarity of this part of his theory with the Freudian interpretation:

> Impulsive conduct is uncontrolled conduct. The structure of the 'me' does not determine the expression of the 'I'. If we use a Freudian expression the 'me' is in a certain sense the censor . . . Social control is the expression of the 'me' over against the expression of the 'I'. It sets the limits, it gives the determination that enables the 'I', so to speak, to use the 'me' as the means of carrying out what is the undertaking that all are interested in.[19]

Mead's 'me' appears and functions in the same social paradigm as the psychoanalytic super-ego. In both theories, super-ego or 'me' is the result of the internalisation of alter's behaviour.

They are also in harmony as regards the bio-neurological source of the dynamic for identification. Identification as a mechanism has not arisen out of thin air or been posited by either of them as an explanatory construct that does not have its base in the sophisticated human nervous system. For Freud and Mead, *identification is a psychological dynamic that is biologically derived*. This is, of course, stating the obvious for those familiar with the psychologies of Freud and Mead, neither of which has any metaphysical underpinning. With the evolution of the human creature who is *per se* a social creature, and the concomitant lengthy and vulnerable infancy and childhood, a personality acceptable to the immediate social group is a simple necessity for social survival – social survival being synonymous with physical survival.

Following Freud and Mead, therefore, identification clearly does not have its dynamic source in any mechanistic sociological explanation; i.e. the dynamic source of the identification mechanism is not derived from a social system's need for stability and, therefore, its constraining imposition of a particular and acceptable social identity upon the infant and then the adult. This kind of explanation, implicit in much sociology, is teleological and reifies the concept of social system. For Freud and Mead, the mechanism is biologically based, though, of course, it meets bio-social needs. Certainly identification is the result of social interaction, but its dynamic source is bio-psychological.

The interesting question arises of whether the drive of the identification mechanism is primary or secondary. 'Primary' would mean that the identification mechanism is biologically programmed into the individual and is simply awaiting the correct trigger for it to come into action; i.e. it actively seeks a meaningful pattern to internalise. Mead's clear anchoring of his theory directly to the human nervous system would seem to favour the primary model. 'Secondary' would mean that the human infant, having discovered by trial and error that identification is a successful mode of resolving primary anxieties and fears and of ensuring primary gratification (food, warmth, comfort, love) becomes so accustomed to using it as a means of ensuring primary gratification that it becomes a drive in itself. As Freud mediated the Oedipus complex between the biological individual and the identification mechanism, it is possible that he would fit the secondary model. Equally, as he is frequently accused of biologism, he might also fit the primary drive model. I shall return to this particular issue when I review Parsons' use of identification, when to understand identification as a secondary drive or 'need-disposition' better fits the sociological approach.

In a sense, however, the demarcation between a primary and a secondary model is an exercise in scholasticism, for whichever it is, without it there would be no social personality – and no survival.[20] Also, whether the drive is secondary or primary, it is inextricably involved in primary gratification. It is through the successful use of the identification mechanism that the infant ensures its acceptance by its immediate social environment and the gratification of its primary needs for basic survival. The infant which does not adapt to the behavioural demands of its immediate social environment will have its feeding and comfort delayed, a hint at more dire and very real consequences. At an older age, a lack of conformity to the social group may mean social ostracism and, equally, death. There are few volunteers for the Robinson Crusoe experience.

Successful identification, then, means successful gratification of primary needs; this is also to say that a *successful ongoing identity is inextricably involved with the gratification of primary needs*. This is not simply an academic proposal, but is a blatantly observable part of the general human experience. It was Erik Erikson who made explicit that feelings of contentment are associated with a secure sense of identity and, equally, that discomfort and personality breakdown accompany any crisis in the sense of identity.[21] A successful and secure sense of identity is, therefore, essentially and unavoidably involved with the gratification of primary needs, with a biologically based drive to survival. This need for a secure sense of identity is as dynamic in the adult as in the infant of the human species. In fact, Freud pointed out that the loss of the super-ego's love was one of the five traumatic situations that caused anxiety. (The loss of the super-ego's love is the introspective interpretation of social ostracism or alienation.) The dynamic adaptive mechanism of identification, then, is associated with the general 'principle of constancy', a fundamental postulate of much psychology which Freud had taken up from Feuchuer and which states that there is 'an inherent tendency in the nervous system to reduce, or at least to keep constant, the amount of excitation present in it'.[22] Anxiety, of course, is a primary experience of this excitation.

In a sense, the infant's very first identification is a remarkable adaptation of the 'megalomaniac creature'. That it should be an ongoing dynamic mechanism is not astonishing.[23] When an individual has passed through infancy and adolescence to adulthood, to suggest that the individual is 'complete' surely misses the reality.

Erikson

It was the psychoanalyst, Erik Erikson, who gave 'identity' a central place in psychological theory and who also brought the term into common usage, particularly in association with the phrase 'identity crisis'. With a particular focus upon the problems of identity formation in adolescence, the major thrust of Erikson's written work was to demonstrate that identity formation was an ongoing process from infancy through to old age, and that it was a progressive and adaptive process inherent within each human.

Though he worked from an experiential base in psychoanalytic practice, his major theoretical concern was psychosocial and his publications display a consistent attempt to define the changing configuration of psychological and social dynamics that go towards forming identity through the human life cycle. He did not put forward a detailed theory of his own concerning the dynamics of the mechanism of identification, but followed Freud and Hartmann.[24] His was careful, however, to make explicit that the continuity of the psychosocial self was, within a psychoanalytic framework, due to the internal organising dynamics of the ego and not due to an external social imposition mediated by a super-ego mechanism. He referred, therefore, to the psychosocial self as 'ego identity' and he underlined this approach by using the phrase 'genetic continuity' with reference to self-representation.[25] In his introductory essay to *Identity, Youth and Crisis*, he was at his most explicit concerning this when he stated that

35

'man's need for a psychosocial identity is anchored in nothing less than his sociogenetic evolution'.[26]

Erikson described identity formation as an *evolving configuration* which gradually integrated 'constitutional givens, idiosyncratic libidinal needs, favored capacities, significant identifications, effective defences, successful sublimations and consistent roles'.[27] According to Erikson this 'evolving configuration' responded to inner drives and social pressures that changed at different stages in the life cycle; moreover he maintained that a failure to hold an integrated and continuing sense of identity led to personality breakdown. Erikson was also the source, though not directly responsible, of both these notions being abstracted to apply to social groups as a whole: e.g. 'the identity crisis of modernisation'.

In describing the different psychosocial configurations of identity formation through the life cycle, Erikson's most detailed focus was upon the period of adolescence when the young individual has most dramatically and explicitly to come to terms with, and to integrate her/his own inner drives with, the expectations of society. It is this period of adolescence which provided for Erikson what was almost a caricature of the inner and outer forces at work. In fact, in a diagrammatic representation of the stages in the life cycle, he characterised the major feature of adolescence as being one of 'Identity versus Identity Diffusion',[28] and he pointed out that this was such a generally recognised phenomenon that adolescents are given a 'psychosocial moratorium' while the young person is allowed to find her/himself. As the young individual emerges from adolescence, society demands that s/he then makes an orientation for life as a full member of that society, a demand explicitly recognised in many societies by rites of passage. Although adolescents *par excellence* pass through crises of identity, the general syndrome of having to synthesise social realities and needs with psychological realities and needs is present in all humans from infancy through to old age.

Resonant with both Freud and Mead, Erikson recognised that after infancy one-to-one identifications were of limited usefulness to the individual:

> [Children's] identification with parents, for example, center in certain overvalued and ill-understood body parts, capacities and role appearances. These part aspects, furthermore, are favored not because of their social acceptability . . . but by the nature of infantile fantasy which only gradually gives way to a more realistic anticipation of social reality. The final identity, then, as fixed at the end of adolescence is superordinated to any single identification with

individuals of the past: it includes all significant identifications, but it also alters to make a unique and a reasonably coherent whole of them.[29]

Mead's 'generalised other' became, then, in Erikson's writing, 'a gestalt which is more than the sum of its parts'.[30] From adolescence onwards, the change in biological circumstances (maturation) may lead to major identity changes, e.g. rogue bachelor *to* responsible young parent *to* middle-aged matriarch/patriarch *to* wise grandparent. If inner biological changes, as they work out externally, do not force a change of identity, then changing historical circumstances will do so. The relationship between inner drives and historical circumstances is dialectical.

Erikson followed Freud and Hartmann in recognising that, due to the crucial link between identification and the gratification of primary needs, any lack of a secure sense of identity (i.e. lack of a successful identification) would trigger anxiety. If the anxiety was not allayed, then personality breakdown would ensue. Erikson saw this as the central adaptive concern of the ego which he underlined, when discussing this issue, by referring to identity as 'ego identity'. Ego identity, however, was held only by reference to the external social world: '

> Ego identity, then, in its subjective aspect, is the awareness of the fact that there is a self-sameness and continuity to the ego's synthesising methods and these methods are effective in safe-guarding the sameness and continuity of one's meaning for others.[31]

Elsewhere, more dramatically, he stated explicitly the crucial importance of ego identity:

> Indeed in the social jungle of human existence, there is no feeling of being alive without a sense of ego identity.[32]

Minimally, then, a prerequisite for a psychological sense of well-being is a secure sense of identity. In fact, Erikson went on to posit that a sense of well-being is 'a symptom' of an increasing sense of identity.[33] And, conversely and crucially, a diffusion of identity, or the inability on the ego's part to synthesise the changing biological and psycho-social configurations, lead to personality breakdown – from anxiety through to acutely disabling paranoid, psychopathic, depressive or other types of disorder.[34] There is thus a psychological dynamic not only to make adaptive identifications, but also to protect and enhance identifications already made. Individuals have a drive to bolster and to defend their identity.

As an infant emerges increasingly from the family into wider society, so the infant is faced with an expanding and increasingly complex world, with which and within which a satisfactory identity must be synthesised. Erikson addressed himself directly to this problem, recognising that 'man, in order to be able to interact efficiently must, at intervals, make *a total orientation out of a given state of partial knowledge*'.[35] Elsewhere, he called this type of orientation 'totalism'.[36] This was not, of course, a conscious psychological mechanism.

This led Erikson to a completely psychological definition of 'ideology'. It was this total orientation, which is a synthesis of historical (already made) identifications with a general mode of behaviour or culture, to which Erikson was referring when he used the term 'ideology'. 'We are speaking here,' he wrote, 'not merely of high privileges and lofty ideals but of psychological necessities. For the social institution which is the guardian of identity *is* what we have called *ideology*.'[37] Elsewhere he wrote:

> Whatever else ideology is (Mannheim 1949; Schilder 1930–1940) and whatever transitory or lasting social form it takes . . . we will view it here as a necessity for the growing ego which is involved in the succession of generations and in adolescence is committed to some new synthesis of past and future: a synthesis which must include but transcend the past, even as identity does.[38]

It is in his exposition of ideology as a psychological necessity that Erikson is also at his most sociological, for he recognised in a Durkheimian sense how society has institutionalised these needs and appropriated them to serve society itself; as ideology harnesses the individual's aggressive and discriminative energies and 'encompasses, as it completes, it, the individual's identity'.

> Thus, identity or ideology are two aspects of the same process. Both provide the necessary condition for further individual maturation and, with it, for the next higher form of identification, namely, *the solidarity linking common identities*.[39]

Ideology, then, while retaining its diffuse meaning as a socio-cultural and political phenomenon, takes on a specific psychological meaning as that generalised identification which is a prerequisite for an 'adult' participation in society. Put *in extremis*, ideology is essentially a psychological function, but its clothing will vary from historical circumstance to historical circumstance; nor is this to gainsay that ideology can be deliberately created, manipulated or appropriated. Thus for Erikson, at a psychological level of analysis, there is a clear continuum between identity, ideology and culture.

A threat, therefore, to ideology or culture is a threat to identity;

equally, an enhancement of ideology or culture enhances identity. Thus a change of historical circumstances – e.g. divorce, revolution, redundancy *et al.* – will threaten the individual's sense of identity by removing and altering the external social coordinates by which the individual recognises her/his own identity continuity. This diffusion of identity, or identity crisis, will trigger anxiety and the crisis will be countered by a dynamic adaptive reaction in which either (a) the already held identity (ideology or culture) is protected, or (b) a new synthesis of identifications is made appropriate to the situation and its constraints. Equally, individuals seek to enhance their sense of identity and the psychological sense of security and well-being that comes with it.

To counter anxiety, to maintain security and to enhance the sense of well-being that is concomitant with reinforced identity – all of which are unconscious motivations – the adult identification mechanism, like that of the infant, is dynamic and not simply a passive adaptation dictated by the environment.

Although not centrally important to Erikson himself, there was a thread running through his writing that gained wide popular acceptability. This was the notion that 'identity', 'secure identity' and 'identity crisis' can be applied to groups. This is logical in so much as identification is, from its inception, a group process even if the group or social system is only parent and child.

Any identification means *per se* that two are involved: the identifier and the identified. Once the infant moves beyond one-to-one identifications, the identifications become generalised. Even, of course, the original one-to-one with parent identifications carry general aspects, as each parent's own identity is made up of generalised ideological and cultural identifications belonging to the wider social environment. To a lesser or greater degree, then, all identifications are social – family *to* baseball team *to* planetary citizen. Equally, to a lesser or greater degree, all identifications are shared.

It follows, therefore, that a change of historical circumstances which affects or threatens a particular *generalised* identification will also affect and threaten the identity of *each individual* within that group. At an individual level, there will be identity diffusion, insecurity and anxiety, and there will also be the behavioural imperative either to protect the already held identification or to resynthesise a new and secure identity. This syndrome, of course, will be shared by all the individuals within the group that share the same identification. Theoretically, each individual may separately resynthesise a new identity or bolster the old one in isolation from her/his fellows who share the same situation. On the other hand, however, by reference to each other the individuals may *together* synthesise a new identification or bolster the old. The degree to which the group will respond as a whole will depend upon certain historical and existential bonds within the group: geographical propinquity, length of time passed together, class, ethnicity, religion, ritual and the degree to which that particular identification is crucial to the general identity. The form that the group reaction to a shared identity threat takes will be determined by a configuration of shared perceptions and commonly accepted communications about the nature of the crisis. Both the perceptions and the communications are, of course, vulnerable to manipulation – particularly so since individuals, and individuals as a group with a shared identification, may seek together to enhance their sense of identity.

The first point to draw out of this is that the individual will, therefore, seek to protect and enhance her/his sense of identity. As with the gratification of hunger or the sexual instinct, the drive to protect and enhance identity may be aggressive.

The second point is that when the sense of identity is threatened, *the individual will either reinforce the already held identification or will actively seek to make a new identification*.

The third point is that the mechanism is unconscious and that unless the individual's social environment has been stable since infancy, the identification drive will be continuously seeking to maximise identity protection and enhancement.

A lack of a secure personal identity is experienced as a threat to survival and is felt as anxiety. Identification, as well as being the initial mechanism for the creation of social identity and the assurance of social survival, is also an ongoing and dynamic adaptive mechanism to changes in the life situation that threaten identity. Without this adaptation, there would be ongoing anxiety – and, of course, the non-resolution of this dynamic is a distressed pathological state.

Talcott Parsons

The identification mechanism is, of course, a lynchpin in Parsons' attempt to bring society, culture, personality and human organism into meaningful relationship for a general theory of social action.[40] The simultaneous discovery by Freud, Mead and Durkheim of the individual's internalisation of social norms and mores was, for Parsons, 'one of the few truly momentous developments of modern social science'.[41] It is with Parsons, therefore, that identification theory moves from being mainly concerned with the formation of individual identity to its position as a fundamental base in any general theory of social structure and action.

In preparing this review of Parsons' position on identification, I have come, however, to share that enigmatic attitude towards him possessed by other students of social science who recognise in him an innovating authority, yet who are simultaneously frustrated by his own theoretical inconsistencies which are further obfuscated by his literary style. In his writing on identification, his major internal contradiction concerns its biological and dynamic nature which, when specifically dealt with, he theoretically abstracted to be purely a sociological function. This abstraction led one critic to suggest that life itself had been removed from Parsonian theory.[42] Parsons, however, self-admittedly wished to redress the balance of psychological theory away from the tendency to biologise. Whether he wished to redress it as far as he did is a relevant question, for it seems that it is precisely Parsons' apparently total sociologisation of a behavioural imperative which has led to so much misunderstanding of his general theory and has particularly evoked criticisms concerning its apparently static quality. To understand Parsonian theory, I suggest that it is necessary to appreciate that, despite the fact that he defined identification in terms of social and cultural environment, he also implicitly posited identification as a dynamic behavioural mechanism of the human organism. His failing was in not making this fundamental aspect of his theory sufficiently explicit. In fact, without identification as a behavioural imperative, his theory of action is not coherent. He tied himself in a knot that is worth unravelling.

Both Freud and Mead, as we have discussed, placed the source motor of identification in the human creature *qua* nervous system. Although Parsons recognised the essential creaturehood of the human organism, he was quick to describe how, from the very earliest stages of infancy, social and cultural systemic influences are brought to bear upon infant and mother.[43] At a sociological level of analysis this was a very necessary form of emphasis; at a level of analysis, however, that was to do with a general theory of action – which is *per se* human – it was to neutralise the behavioural dynamic. Yet Parsons took his theory of identification directly from Freud. So how did he neutralise its dynamic biological nature?

Appropriating Freudian identification, he actually changed the essential nature of the psychoanalytic map of id, ego and super-ego so that it became a more useful tool for his general theory. Requiring the

41

incorporation of collective identifications into the general social scheme, Parsons – although using Freudian terminology and the same basic understanding of identification – described a completely different human psyche. In this new Parsonian psyche, both the ego and the super-ego were culturally determined; but more importantly the id lost its primitive sovereignty to become a 'subsystem primarily, differentiated with reference to the function of mediating relations with the individual's own organism'.[44] In explicit theory, therefore, Parsons reduced human instinctual drives to such an abstracted theoretical state that the biological organism had become predominantly a tool of the personality. Thus the human creature was subject to society and society's needs. Most analysis of Parsonian theory stops at this point. Apparently, Parsons has created the 'social dupe'.[45] This is not, however, the full picture, for Parsons was also fully aware of the need to incorporate human motivation, which he did through the notion of human 'need dispositions', which were the result of the dialectic interaction between primary drives and internalised values.

Parsons defined three major types of need disposition: those which mediated person-to-person relationships; those which mediated between the person and cultural standards; and those which mediated between the person and society, society being here defined as a conglomerate of role-expectations.[46] It was in dealing with need dispositions and primary drives that Parsons was at his most self-contradictory. On the one hand, he admitted the intrinsic biological and crucial nature of the drives; on the other hand, he abstracted them conceptually to become malleable servants of society. The drive, once it became a need disposition, was no longer a human dynamic but a defining *relational* factor mediating human to human, human to culture and human to society. Moreover, resonant with this, Parsons also dismissed the 'tension reduction' hypothesis with regard to the relationship between drive and action, accusing it (a) of taking no account of the sociologisation of a drive into a need-disposition, (b) of being tautological and (c) of oversimplifying action. Any behavioural *imperative* thus seemed totally dismissed, but Parsons went on to say:

> However, whether formulated in terms of tension reduction or otherwise, the careful study of the process of gratification of particular drives has made important contributions to our understanding. *It has produced a first approximation to an analysis of the motivation of human behavior.* Our concern here, however, is to consider the problem on more complex levels of organization of motivation in human action.[47] (My italics.)

He thus begrudgingly, but at least explicitly, accepted tension reduction at one level of analysis, but as it seemed to him irrelevant to his more sophisticated levels of analysis, he abstracted it beyond his own paradigm. A few pages later in the same paper he repeated this syndrome when, discussing the essential prerequisites of the personality system and its persistent tendency towards an optimum level of gratification, he stated that the discussion concerning this persistent tendency 'simply asserts that at any given time, and with a given set of need-dispositions, mechanisms will be in operation which will adjudicate among conflicting need-dispositions and will tend to reduce the state of dysphoria (the subjective experience of deprivation) to tolerable limits'.[48] Thus, again, he acknowledged a biological basis whilst dismissing it from being a central concern of his own theory.

Throughout Parsons' discussion of personality and psychology, pace his specific attention to deviance, there is a consistent tendency to place the human creature in a theoretical space where it is incapable of upsetting the apple cart – the apple cart of society and the apple cart of Parsonian theory. The truth, of course, is that human behaviour frequently does upset both apple carts. The irony is that while Parsons was dismissive of biological drives being relevant to his theory, they are, in fact, essential to it in order both to avoid the criticisms of stasis and social determinism, and to understand human motivation.

Moreover the irony is doubled because the whole Parsonian paradigm of need disposition is necessarily and, in fact, explicitly posited upon a basework of human drives which are repressed and successfully controlled by successive identifications: each successive identification taking the individual ever further into a social/cultural correlation and ever more distant from her/his biological source. Yet, whatever the distance conceptually from the biological source, the mechanism itself is always rooted in the earliest infantile behaviour. Although in theory the human identity and personality is abstracted by Parsons to several removes from its biological base, yet it still inalienably inhabits its structure of flesh, bone and nervous system.

It is probable that the major difficulty that many experience in coming to terms with the central core of Parsonian theory is based in the fact that, having abstracted almost completely away from human drives, the system is purely interrelational and tautological in the grandest sense. The interrelational systems of society, culture, personality and organism exist only to support their own gestalt; their purpose is apparently to be a general system. The teleology is obvious, and it is interesting to speculate why Parsons missed this obvious

43

methodological fault, not only to clarify his own inconsistencies but also because it may give some insight on to a more general blinkering in social theory. It is possible to speculate that Parsons held a *Hobbesian* world-view – that human nature is essentially savage and society has evolved in order to keep savage man in due bounds. By this view, it must be the constraints of fellow humans that evoke identification, socialisation and acceptability; it is society that constrains identity. If this is not so, then humans are to be understood as essentially cooperative which is *per se* beyond the Hobbesian paradigm. And indeed, in Parsons' detailed analysis of the personality in *Family, Socialization and Interaction Process*, he stated explicitly that organic need-motives or primary drives *'cannot* serve as the primary basis for the organisation of personality as a system'. He went on to say:

> We can put it that, if this were the primary structure, there would be no adequate way of 'matching' motivational components with object-categorisations and value-systems in roles. The functional exigencies of systems of social interaction *must* have primacy over the functional requirements of the organism as a physiological system, if this is to happen. These latter must be adequately 'met', but they must not be controlling. This is why the *first* fundamental necessity of socialisation is to establish *control* through social interaction over the significant organic need system.[49]

Yet his whole classification of need-dispositions was presented as a tree in which every branch and twig had its source in the trunk of oral dependency and thus primary need gratification.[50] One can suggest that there was no epistemologically sound reason, other than a Hobbesian world-view, to give society such deterministic pre-eminence over the individual human and to create that 'social dupe'.

The problem is fairly obvious. Though changing, social systems display stability. Whence this stability? If human nature is essentially savage, then the source of the stability must be in the reified system itself and society, therefore, has primacy over the individual; by a Hobbesian view of human nature, stability *cannot* have its source in the individual. This *philosophical* stance, however, creates an unreal and total gulf between human nature and the stability of social systems – a gulf which is bridged by an identification mechanism that is dynamic.

Inherent in the notion of identification as a behavioural imperative is that human beings actively seek to identify and to secure, to adapt to and to enhance already made identifications. Writ sociologically, this is to say that humans actively seek to glue their cultures and social

44

systems together – and do not have to be constrained or coerced into so doing.

Philosophically, identification may be intrinsically a selfish drive – and, practically, it may be conducted aggressively and sometimes fatally – but socially it is by its very nature cooperative and adaptive. This is not to deny either power interests or socio-economic exigencies; it is merely to posit a psychological factor which has to be theoretically integrated.

Ironically, elsewhere Parsons showed himself to be fully aware of the adaptive nature of identification. In a very carefully worked passage in his chapter 'The Mechanisms of Personality Functioning' in *Family, Socialization and Interaction Process* he describes this adaptive function. Because of its clarity it is worth quoting from it at length:

> We conceive the process with which we are concerned in a broad way to be analogous to the processes of transformation between matter and energy, which have been so important in physics, only here the relevant terms are 'structure' and 'motivation'. Starting as we have from an initial stable state, we assume first the old 'structure' of that stable state has to be broken down. This breakdown results in the 'release' of energy, i.e. of motivation . . .
>
> After the imposed situational change which in its beginnings marks the transition from the stable state of the old system (T_1) into the new adaptive phase (T_2), the primary 'problem' of the system is that of adapting to an altered situation and developing a meaningful cognitive orientation to the definition of *what* it is that has changed . . . It is not only change, but frustrating change, as we have argued above, so that this is the phase in which the most immediate consequences of frustration develop. The primary cognitive starting point is what we will presently call the 'perception of error' in the sense that the presumption of gratifying experience within a certain situation proves to be in error, and first this has to be 'taken in' as a 'fact'. We may call these mechanisms in this phase those of 'primary adaptation' – primary because from a broader point of view the whole process is one of adaptation.
>
> If we were dealing with an ordinary process of 'learning by experience' on a fully autonomous basis there would be no significant changes in the situation from here on except as controlled by the ego. But we assume that in this case the order of frustration is too great for the ego to cope without help. The first order of help he receives is permissiveness toward the manifestations of his disturbance, but then (in T_3) a more positive help which we have called 'support'. This consists in giving enhanced positive gratification to *part* of the old motivational system, which is allowed by a set of reactions to the selective character of this gratification within the personality system

45

and in its relations to objects. We may refer to this cluster as the 'mechanisms of relative deprivation'.

The third phase (T_4) is that in which the new structure definitely emerges as part of the personality. It involves the reconversion of 'free-floating' motivation into structure, this time, however, *new* structure. For the first time the new objects . . . are positively cathected. We may call this cluster, then, that of the 'mechanisms of internalisation'. Finally, in the last phase (T_5) the newly internalised structure is consolidated and reinforced. We presume that it is stabilised by its main structural outlines taking on definitely *normative* character in the sense that there is a progressively increasing independence of the continual presence of the older situational stimuli, hence an increase in the capacity for self-regulation of the personality system. It involves the growth of motivation to reorganise positive activity in terms of the new goals and values. We may adopt the psychological terms and speak of this cluster as that of the mechanisms of 'reinforcement'.[51]

Parsons, therefore, presented his own coherent model in opposition to the primacy of social exigencies and this was complemented by a perceptive listing of the cognised signals which set the whole process in motion.

It seems, then, that if Parsons' world-view had encompassed the notion that there could possibly be an innate drive in man that was essentially – if only by an accident of evolution – cooperative, he would have integrated his knowledge of a dynamic identification mechanism with his general theory of action. Had he done so, he would have avoided both a major source of internal contradiction and also the criticisms that his models are static.

What is important for this thesis, however, is the central and crucial role of identification in all Parsonian theory. Although overtly, and for the purposes of his world-view, identification is a social function, covertly he well recognises its source in a biological drive.

Habermas

For Habermas, a dynamic identification mechanism is a central plank in his attempt to formulate an agenda for reconstructing the base assumptions of the social sciences. He posits that satisfactory group identification is the essential prerequisite for a cohesive social system. In contradistinction to Parsons, his view of human nature is essentially more sympathetic: humans are positive actors on the social state. A *dynamic* identification mechanism is, therefore, crucial to his philosophy. Although he explicitly derives his use of identification from Freud, Mead and Parsons, he does not, however, expand upon their theory of the identification dynamic itself – nor does he spell out the behavioural imperative involved in identification. Thus, as with Parsons, he has also been criticised for creating static models with an overemphasis on shared values.

Interestingly, his epistemology for identification is, in fact, derived from a philosophical and not a social psychological basis. For Habermas, the whole problematic of identity and identification is the major concern of philosophy – as human and community seek, through the self-reflective symbolism of identity, meaningfully to locate themselves in their profane and cosmic environment. In fact, he holds 'this problem of identity to have been the actual impetus of Hegelian philosophy' in whose broad wake he locates himself as an inquirer.[52] Within this tradition, the central theme is that humans and society seek *actively* to 'find' – both in terms of locating and creating – their 'proper' and 'true' identity and this, in a sense, is the true thrust that works within history. Within this philosophical framework, then, the psychological mechanism of identification has necessarily a dynamic base. This philosophical argument is complemented by anthropological observations of man's need to make meaningful sense of his environment through appropriate identifications. In *Legitimation Crisis*, Habermas quotes a lengthy and dramatic passage from Peter Berger's study on the sociology of religion *The Sacred Canopy*; the quote ends:

> To be in society is to be 'sane' precisely in the sense of being shielded from the ultimate 'insanity' of such anomic terror. Anomie is unbearable to the point where the individual may seek death in preference to it. Conversely, existence within a nomic world may be sought at the cost of all sorts of sacrifice and suffering – and even at the cost of life itself, if the individual believes that this ultimate sacrifice has nomic significance.[53]

Habermas is here using Berger in dramatic form to restate Erikson's point that identity diffusion leads to personality breakdown.

Habermas is particularly concerned with that generalised identification which is made between an individual and the most diffuse culture of which s/he is a member. The term which he uses to describe Erikson's 'ideology' and Mead's 'generalised other' is *identity-securing interpretive system*. In the final analysis, for Habermas, it is the match between the identity-securing interpretive system and the realities of social existence which legitimates the structure of any social system. This is to say that if there is not an appropriate symbolic mediation (the identity-securing interpretive system) between the individual or the group and the social structure, the anxious need for a secure and meaningful identification will manifest itself in either the change of the interpretive system or a demand for a change in the social structure. If the interests inherent in identification are not met, then the social system is not legitimated.

Habermas is explicit that legitimation crises are to be understood and analysed within the identification paradigm. 'Only when members of a society experience structural alterations as critical for continued existence and feel their social identity threatened can we speak of crisis.' He continues:

> Disturbances of system integration endanger continued existence only to the extent that *social integration* is at stake, that is when the consensual foundation of normative structures are so much impaired that the society becomes anomic. Crisis states assume the form of a disintegration of social institutions.
>
> Social systems too have identities and can lose them; historians are capable of differentiating between revolutionary changes of a state or the downfall of an empire, and mere structural alterations. In doing so, they refer to the interpretations that members of a system use in identifying one another as belonging to the same group, and through this group identity assert their own self-identity. In historiography, a rupture in tradition, through which the interpretive systems that guarantee identity lose their social integrative power, serves as an indicator of the collapse of social systems. From this perspective, a social system has lost its identity as soon as later generations no longer recognise themselves within the once-constitutive tradition.[54]

In order to demonstrate the historical continuity of this interrelationship between individual identity, interpretive system and social structure, Habermas paints an enormously broad canvas of its basic features through four social formations – 'primitive', traditional, capitalist and post-capitalist.[55] His approach can be easily criticised as impressionistic, but his purpose is to delineate that, at the most diffuse level, identity-securing interpretive systems are analytically meaningful. Moreover, an historical understanding of the evolution of the most diffuse identity-securing interpretive systems makes it easier to locate oneself contemporarily.

In 'primitive' societies whose structure is determined by kinship ties and in which the physical environment is directly threatening, there emerge mythical world images as the identity-securing interpretive systems. In these systems, world image and norm are scarcely differentiated, interpenetrating in rituals and taboos that require no independent sanctions.[56] The mythical world image assigns a meaningful place

> to every perceptible element; in so doing it absorbs the insecurities threatening a society which, due to its under-developed productive forces, is barely able to bring its environment under control. Almost every contingency can be dealt with through the medium of interpretation: it can be 'interpreted away'. The mythical world comprehends all its entities as analogues, men are substances in the same way as are stones, plants, animals and gods.[57]

On the other hand, traditional societies or early civilisations display principles of organisation in terms of class hierarchy and 'a form of centralised political organisation which requires legitimation and must hence be assimilated into religious narratives and secured by ritual'.[58] Two changes in the mythical world image of 'primitive' societies, therefore, take place, both linked by a humanisation of the gods. Paralleling the desacralisation of the natural environment and man's growing control of his physical ecology, first, the gods become less absolute and more propitiatory and, second, new patterns of interaction between human and divine develop in modes of prayer, sacrifice and worship.

With the further development, however, of institutionalised systems of unequal distribution, social hierarchy and the imperial development of ancient civilisations, the need for further legitimation grows. Habermas observes that this phase coincides with the rise of 'cosmologically grounded ethics, higher religions and philosophies which go back to the great founders: Confucius, Buddha, Socrates, the prophets of Israel and Jesus'.[59] Then with the substantial expansion of state and government into economic steering and other realms, so the size of the state's domination or authority that requires legitimation has also necessarily increased. It is a major feature of Habermas's work to analyse both the elements of these new relationships and how crises in any part of the system overspill and link into crises of identification:

> The state does not, it is true, establish the collective identity of the society; nor can it itself carry out social integration through values and norms, which are not at its disposition. But inasmuch as the state assumes the guarantee to prevent social disintegration by way of binding decisions, the exercise of state power is tied to the claim of maintaining society in its normatively determined identity. The legitimacy of state power is then measured against this; and it must be recognised if it is to last.[60]

There may thus be a great historical and social distance between 'primitive' and industrial societies, but still humans manifest the same psychosocial syndrome: social (and cosmic) reality must be satisfactorily mediated to them through a myth or ideology or identity-securing interpretive system which meets the behavioural imperative to identify. People require a cognitively accessible interpretation of cosmic and social reality, so that they know how to relate themselves to this environment – thus they have identity. If, then, the dynamic mechanism of identification is not suitably gratified, the result is anxiety and breakdown, both individual and social.

Habermas may have overstressed the consensual nature of social cohesion, but even his most severe critics admit that while he may have 'an inadequate conception of the way societies cohere', his model *is* valid when applied to a state in times of international conflict and to its citizens' general adherence to nationalism.[61]

SUMMARY AND POLITICAL IMPLICATIONS

Through an exegesis of Freud, Mead, Erikson, Parsons and Habermas, this chapter has established the following propositions:

1 Identification – the mechanism of internalising the attitude, mores and behaviour of significant others – is a psycho-biological imperative based in the earliest infantile need to survive.

2 Identification is a dynamic adaptive mechanism as much at work in adults as in infants.

3 A satisfactory synthesis of identifications, or identity stability, is crucial for a sense of psychological security and well-being. Identity enhancement leads to a greater sense of well-being; identity diffusion leads to anxiety and breakdown.

4 As life circumstances change, individuals may make new and appropriate identifications. Individuals may also seek to protect and enhance identifications already made.

5 As the individual enters more fully into society, identifications are made with more diffuse symbolic entities than the simple identification with mother or father. These are Mead's 'generalised others', Erikson's 'ideologies' and Habermas's 'identity-securing interpretive systems'.

6 Insomuch as a group of individuals shares a common identification, there is the potential for that group to act together to enhance and protect that shared identity.

In terms of political analysis, these propositions concerning identification theory lead to the clear corollary:

50

Mass mobilisation is possible when the individuals in the mass share the same identification.

From a power political perspective of internal political control it is advantageous, therefore, (a) to evoke a common identification and then (b) to possess a monopoly of power in terms of manipulating the symbols of that identity.

How this evocation of a mass shared identification happens is obviously a crucial issue for political integration and nation-building within a state. Following Freud's insight that identification could be of two types – the anaclytic and oedipal – it is possible to propose a useful parallel classification which can be applied to the evocation of a group identification.

(a)   In the anaclytic or sympathetic mode, the identification is made with the direct materialistic benefactor. In the infant's case this is with the parental provider of warmth, nurture and care. In groups, this is paralleled by a general identification being made with a social or political entity that directly and materialistically benefits the group, there, of course, being certain clear symbols which represent that entity.

(b)   In the oedipal mode, the identification is made not with a directly materialistic benefactor, but with a model who provides the right mode of behaviour in a situation of threat. According to Freud, the prototype of this kind of identification is based in the fact that one parent, the father, himself represents the threat and that psychological security is achieved by internalising this threatening parent's behaviour. In groups, this syndrome can be applied when a general identification is made with an entity which presents an appropriate mode of behaviour and attitude in a situation of threat.

What is clear from this whole discussion of identification is that the evocation of a shared group identification can be triggered only by meaningful and real experience. This is to say that any identification is only made if, in the first place, the dynamics of the situation are such that it is positively, psychologically beneficial for the individual so to do. This point may appear self-evident, but it requires to be bluntly stated lest it be thought that an image or a set of symbols can evoke identification simply because they are presented – logically, attractively or otherwise – to an individual. For an identification to be made, the symbols have to be *appropriate* as a mode of behaviour and attitude for a particular and real experience. An infant makes an identification with parental behaviour because of its vulnerability and because of the

51

total *appropriateness* of internalising the images and behavioural symbols of the parents. To behave like the parent is the totally appropriate way for the vulnerable infant to deal with the threatening environment. Later in life, when appropriate behaviour is required in more general social environments, identifications are made that are equally appropriate for achieving security. Following Erikson's use of the term, ideologies provide appropriate behavioural patterns and attitudes for more diffuse life situations. And one of these ideologies or identity-securing interpretive systems may be the nation which gives the identity of nationality.

To anchor this theory, then, in practical political realities: political ideologies and ideas of nationalism cannot of themselves evoke identification. Political ideologies do not work in a psychological vacuum. They must provide appropriate modes of behaviour, appropriate attitudes, appropriate ideologies, appropriate identity-securing interpretive systems, for dealing with real, experienced situations. Popular support – i.e. identification with such an ideology – comes only if it interprets and provides an appropriate attitude for an *experienced* reality. This experience may, of course, be politically manipulated – but a symbol or an ideology *without* a relevant experience is meaningless and impotent in terms of evoking identification. The next chapter examines in detail the evocation of a shared national identification. The chapter following that examines how it can be manipulated.

What should be clear from the whole of the preceding discussion is that it is now possible for the phrase 'National Identity' to be discretely and theoretically meaningful:

> *National Identity* describes that condition in which a mass of people have made the same identification with national symbols – have internalised the symbols of the nation – so that they may act as one psychological group when there is a threat to, or the possibility of enhancement of, these symbols of national identity.

This is also to say that national identity does not exist simply because a group of people is externally identified as a nation or told that they are a nation. For national identity to exist, the people *en masse* must have gone through the actual psychological process of making that general identification with the nation.

It is helpful at this stage to introduce another phrase which will facilitate analysis, but which requires definition. The phrase is *National Identity Dynamic*.

National Identity Dynamic describes the potential for action which resides in a mass which shares the same national identification.

If a mass of people exists whose individual constituents share the same national identification, then it can, with a clear methodological base, be stated that this mass may act as one unit in situations which affect the shared identity. They may act together to make new identifications, or they may act together to enhance and protect identifications already made. Identification theory, therefore, provides a theoretical tool which can explicate the relationship between individual action and the aggregate and thus investigate at a psychological level of analysis mass national mobilisation.

CONCLUSION

This chapter has delineated an identification theory which is dynamic and which states that identification is an inherent and unconscious behavioural imperative in all individuals. Individuals actively seek to identify in order to achieve psychological security, and they actively seek to maintain, protect and bolster identity in order to maintain and enhance this psychological security which is a *sine qua non* of personality stability and emotional well-being. This imperative works from infancy through adulthood and old age. Moreover, identifications can be shared, with the result that individuals who share the same identification will tend to act in concert in order to protect or enhance their shared identity.

The next chapter is concerned with how the evocation of a mass identification happens on the scale of the nation. Chapter 4 is then concerned with an analysis of the national identity dynamic in relation to international politics.

3 NATION-BUILDING

INTRODUCTION

Can identification theory be applied to political analysis? And, if it is applied, is the practice theoretically sound? The argument of this chapter follows on directly from the previous chapter and describes how identification theory can be used to analyse the question of political integration or nation-building.

The overall purpose of the chapter is straightforward: if the identification imperative can be coherently demonstrated as a major dynamic in nation-building, then it can be logically suggested that the mass general public which has made such a national identification will tend to act together to defend or enhance that identity. The basic theoretical building blocks will thus have been laid for using identification theory as an analytical tool for investigating the behaviour of the mass national public in relation to international politics and its country's foreign policy; this investigation is the subject matter of the next chapter.

The previous chapter presented a clear theoretical mode for investigating, at a level of analysis concerned with indentification, the nature and dynamics of the psychological link between an idividual and her/his nation. This chapter is now concerned with spelling out the circumstances which will tend to evoke this identification with the nation.

Its major focus, then, is upon the mass psychological aspect of political integration. This requires that the mass psychological aspect be disengaged from the more complex issues of political participation and social mobilisation. It, therefore, opens with a discussion and definition of nation-building. This also requires a discussion of nationalism in order, so to speak, to clear the theoretical decks. Following identification theory, the two sets of circumstances which evoke mass national identification are then delineated. The nation-building process of mediaeval England and France is then used to illustrate how this level of analysis can be applied. It is proposed that this process in mediaeval England and France provides a paradigm which has validity for nation-building generally. Potential theoretical criticisms concerned with psychologism, eurocentrism, falsifiability and internal consistency are addressed in the final chapter.

DEFINITIONS

Political integration is, of course, a major practical concern of all political study. Without integration there is little hope for the continuity of a state. It is quite beyond the scope of this research to discuss the historical circumstances which led, at least from the nineteenth century, to the notion – both practical and normative – that an essential component of political integration is that the constituents of a state should form, or feel themselves to be, a 'natural' community concordant with the state. Certainly since its introduction into political analysis by Deutsch in the early 1960s, the phrase 'nation-building' has been synonymous with the process of achieving political integration.[1]

Put at its most simple, 'nation-building' describes the process whereby the inhabitants of a state's territory come to be *loyal* citizens of that state. 'By "nation-building" we mean both the formation and establishment of the new state itself as a political entity, and the processes of creating viable degrees of unity, adaptation, achievement, and a sense of national identity among the people.'[2] Inherent in its usage is the fact that a *state* has already been created and that the nation, or community of solidarity, is to be built within it.[3] Nation-building, as generally used in social theory, is not, as such, concerned with how a community of people may come to perceive themselves as a nation and then perhaps demand a state.[4] It is concerned, in Toennies' classical terms, with how a *Gesellschaft*, or functional society, may become a *Gemeinschaft*, or homogeneous community.[5] Lustick makes this clear in his description of the two processes involved in state-building:

1　The acquisition, violent or otherwise, of new territory by a state-building core.
2　The elicitation within the new territory of loyalties and political commitments reflecting the ascription of legitimacy by the indigenous population to the authority structure emanating from the core.[6]

Again, that the state precedes the nation is analytically important, for any swopping of the two – i.e. that the nation might precede the state – can be highly misleading. This is so because, as Walker Connors pointed out, more often than not nation-building requires first of all the *destruction* of nations. Commenting on the new post-war, post-colonial states, he wrote, 'Since most of the less developed states contain a number of nations, and since the transfer of primary allegiance from these nations to the state, is generally considered the *sine qua non* of successful integration, the true goal is not "nation-building" but "nation-destroying".'[7] This, of course, is equally applicable to the origins of the vast majority of contemporary states, as each of them also needed to manipulate the transfer of allegiance from its constituents.

The assumption behind this view of political integration is that coercive political power alone cannot be the determining factor in the *continuation* of a nation-state. 'The supremacy of that coercive power itself', Emerson wrote, 'rests upon the fact that men in the mass acknowledge the legitimacy of the demands which the national state makes upon them and accept the nation as the community which makes the nearest approach to embracing all aspects of their lives.'[8] The attitude which Emerson here describes is rarely one that is intellectually self-aware. The nature of the relationship which leads 'men in the mass' to acknowledge that legitimacy is based in the more instinctive and less conscious psychological dynamics of identification.

Power politics create a state, but its endurance is guaranteed only if the psychological nation is built. Lucian Pye stated this clearly in his analysis of nation-building in Burma. 'The real problem in political development is therefore the extent to which the socialisation process of a people provides them with the necessary associational sentiments so that they can have considerable conflict without destroying the stability of the system. When these sentiments are lacking, a polity cannot even endure moderate levels of controversy. In short, it is associational sentiments which make it possible for organisations to endure, and to thrive upon, many forms of controversy.'[9] To endure, the state requires not only deference, but also devotion.[10]

Although building the concord between a culture and its polity – or, to put it another way, constructing the legitimating cultural structure between a state and its society – is a core issue for social theory,[11] 'nation-building' arose as a major academic issue mainly in the post-World War Two years, when the withdrawal or ejection of colonial powers thrust statehood upon many territories in which the cultural match between the new state and its society were tenuous, if not totally missing. Rather than investigating the structure and functions of social solidarity as it already existed in western states or in tribal communities, social theory became concerned with how social solidarity was actually to be brought about in these new states.

This problem of creating an homogeneous and integrated citizenry coincided, however, with the apparent need for these new states to catch up economically with the already industrialised countries. Industrialisation and rapid economic growth were seen as prerequisites for modern statehood. The academic problematic of nation-building thus became inextricably involved with the whole question of modernisation and theories of development. Modernisation theories, however, never achieved any satisfactory coherence;[12] in fact one distinguished commentator described the whole analytical bundle as 'an embarrassment of the sixties'.[13] The lack of success of these approaches was not simply because of their Eurocentric cultural bias and the use of western value-laden methodologies in which western academics argued that 'non-Western societies must travel the path trod by Western societies in their confrontation with industrialisation'.[14] The fact, surely, is that these issues, if writ large, are precisely the same major theoretical concerns of the *whole* historical process of modernisation and industrialisation beginning seven hundred years ago, for which social theory as a whole lacks an overarching paradigm.

Karl Deutsch made a major attempt to put forward an overall pattern of nation-building in which he suggested a five-fold process which ran from the independence of internal subcultures through to assimilation.[15] By the final stage of assimilation all groups within the state are 'indistinguishable'. The various factors involved in the process, however, are extremely complex, involving levels of social mobilisation, political participation and communications systems. Stein Rokkan, the other major recent worker in the field of nation-building, also worked with an approach that was sophisticated and complex as it sought to integrate socio-economic and political factors in a general centre–periphery model.[16]

The approach adopted by this research, however, is to disengage the social–psychological aspect from the vast kaleidoscope of political and socio-economic factors. This can be justified insomuch as that regardless of multifarious political and socio-economic variables, the end result of successful nation-building is an *ideal type* of political situation whose fundamental feature is social–psychological. This is not in any way to deny the importance of socio-economic and political factors as determining variables in evoking identification. It is only to state that if identification theory as an analytical tool is used with methodical consistency, then a clearly discernible social–psychological level of

57

analysis is defined. What it may appear to lack in holism, it makes up for in clarity and parsimony. Moreover it is careful not to exclude political and socio-economic factors for they are indeed the essential environmental factors that make for identification.

Regardless of a state's political and historical circumstances, nation-building suggests a clear norm for the psychological relationship between the mass citizenry and the state. This norm can be made explicit both in terms of its *internal* and its *international* functions.

Internally, the congruence between culture and polity has been sufficiently achieved when internal political conflicts – no matter how fierce – do not intrinsically threaten the existence of the state itself. 'They threaten governments', Clifford Geertz wrote, 'or even forms of government, but they rarely at best . . . threaten to undermine the nation itself, because they do not involve alternative definitions of what the nation is, of what its scope of reference is. Economic or class or intellectual disaffection threatens revolution, but disaffection based on race, language, or culture threatens partition, irredentism, or merger, a redrawing of the very limits of the state, a new definition of its domain.'[17] Internally, then, nation-building has been successful when the nation-state has the ultimate or transcending claim on its people's loyalty. There may still be regional, religious or ethnic ties, but these loyalties cannot be mobilised against the nation-state itself although they may compete *within* the nation-state.[18]

Internationally, this internal coherence is reflected in a clear political solidarity in relation to the external environment. Nation-building has been successful when the state can rely upon the mass support of its citizenry in a situation of competition with external actors. This mass support manifests itself most dramatically in the mass mobilisation demonstrated in times of international conflict. More generally it manifests itself in situations where symbols of national identity are perceived to be threatened. Provided that state foreign policy initiatives can be perceived to be defending or enhancing national identity, then the state can take an initiative in foreign policy in the confidence that there will be an initial and automatic response of support from its citizens. Government can take international action with the expectation of a period of domestic political grace before its actions are subject to scrutiny and criticism. Loyalty will precede criticism, and any immediate political criticism – no matter how well founded – may be interpreted as unpatriotic and treacherous. Here the state has the benefit of successful nation-building as summed up in the crude cliché of 'my country right or wrong'.[19] National sentiment is a major power resource for any state and a prerequisite for a credible foreign policy. This international dimension is discussed in full in the next chapter.

That successful nation-building has both internal and external functions is most clearly demonstrated in those situations where countries in a state of domestic revolution or civil war are attacked from outside. Instead of further fragmentation within the revolutionary situation, the external threat evokes the overarching sense of national identity and the country binds together to rebuff the attacker.

NATIONALISM

Before proceeding to describe the general dynamics whereby the mass of people come to internalise symbols of the nation-state as a major identity-securing interpretive system, it is necessary to achieve some clarity concerning the issue of nationalism.[20]

The previous chapter ended by pointing out that the *idea* of a nation, or even its actual existence, do not as such lead to an identification with it. This is in direct contradiction to any notion that nationalism, as an idea or an ideology, has some kind of *intrinsic* structural appeal.

For the individual to internalise the symbols of the nation, the nation – in one representational or symbolic form or another, direct or indirect – must impinge upon the actual experience of the individual. Not only must it directly touch the individual, but the experience of this contact must be such that it actually benefits the individual, in terms of psychological security, to make an identification with the nation. Thus the propagandist or prophet might incessantly sell the nationalist notion – i.e. that there exists this nation and this nation should have an independent state of its own – but the sale will not be made unless the purchaser experiences a direct psychological benefit from the transaction.

It is important to pursue this point lest the assumption that there are such entities as 'natural' nations cloud the psychological, and the political, reality. This is especially relevant when discussing the first modern nation-states, those of western Europe, because some history has been presented in such a way as to make it appear that these states did not experience the problems of nation-building because the state emerged territorially resonant with an already existing nation. This is implicit, for example, in Seton-Watson's writing when he calls the western European states 'the old continuous nations'.[21] There can be no interpretation of this other than that those particular nations are some kind of purposeful organic or metaphysical entities which have actively sought statehood as a predestined stage of their evolution. And, indeed, this is explicit in the nineteenth-century romantic writings, for example, of Herer, Mazzini, Hegel and Fichte,[22] and more recently in the mystical expositions of theosophy, anthroposophy and Jungian psychology.[23] This romantic and mystical nationalism receives some non-metaphysical theoretical support from the perspective of historical ecology and social anthropology. This perspective can demonstrate that a particular geographical situation and a particular ecological relationship do indeed work to form definable parochial cultures.[24] Whether, however, this is the outcome of divine intent or purely fortuitous is not relevant. The fundamental question is about the nature of the forces that then take a culture, or group of cultures, and create a political entity.

A glance at any historical atlas[25] shows that any contemporary state, even 'an old continuous nation', was previously a patchwork of cultures and smaller political groupings. There are currently only 160-odd states, but there have been, and are, many thousands of distinct geographically defined cultures. Unless, then, one possesses that divine inside knowledge about which particular cultural group, i.e. nation, is destined to become a state, one must recognise that there is no internal intrinsic force within a natural culture that determines its emergence as a state. This is not to argue Lord Acton's case against nationalism *per se*: 'A state may in the course of time produce a nationality but that a nationality should constitute a state is contrary to the nature of modern civilisation.'[26] It is, however, to state that if one's world-view is not romantic or mystical, then any assumption that a particular state is the natural result of a particular nation is purely *ex post facto*. It has no methodical justification.

Equally, it needs stating clearly that there is no justification in the psychologism that a nation seeks to secure its identity in statehood. This can only be justified if the nation is understood as an anthropomorphic entity. Which particular nations make it to statehood is a matter of power political realities in which the psychological dynamic of identification in terms of a national culture is but one of several resources.[27] The creation of a state is historically based in nothing so innocent as a mystical or psychological dynamic, but in power political competition. Raymond Aron's statement that 'War is the midwife of nations'[28] puts the case *in extremis*.

All of this is to clarify that the nationalist cry – 'this nation demands an independent state' – does not emerge as a natural expression of the nation. It emerges as the utterance of certain particular political activists who already identify with the nation. The cry for nation-statehood will not then *of itself* evoke any response from a national people – it being supposed that these people are mystically or subconsciously awaiting this call to bring their nation to the Hegelian fruition of statehood. Those people, in whose psychological interest it is to be moved will be moved; for these people, nationalism provides an appropriate ideology or identity-securing interpretive system. As an idea, nationalism has no intrinsic power to create any national identity. It may, however, be appropriate to, and harness, a sense of national identity which already exists.

In terms of nation-building, this is crucial, for it clears away any notion that the idea of nationalism may of itself evoke loyalty. Identification with, and loyalty to, the nation is evoked from actual experiences in which it is psychologically beneficial to make the identification. The next section describes how this process of evocation takes place.

THE PROCESS OF NATION-BUILDING

Nation-building requires that the mass of individuals make an identification with the nation-state. Following identification theory, this requires:

1   That the individual actually experiences the state
  and
2   That this experience is such as to evoke identification.

This evocation will come about if symbols of the state – be they individuals, ideas, or rituals – present a mode of behaviour or a set of attitudes the adoption of which will enhance identity and psychological security.[29] Again, following the theory presented in the previous chapter, internalisation and identification will occur if:

1   Symbols of the state present an appropriate attitude in situations of perceived threat, or
2   Symbols of the state behave beneficently towards the individual.

The symbolic representatives of the state may be formal individuals, institutions and ideas – e.g. monarchs, structured benefit systems and constitutions. They may also be informal individuals, institutions and ideas – e.g. tavern patriots, longbows and ballads. It is crucial, of course, that the symbol is clearly associated with the state. The symbol associated with the state may then be a single prominent individual, or it may be a far more complex set of behavioural mores represented by a more general social group. An identification made with such a symbol may then be reinforced by informal and formal social rituals in which people communicate together about the commonly held identification. In states where the nation is already 'built', it is, of course, these rituals and communications which, from infancy, socialise the child into being a national citizen.[30]

In studying states where there is the appearance of successful nation-building, we should, therefore, be able to discern clear historical circumstances which would have evoked identification with the nation-state. There should be features of the state acting to defend against threat, or features of the state acting as a materialistic benefactor – or both.

For the purposes of illustration, the features of nation-building in late mediaeval France and England are now examined. I chose these two countries because it is generally held that they demonstrate, along with a few other western European countries, the first examples of the modern nation-state. Had I, as a scholar, been located for example in America, Africa or Asia, then perhaps my choice would have been different. But, if the theory is structurally sound it can be universally applied.

NATION-BUILDING IN MEDIEVAL ENGLAND AND FRANCE

To modern perceptions, contemporary Britain and France provide apparently classical examples of states in which the nations are fully built. Political culture mediates successfully between the state and the national population. Both states display a history of political integration and an internal coherence which is reflected in a clear political solidarity in relation to the external environment. This coherence, however, is by no means perfect. Observed closely, both states also display disintegrative dynamics in terms of ethnic groups and sub-nationalities seeking greater political self-determination. In Britain the relationship of Scotland, for example, to the United Kingdom is continuously in flux and evoking special treatment from Parliament and Whitehall. In France there are also peripheral nationalities, such as the Bretons, continuously evoking special attention from Paris; also in France, albeit perhaps only superficial, is the centuries-old cultural gap between north and south which seemed to reappear during the Second World War as the division between German-occupied France and Vichy France.

The comments of the preceding paragraph are to underline that in discussing successful nation-building, we are, in actual fact, discussing not a theoretical ideal model but an existential, dynamic and changing socio-political organism. In discussing, then, the nation-building that took place in mediaeval England and France, we are not focusing upon a process with an empirically observable completion. Instead we are delineating those historical features which, within the methodology provided by identification theory, explain the nation-building which has taken place.

Nation-building, as an ideal model, is never complete, for two reasons: First, there are always individuals and groups who, for one reason or another based in previous identifications, do not identify with the nation-state. Second, historical circumstances change and there may, for example, be policy trends in government or changes in international relations which actively alienate groups and individuals from the nation-state.

Even a casual study of English and French history indicates that the two countries are definitely not Seton-Watson's 'old continuous states'. In terms of power political realities, the English state did not territorially approximate to its contemporary boundaries until after the Norman conquest in the eleventh century; equally, the French territorial state was arguably not complete until the 1600s. The appearance of continuity comes perhaps from a sense of natural boundaries, but perhaps more so from the images learnt in the study of Latin and of Roman history. From ancient Rome's perspective, the different clans, tribes and kingdoms had a virtually irrelevant profile. What existed were two territories, *Britannia* and *Gallia*, Britain and Gaul. Before the Romans, these two territories were definitely not, either formally or informally, coherent political or cultural entities. It might, then, seem that contemporary Britain and France are the direct descendants of those two Roman provinces – the political arrangements continuing under new masters across the whole of the two territories – but that is also wrong. After the collapse and withdrawal of Roman power, the two territories fragmented into warring kingdoms with no sense of an overarching identity or even of pragmatic forms of political integration. This is not to deny that there was sometimes cooperation in the face of invasion, but this cooperation had no staying power that was demonstrated in political and territorial arrangements.

Moreover, many of the invasions were successful. The genetic stock of the British and French nations is substantially different from that of the two territories two millennia ago. In Britain, the Angles, the Saxons, the Vikings and then the Normans came. In France, there were also great invasions, the greatest of which is symbolised in the change of the country's name from Gaul to France; one can still argue today about who are the genuine Frenchmen – the Gauls or the Francs.

Although the territory of France was consolidated later, and more gradually, than that of England, both countries began to manifest an increasingly authoritative and centralising monarchy during the same period; furthermore, these new governments implemented policies which reached beyond barons and feudal lords to touch the mass national peoples. Certainly at Runnymede in the signing of the Magna Carta, the English monarchy had *de jure* acknowledged the actual power relationship between Court and barons. But, having made that acknowledgement of power, the monarchy reached over the heads of the barons to give protection, and social and economic justice, to the peoples. Whether the impulse for such a policy was idealistic and Christian, or whether it was based in the instinctive creation of a third force – the people – in order to create a new balance of power with the barons, is not here important. What is crucial, however, is that the new policies – introduced from the twelfth century onwards – touched the people and evoked their identification with the nation-state. These policies were introduced over several centuries and, certainly by the 1500s, it was expected that monarchs would not be concerned simply with their own privileges and powers – for which they might perhaps need to barter with barons and feudal aristocracy – but that they would be concerned with the total good of their country and of their people. There are many interpretations, Marxist and power political, that can be made of this change in regal attitude. It might, however, be easiest to adopt an interpretation which sees that a certain degree of territorial stability allowed the monarchy to return to the implicit social contract that had always existed between chief and tribe in more 'primitive' historical situations – that of mutual benefit and reciprocity.

If warfare and political contract rearranged the territorial patterning of western Europe, what were the actual factors that led the parochial loyalty of individuals to village, town or shire to be transferred to the emerging mediaeval state? To answer this question, the focus will be first of all upon those features of relationship with the external environment which evoked identification, and then upon domestic policies and realities.

EXTERNAL REALITIES

In the period under focus, certain clearly observable national identities had already begun to emerge at a social level which were not directly involved in court rivalry. 'I tell you confidently', the Bishop of Seez, for example, wrote to Pope Innocent III about the impending

Crusade, 'and I believe there are many who agree with me here – that it is very important for this business that the Germans should not march with the French; for we cannot find in history that they were ever in accord in any momentous common enterprise.'[31] The conflict and rivalry between nationalities was actively in evidence not only in the armies of the Crusades, but also within the monasteries, within the hierarchy of the Roman Catholic Church and in the universities.[32] In fact, 'it is clear by the end of the eleventh century that the Europe of the future is not going to be built up politically as an empire, and that the ultimate development of some form of national state is assured . . . In the twelfth century, though the sense of a common Christianity is the predominant characteristic of the age, the development of national characteristics proceeded apace.'[33]

This is particularly interesting because national identities were manifesting themselves more strongly than the European identity of being fellow citizens of Christendom, even though the language, Latin, and the religion, Christianity, were shared. This conflict between nationalities could be observed at its most extreme in the university towns, as national gangs of students roamed the streets seeking, often fatally, conflict with each other.[34] This sense of national identity manifested itself when individuals of different cultures came into contact. Psychologically threatened by the alien culture, the individuals sought security with those who shared the same culture, with those with whom there was a shared sense of identity. The individuals, then, actively pursued the defence or enhancement of their shared identity by formal and informal group rituals, of which the university street gangs were but the most extreme example.

The loyalty, or degree of national identification of the feudal lord, however, might be purely instrumental and based in political considerations; but it can be clearly observed that there was an emerging sense of national identity in the clerical, monastic and warrior class.

This evocation of national identity in the face of external threat, in the face of 'other' actors was amplified immensely by the Hundred Years War. In England and France, it is certain that a sense of national identity spread from the elites who were directly involved in the affairs of Christendom through to all those who were directly and indirectly touched by the Hundred Years War.[35] It was this protracted conflict, Trevelyan wrote, which brought England 'strong national self-consciousness; great memories and traditions; a belief in the island qualities . . .'[36] A similar process also took place in France throughout the same period,[37] the psychological reality personified in charismatic and mystical form by the Maid of Orleans, Joan of Arc.

It is necessary, of course, to be explicit about how the Hundred Years War evoked this general national identification. At first study it may appear peculiar that this general sense of nationality was, in fact, evoked, for the numbers involved in the actual warfare were relatively small – the largest army fielded was barely some thirty thousand men[38] – and there was no modern mass media to communicate about it. Moreover, the companies of soldiers were originally organised on a basis of loyalty to their feudal lord and not on a basis of loyalty to the general cause. Indeed, as Finer nicely pointed out, the whole operation would have a contemporary parallel if modern armies were arranged so that each officer financed and brought along his own retinue, tank and airplane.[39] As the war progressed, different methods of conscription, recruitment and organisation were used.[40]

The important point, however, is that, regardless of conscription methods, all across a specific geographical territory – in this case England and France – men were engaged in a similar endeavour, an endeavour which was defined by opposition to an outside culture. The fighting men themselves – whether fighting for wages, for feudal obligation or for glory – had acquaintances, friends and relations. The fighting men came from, and returned to, local communities. Even though the largest force fielded was only thirty thousand, over time – and the duration here was that of a century – no local community in France or England would have been excluded from some form of contact with the war. This contact would have included the formal rituals associated, for example, with the death of a relative, neighbour or landlord – or associated with a victory; it would have included the semi-formal rituals of ballads, poems and stories;[41] and it would also have included the informal rituals, for example, of gossip and drunken boasting. In these situations, the mass of people would have experienced being communicated about as members of this one national group threatened by another national group. They would also have experienced the psychological security of being identified with the individuals who were actually communicating about the experience. Therefore, although not having actually fought in the war, the mass of people experiencing these various social rites were able to share in a group security and enhanced identity – the national identity of being English or French.

The communication about the war was similar regardless of the shire or province in which the communication took place; its basic structure was that of a common endeavour against a common enemy performed by a people sharing a culture and *sharing the same monarch*. This point about 'sharing the same monarch' is crucial, for the fighting monarch is here the supreme symbol of the nation. The monarch is also, of course, the supreme head of state. Moreover, it is the state apparatus which actually organises the defence of the nation. The identification made by the mass of people was simultaneously with the English – or French – nation and state.

This experience of shared communication about the war was reinforced by other common experiences initiated by the emerging state structure and concerned with the war, such as shared economic measures to pay for the protracted adventure, and active court encouragement of martial arts. For example in England, 'in the fourteenth century the longbow became more and more the prescribed weapon, and the practice at the butts behind the churchyard became the chief sport and excitement of village life. Edward III encouraged it by royal proclamation, *prohibiting by pain of imprisonment* – handball, football, or hockey; coursing and cockfighting, or other such idle games.'[42] So effective was this building of a sense of nationality that by the time of Henry VII, the Venetian envoy to London could write: 'They think there are no other men but themselves, and no other world but England; and whenever they see a handsome foreigner, they say "he looks like an Englishman".'[43]

It is clear, then, that the Hundred Years War was a protracted event that created all the circumstances likely to evoke national identification with the nation-state from the mass of people in England and France.

DOMESTIC REALITIES

During this same period, there was a clearly discernible general trend for the policies of the newly emerging state – edicts from the King's Court – to be directed at all social levels and to cover the whole territory. These policies could be experienced as directly beneficent and, therefore, evoking identification. They directly touched an increasing number of subjects whose previous experience of government had been limited solely to parochial landlords and barons. Most importantly, these emerging state policies were not complied with because of the threat of naked force, but because they worked towards what Oresme called *publica utilitas* and the ordinances of France called *la chose publique*.[44] The purpose of these policies was not simply to benefit a landed and Court elite, but for the *public*. It is beyond the scope of this work to provide a complete picture of those policies which benefited the people generally and evoked national identification; any reasonable economic history of the period provides a full picture. It is, however, possible to pick out certain highlights:

Taxation. The new approach was particularly noticeable, for example, with regard to taxation. The whole ethos and purpose of taxation changed, away from a demanded, which was at its worst nothing but 'protection', money to revenues necessary for effecting policies to the general good. Previously, as Thomas Aquinas noted, 'the revenues of the land [were] intended to prevent those living on them from plundering their subjects'.[45] Now taxation became a necessary donation to the *publica utilitas*.

(Taxation, in fact, provides an enlightening example of how the experience of state directives can evoke either identification or alienation. If the perception of taxation is that it fulfils a materialistically beneficent role, then identification with the state will be evoked. Contrarily, if the perception is that taxation is an unnecessary imposition, then alienation will be evoked. Which perception applies will be partly due to actual experience and partly due to natural or politically manipulated communication about the taxation. This dichotomy between beneficent and negative intervention by the state is well illustrated by the mythical distinction between 'bad' King John and 'good' King Richard within the Robin Hood fable. One king has no interest in the people other than using them to enrich himself, for which he employs as his agents equally greedy men. King Richard, on the other hand, loves his people – even if he is a thousand miles away he is at least at the national sport of war – and whatever money he takes is for the public good, if only the enhanced sense of national identity that comes from prestigious endeavours abroad. King John, of course, does not evoke identification with the nation-state and is the destroyer of a sense of national community. King Richard, on the other hand, is the successful nation-builder. One can see this syndrome illustrated during the Hundred Years War: the English were happy enough to pay for it while victories were being achieved in the field, but, by 1381 when the war was going badly, widespread tax evasion was evident.)[46]

This *publica utilitas* was not simply the protection of national sovereignty via the monarch's army, but also included various state functions bringing social justice and economic benefits.

Law. This period saw the emergence of legal systems propagated by the Central Court. The King's peace, the King's courts and Common Law all emerged in England in the Middle Ages. Whereas, for example, in Canute's time the monarch's rule of law covered only his own household, a few great highways and the great Church festivals, 'by the end of the twelfth century . . . all serious offences involving a breach of the peace are now Pleas of the Crown, and most Pleas of the

Crown are now heard in the Royal Court'.[47] This meant that the ordinary inhabitant of the land was now protected by a law that emanated from the central organs of the state and it was a law to which they had direct access; pleas could be, and were, brought, for instance, by 'quite humble persons in respect of quite small plots of land'.[48] The reign of Henry II – 'The Lawgiver' – was particularly associated with this emergence of Common Law and Trevelyan suggests that it was this sense of justice which, for example, allowed Henry II to have no standing army and even to encourage his subjects to be armed.[49] This is certainly indicative of successful nation-building. In France, Louis VI, for example, became famous as a defender of law and justice, thereby extending the influence of Paris by drawing upon common sentiment.

Trade. Although personal taxation could evoke either identification or alienation, central economic interference in international trade worked in two ways to evoke identification. First, by the imposition of tariffs at national boundaries, 'real' frontiers were created. Economic competition, previously between individual entrepreneurs, was now framed by the edicts and borders of the nation-state. What might previously have been a rivalry between cultural trading groups was now formalised by political decision and state intervention. This formalisation of economic competition between geographical territories made what had previously been the business of the individual entrepreneurs into a communal/national interest. As a competitive game, it *per se* evoked identification within the in-group/out group syndrome.

But the purpose of this central interference in trade was not simply to raise money for the Exchequer, but was designed also for the general good and economic protection of the country. Thus the state was acting as the parental and materialistic benefactor. The ordinances on international trade were preceded by central directives that affected domestic modes of production and the trading of wool and cloth; the first great measure of government control of the English cloth industry was the Assize of Cloth in 1197 which, for example, confined the manufacture of cloth to the towns and laid down comprehensive regulations for its size and quality.[50] The geographical distribution of sheep-rearing and the wool industry, and the use of wool by everyone for their clothing and blankets, ensured that these ordinances affected every member of the population. On the international stage in 1275, for example, Edward I imposed export duties on all wool, wool-fell and hides. Two years later in 1277, the French replied by prohibiting all wool exports.[51] Later, when Edward I had settled his differences with

69

Philip the Fair, the Flemish were excluded from trade in England in return for a ban on Franco-Scottish trade.[52]

Labour. State interference in production and trade was paralleled by edicts concerning labour. In 1349, for instance, maximum wages were fixed by law in England; at the same time, standardisation of the fees of craftsmen and artificers was introduced. And three decades later it was laid down that anyone who had served in husbandry up to the age of twelve had to continue to do so; similarly legislation was enacted to mobilise vagrants and beggars into the labour market.[53]

Communications and public health. The state also interfered in communications, public health and to alleviate dearth. France in particular embarked on a programme to improve communications by building new roads and by simplifying the systems of tolls. There was direct intervention in urban living conditions. Severe measures were introduced to prevent streets from becoming increasingly narrow, paving was introduced and monumental fountains for hygiene were constructed.[54] In fact, in France, the welfare, rather than the authoritarian role of the French monarchy, was so evident that in an ordinance for pastry cooks, Charles VI announced that he had the right 'to dispose and order the estates, trades, crafts and other activities in which our subjects are engaged day by day for the common good and their own sustenance, so that by good governance . . . each may be preserved, maintained and conserved by our edicts . . . whereby each one of them can remain and live in good tranquillity and peace under us'.[55]

In measures that could only be interpreted as being for the public good, the new central state organs also took measures against dearth and the threat of famine. In France, grain exports and inter-regional trade were banned on several occasions. In England, the regulation of the food trade included the control of the prices and standards of quality of the prime necessities; and in actual times of dearth the Court facilitated the import, for example, of Baltic wheat.[56]

The preceding discussion demonstrates that there were considerable factors which, over a long period of time, provided the appropriate circumstances for evoking mass identification with the nation-states of England and France. There are clearly observable state actions and events which impinged directly upon the experience of the inhabitants of the state's territory.

There was no natural community of an English or French *volk* which produced, as if out of a Hegelian conjurer's top hat, the nation-states of Shakespeare's England and the Sun King's France. The expansion of the domain of the principality of Wessex over England, and that of the Ile de France over France, were power political processes. Protracted international conflict and beneficent state actions evoked the national community. A sense of national community identified with state symbols – the concordant identification of culture and polity – was the result of a lengthy shared experience in which actions of the state, domestically and internationally, directly touched the mass of citizens and evoked their identification.

These various actions of the nascent French and English states were, of course, only the beginnings of an expanding process of inter-state relations and central government interference in the lives of its citizens. By the mid-twentieth century, the land surface of the planet was covered only with competing nation-states, and domestic state interference in the developed countries had evolved to become the fully-fledged welfare state in which the central organs of government had taken over the multiple provisions for community care which had previously been a far more parochial responsibility.

THE ONGOING NEED FOR NATION-BUILDING

Once the mass of the people have made an identification with their nation-state, then family and other social groupings will tend to socialise new generations into that same identification. It is necessary to clarify, however, the fact that nation-building is not a finite business. It is not just that every new generation requires socialising into the national community. It is also that during the lives of individuals, the constellation of socio-economic and political realities is constantly changing. As the identification imperative is always seeking to maximise psychological security, new identifications and new loyalties may come about. Apparently dead peripheral ethnic identities may turn out to have been only slumbering, and regional demands may suddenly put severe pressure on central government. Equally, revolution may threaten the state which disregards the identification dynamic across a whole class.

Nation-building is a problem, therefore, not only for developing states, but is also a prime, ongoing necessity of contemporary politics in all developed states. Much of the art of contemporary mass politics is in attuning to, playing to and orchestrating this dynamic. Indeed, this is the very stuff – philosophically, theoretically and practically – of legitimacy in the modern state.

WHY THE NATION-STATE AND NOT THE TRIBE, CLAN OR SECT?

The whole of the above discussion has been concerned purely with the identification made with the nation-state. But the individual can, of course, make other identifications – many other identifications. These identifications can be on any scale from that of a one-to-one identity (e.g. student with sympathetic teacher) through to that with the whole of humanity (planetary citizen). From the perspective of this book, the interesting and most important other identifications are those which might compete with the state.

Given the right images and communications, citizens are prepared to fight and to die for their country. It is part of the ideology of the nation-state, part of the nation-state's identity-securing interpretive system, that citizens defend it, if necessary by force of arms. It is, equally, part of the ideology of the clan, the tribe, the nation (without a state) and of many religious sects that they too be advanced and defended.

Identification theory, as such, has nothing to say about the outcome in a situation where there are divided loyalties. The human being seeks physical and psychological safety. In some cases, an individual will betray a belief (an identification) rather than die. In other cases, the individual is prepared to die rather than betray the belief and negate an identity. Individuals are unique beings with unique histories. Some are brave, some cowards; some introvert, some extrovert; some calm, some excitable; some guilt-ridden, others liberated, and so on. Many personality factors need to be taken into account before one can define or suggest how an individual will behave in relation to her/his identifications in any given situation. Moreover, there is a constellation of dynamic external factors which bear down on each unique situation. What are other people doing? What communication is believable? Is there a perception of genuine threat? Is the threat immediate and potentially lethal, or distant? What do colleagues/friends feel and plan?

In a situation where there is a conflict of loyalties, actual behaviour will depend upon the psychology of the individual and upon the environmental input. The inability to be more precise is shown up by suggesting two scenarios. In one, the individual is strong-willed and *ignores* forceful propaganda and crowd hysteria (on behalf of clan, tribe, nation or sect) even though s/he may be identified with the cause. In the other scenario, the individual is weak-willed and simply carried along by the group's enthusiasm even though s/he might not be identified with the cause.

The degree to which the nation-state itself holds the loyalty of the inhabitants of its territory will depend exactly upon what degree it has implemented or appropriated nation-building. If there has been no nation-building, then obviously other identifications and loyalties will prevail. Equally, if the state, having previously nation-built, then implements, or is perceived to implement, policies that disadvantage and alienate, other loyalties will again prevail.

The state, however, does possess – or theoretically should possess – one overwhelming existential advantage over other entities that would compete with it for the citizens' loyalty: within its territory, the state possesses, ultimately, the monopoly of force and power. It possesses also, ultimately, control over the media. The nation-state also owns an ideology which goes virtually unquestioned, that it is normal and good to fight to preserve it. In a very different dimension, the nation-state can be seen to possess the ethos and the constraints of the mafia; conscientious objection is the pariah's choice. Thus, although there may be competing identifications with the nation-state, the nation-state controls an array of communications and functions which bear down heavily upon citizens. So powerful is this array, that rarely nowadays will the church, sect or clan go against the state; although the state, as a matter of political pragmatics, may well adjust its policy to take account of the church, sect or clan.

One can, then, look at the various factors which will affect loyalty in any given situation.

a   Individual psychological traits.
b   Degree to which identification has been evoked. (Some interesting empirical questionnaire research could be pursued here with questions such as: 'I would be prepared to die rather than see my (delete as appropriate) family/village/church/country disappear.')
c   Intensity and perceived reality of communications and propaganda.
d   The general reaction and discourse of fellows who share the same identification.
e   The sanctions and constraints possessed by the entity claiming the individual's loyalty.

NATION-BUILDING AND INTERNATIONAL IMAGES IN THE CONTEMPORARY WORLD

It is worth underlining that the nature of the contemporary world is such that *explicit* conflict and external threat are not necessarily required for nation-building. This is because the modern international system provides ever-present images of competition and threat.

Statehood in the modern world context involves certain realities which are unavoidably constrained by the nature of the international environment. These external realities, regardless of any state's unique internal social system and political culture, tend to define and highlight the relationship between a state and its external environment as a relationship of threat, competition and conflict. Various factors work towards this effect.

The primary images inherent in the international environment are those of international competition and conflict. Every infant is born a citizen of a state and the infant's nationality is necessarily defined by contradistinction to the external environment.[57] Historical and contemporary realities, from warfare through to sport, demonstrate a scenario of competition. Power politically, each state has emerged from a usually bloody political history of either conquest or liberation. Moreover, despite the degree of international law and cooperation that does exist, force remains the potential final arbiter of all international disagreements. And economically, of course, statehood immediately places the polity into an internationally competitive system, as each state competes in a world economic system to achieve internal economic growth and successful balance of payments figures.

This means that there is a natural dynamic, in terms of images and realities, which works towards identification with the nation-state. The nation-state into which the infant is born as citizen is in a state of permanent competition with its international environment. Other countries are competitors in the great international game. It is clear, therefore, that there is a further inherent dynamic in the contemporary images of international political competition to create us/them, in-group/out-group perceptions and attitudes in terms of domestic national citizens versus international aliens. To avoid citizenship and national identity is extremely difficult – so difficult, in fact, that in the contemporary world, to be without nationality is to be perceived as almost without identity.

SUMMARY

Let me make clear the basic propositions of this chapter:
1 Nation-building can be investigated at a purely social–psychological level of analysis defined by identification theory.

2   Nation-building only occurs if the mass of citizens, directly or indirectly, actually experience the actions of the state.

3   These actions will evoke identification and, therefore, nation-build only if:

   a   The state is perceived as being involved in a common endeavour in relation to an external threat; or if

   b   the state acts beneficently towards its citizens.

4   The nation-building experiences of mediaeval England and France provide a model which can be generalised.

5   Nation-building is a dynamic process and not finite.

6   The images of the contemporary international system work towards nation-building insomuch as they present a picture of international competition.

In the next chapter, the relationship of nation-building, mass mobilisation and foreign policy will be examined, and in the final chapter there will be an examination of the policy implications for nation-building.

4 THE NATIONAL IDENTITY DYNAMIC AND FOREIGN POLICY

INTRODUCTION – THE MASS PUBLIC AS FOREIGN POLICY VARIABLE

It is important to understand clearly the relationship between the mass national public and government decisions, not simply for the sake of political analysis. It is also important that we should be able to think clearly about 'what is the proper relationship between a society and those professionally responsible for its external affairs'.[1] Because of the methodological difficulty, however, in generalising from the individual out to the group,[2] there has existed a specific difficulty in foreign policy and international relations theory in understanding the role of the mass public, or in using the mass public as a theoretically integrated variable. There have, nevertheless, been two lines of approach to the subject, the first of which has been unconcerned about the methodological difficulties, and the second of which has self-consciously floundered in them.

The first approach has been that of the strategists and realists who have straightforwardly recognised the mass population as being one of several resources available for foreign policy and, in the final analysis, war.[3] If war is diplomacy conducted by other means, then those means include the men and women prepared to take up arms. Put at its most basic, this is a recognition of the mass public as cannon fodder, as another power resource. This approach to the populace can be made slightly more subtle by the further recognition that it is not only the quantity, but the quality that matters.[4] As Francis Bacon wrote, 'Walled towns, stored arsenals and armories, goodly races of horse, chariots of war, elephants, ordnance, artillery and the like; all this is but a sheep in a lion's skin, except the breed and disposition of the people be stout and warlike. Nay, number itself in armies importeth not much, when the people is of weak courage; for as Virgil saieth: "It never troubles a wolf how many the sheep be".'[5]

In an age of 'total war', this requires, in strategic terms, that the people as a whole must be capable of being mobilised and of remaining mobilised. This, of course, is only possible if there has been successful nation-building. (It is, of course, irrelevant in the case of nuclear holocaust triggered by a few individuals.)

Hans Morgenthau was fully aware of the necessity of nation-building, but his understanding of the mass national public was distinctly coloured by his Hobbesian vision of human nature. Thus, he saw the mass public which has identified itself with the nation as an amorphous force, prey to the primitive dynamics of nationalism and actively seeking foreign aggression. In fact, Morgenthau understood the highest feat of statesmanship as 'trimming his [the statesman's] sails to the winds of popular passion while using them to carry the ship of state to the port of good foreign policy'.[6]

At the very least, Morgenthau had a clear theory about the mass public as an actor in international relations. The mass public has passionate public opinions which work directly upon those in government, and public opinion is 'a dynamic, ever-changing entity to be continuously created and recreated by informed and responsible leadership . . . it is the historic mission of the government to assert that leadership lest it be the demagogue who asserts it'.[7] According to Morgenthau, then, the mass public is instinctively aggressive, but plastic and capable of being manipulated. The statesman thus stands as 'superman' reigning in the primitive beast. It is important to note that Morgenthau has had an immense influence on the post-1945 study of international relations, and his understanding of mass national publics is, therefore, part of the subliminal intellectual baggage carried by students and practitioners who have been persuaded by Morgenthau's realist paradigm. Morgenthau, however, never provided any clear analysis of his basis for making such an assumption about human nature and mass national publics.

Governments, however, do have to be sensitive to the general *will* of the mass national public – acknowledging the norms of democracy (and all states claim democracy) and acknowledging the practical consequences of pursuing unpopular policy. The relationship between the mass national public and the government exists, but it is difficult to analyse. Kenneth Younger, for example, wrote of British foreign policy that although he could think of no occasion when he or his superiors had been greatly affected by public opinion in reaching important decisions, nevertheless, 'the government tends to identify itself almost unconsciously with a vaguely sensed general will, and no clear formulation of the pressure of public opinion upon government policy ever occurs'.[8] And, as Kurt London wryly remarked, 'There is no constitutional provision in any country, democratic or totalitarian, which would include public opinion as a co-determinant in [foreign] policy-making.'[9]

There is not only a problem in analysing the relationship between public opinion and policy-making – 'Probably no aspect of foreign policy', wrote Holsti, 'is more difficult to generalize about than the relationship of public opinion to a government's external objectives and diplomatic behavior.'[10] There is also the severe difficulty of building consistent theory about public attitudes. Although, for example, there has been an immense amount of research into public opinion, especially in the United States,[11] the problem has been to find any consistent causal relationship between environment and attitude. Rosenau produced a suggestive framework for analysis, but no consistent variables that were capable of being operationalised.[12] And one researcher in this field was finally led to describe the connection between public opinion of foreign policy and the electoral behaviour of the same public as 'chaotic'.[13]

Even those writers, however, who sought to take a behaviouralist or scientific approach to the problem, had a distinctly cynical view of the mass public and public opinion. Although lacking the Hobbesian 'realism' of Morgenthau, they perceived the major features of public opinion in relation to foreign affairs to be emotionalism and unpredictability. James Rosenau wrote that the mass public's response to foreign policy matters was 'less one of intellect and more one of emotion; less one of opinion and more one of mood, of generalized, superficial, and undisciplined feelings which easily fluctuate from one extreme to another . . . The most predominant mood of the mass public is, of course, indifference and passivity – except for acute peace-and-war crises.'[14] Even more brutally, Rosenau went on to quote Gabriel Almond, stating that the cumulative effect of public opinion could be 'under-stood in terms of the analogy of loaded pistols which are triggered off by special issues which bring generally inattentive and uninformed groups into a sudden impact on the policy-making process'.[15]

There has been a general tendency, then, to divide the public into two sections: (1) a small, thoughtful and attentive group 'which is informed and interested in foreign policy problems, and which constitutes the audience for foreign policy discussion among the elites'; and (2) a much larger general public which 'reacts to general stimuli'.[16] There has been no analytical success, though, in defining the nature of the attitudes of the general public, nor of the relationship between the general public and government decisions. There is certainly the recognition of such a relationship, but the only clarity to be found is in the Morgenthau view of the 'super-statesman' taming and harnessing the beast.

Identification theory, however, provides a precise tool for defining and investigating a general level of analysis for the relationship between the mass national public and foreign policy decisions. Identification theory can demonstrate several consistent features in (1) the mass national public's attitude to international relations and (2) the relationship between the mass national public and actual foreign policy decisions. The next section of this chapter is concerned with making these general features explicit. It is then followed by illustrative case histories.

THE NATIONAL IDENTITY DYNAMIC

If nation-building has been successful, then identification links the individual citizen with his or her mass of fellow citizens through the shared national identity. Thus:

> If there has been a general identification made with the nation, then there is a behavioural tendency among the individuals who made this identification and who make up the mass national public to defend and to enhance the shared national identity.

This tendency as it works through the mass national public may be called the *national identity dynamic*.

If, then, images and experiences concerning international events are presented to the mass public in such a way that either (1) national identity is perceived to be threatened, or (2) the opportunity is present to enhance national identity – then the identification imperative will tend to work through the mass public as a national whole. The mass national public as one group will seek to secure, protect and enhance their general national identity. The *national identity dynamic*, therefore, describes the social–psychological dynamic by which a mass national public may be mobilised in relation to its international environment.

This is to state explicitly that the mass national public has a clear and psychologically coherent relationship with international affairs.

> The mass national public will mobilise when it perceives either that national identity is threatened, or that there is the opportunity of enhancing national identity.

79

Moreover, identification theory makes explicit the structural features of the relationship between the national identity dynamic, the state decision-makers and the international environment. It is possible to delineate a triangular relationship between:

1 The mass national public.
2 Government foreign policy decisions.
3 Images of the relationship between the nation and the international environment which threaten or provide the opportunity of enhancing national identity.

The logic of the relationship is as follows:

1 Images of the international environment can mobilise the national identity dynamic.
2 Government may create/manipulate these images in order to mobilise the national identity dynamic.
3 Factors beyond government control may create/manipulate these images. The mobilised national identity dynamic may then affect government foreign policy-making.

This can be summed up:

> The state, in terms of its foreign policy decisions, may trigger, manipulate, appropriate – or be manipulated by – the national identity dynamic.

and

> The national identity dynamic can be triggered by international images manipulated by the government *or* by other actors.

The mass national public is thus shown to be a discrete actor in the foreign policy decision-making process:

> The mass national public will always react against policies that can be perceived to be a threat to national identity.
> The mass national public will always react favourably to policies which protect or enhance national identity.

DOMESTIC POLITICAL COMPETITION AND THE NATIONAL IDENTITY DYNAMIC

The national identity dynamic is triggered by political circumstances, and it is necessary to look at the general nature of these circumstances. It is, of course, in the very nature of domestic politics

that there should be competition to trigger, manipulate and appropriate the national identity dynamic. The political attractiveness of the
national identity dynamic, of the mobilisation of mass national sentiment, is that *it is the widest possible mobilisation that is available within a
state*. It theoretically includes the total national population, transcending political, religious, cultural and ethnic factions. If a politician,
therefore, can symbolically associate her/himself with national identity
and mobilise it, s/he will then possess a virtual monopoly of popular
support.

As the national identity dynamic, based in the identification imperative, is constantly seeking enhancement and is therefore volatile, *it is a
permanent feature of all domestic politics that there be competition to appropriate the national identity dynamic*. This is to say that political factions
compete with each other to be perceived as the party whose policies
and utterances most enhance national identity and protect it from
foreign threat. No politician seeking popular support can run counter
to this dynamic.

Furthermore, there is that other political reality – that, in the face of
continuously changing political and socio-economic realities (which is
in the nature of contemporary life), nation-building is an ongoing
necessity. It is a necessity in order to maintain political integration and
stability. Thus, there is ever-present the temptation for government to
nation-build by mobilising the national identity dynamic in relation to
the international environment.

These two dynamic political factors – (1) domestic competition and
(2) the ongoing necessity of nation-building – mean that no government can afford to ignore the national identity dynamic lest it be
triggered or appropriated by political opponents.

In relation to international affairs, then, this means that every
government must be concerned about how its actions are perceived by
the mass national public in relation to the national identity dynamic. A
government's foreign policy may thus be dictated by internal domestic
political realities as much as by the actual nature of its international
relations.

FOREIGN POLICY MANIPULATION

The key to foreign policy as a tool for nation-building is that
foreign policy can create a situation in which the mass of people can
perceive a threat to their communal identity, or an opportunity to
protect and enhance it. The government *qua* state then acts as the
parental or significant symbolic figure which is fully involved in the

protection and enhancement. The government-as-state thus is perceived, and psychologically experienced, by the mass national public as being one with the national community. Government, state and national community are entwined as one bundle of symbols representing national identity.

Foreign policy can create a situation in which the whole national community can be perceived as sharing the same experience in relation to a foreign actor.

Whether the social–psychological theory is self-consciously understood by the decision-makers or not, the opportunity is always present for a government deliberately to use foreign policy as a method of mobilising the mass national public sentiment away from internal political dissension, and achieving political integration. In these situations, the government appropriates the mobilised national support on behalf of the nation and, at a very practical level, any anti-government behaviour can be interpreted as anti-nationalist, unpatriotic and treacherous. It is, therefore, of course, a well-remarked syndrome for governments to distract attention away from domestic crises by creating involvement in international crises.[17] The social–psychological dynamics of this syndrome, however, have not previously been analysed. The reality is not simply that 'attention is being distracted' – but that a deep psychological motivation has been tapped and triggered.

It should also, of course, be noted that even if the national identity dynamic is purposefully triggered and manipulated by government, it can still, like the forces unleashed by the sorcerer's apprentice, run out of control. A government's international posturing may trigger a mobilisation of the national identity dynamic that forces the posturing into real action – for if there is no action, the government will lose credibility and fall prey to internal political opposition.

The national identity dynamic can, of course, be triggered and mobilised by sources other than the government or state. Once triggered it has a powerful momentum which has to be acknowledged by government in terms of its foreign policy. This is simply based in the practical fact that no government can afford to ignore the pressure of such a substantial political force. This, of course, is the art of politics, the art of adept response to the general will. It is not capable of the kind of scientific measurement which would be sought by a behavioural approach to politics, because it concerns the images that politicians and statespeople have of their domestic political environment, and the calculations they make of how they can affect that environment.[18]

There are clear historical examples of the mobilised national identity dynamic, of public opinion, forcing governments into aggressive international behaviour. Public opinion, for instance, clearly took the United States into the Spanish-American War. The Anglo-Spanish War of 1739 was more popularly known as the War of Jenkins' Ear, for it was the severing of the English sea-captain's ear which mobilised the English people (the said English ear being the symbol of the English national identity) so that Walpole, against his better judgement, was forced to war with Spain.[19] The Crimean War was also precipitated by public opinion in Britain and France, as the two countries competed with each other to force Russia to back down over the guardianship of certain holy places in Jerusalem.[20] And in Japan, at least since the Meiji Restoration, public opinion and spontaneous mass mobilisation have been central factors in the making of an aggressive Japanese foreign policy; it was, for instance, specifically public opinion which took Japan into Korea in 1894 and into the war with China in the same year.[21]

NATIONAL INTEREST, NATIONAL PRESTIGE, HIGH AND LOW POLITICS

National interest. This clarification of the nature of the national identity dynamic and its general effect on foreign policy, also allows for a certain clarity with regard to the notion of *national interest*.

It is possible at a social–psychological level of analysis defined by identification to state:

National interest is that which:
(a) can be perceived as being a part of national identity
and thus
(b) is capable of triggering national mass mobilisation to defend or enhance it.

Such a definition, if accepted, clears up the difficulty over whether or not national interest is a useful analytical term or a term that is so diffuse in its meaning as to be useless. Classical definitions of national interest, for example, state that national interest is the preservation and enhancement of security of a state's territory and of the core values and culture of its citizens.[22] As an academic tool for analysing foreign policy, however, the concept has had apparently little use as it is bound by value ideas of what is 'best' for the nation and, as Furniss and Snyder stated, national interest is frequently 'whatever the decision-maker says that it is'.[23]

But this is exactly the point, for national interest defines that political arena of discourse in which those factors that affect the national identity dynamic are communicated about. The political rhetoric, therefore, in which the domestic power competition for control of the national identity dynamic is communicated, is framed, rationalised and legitimated by the concept of *national interest*. Certainly, national interest may be whatever the decision-maker says it is, but we can be clear that the decision-maker's purpose in so saying is to mobilise the national identity dynamic. Certainly, the actual content matter of national interest may be redefined, but the redefinition concerns what may or may not mobilise the mass national public. Politicians and decision-makers may attempt any number of ruses to harness the national identity dynamic. National interest is the basket which contains issues that mobilise, or which politicians assume or think should mobilise, the national identity dynamic.

In terms of political analysis then, national interest has no conceptual use as a tool for ranking foreign policy priorities. It does, however, describe a discrete social–psychological structure – the arena of communication and discourse for mobilising the national identity dynamic.

National prestige. Equally, 'national prestige' as a factor in contemporary international relations[24] receives some methodological clarity from identification theory. Following the *Oxford Dictionary*'s definition of prestige as 'influence exercised or impression produced by a nation's or institution's or person's reputation', and following identification theory, it can be stated:

> National prestige describes the influence that can be exercised or the impression produced by virtue of events and images that devalue or enhance national identity.

Thus, an increase in prestige is synonymous with any circumstance that enhances national identity; a decrease in prestige is any circumstance that devalues national identity. National prestige is, therefore, of course, a matter of perception and communication, and political leaders will seek to associate themselves with it as a way of appropriating the national identity dynamic.

It can be said, therefore, that states compete with each other for prestige, not because it is inherent in the nature of the international system so to do, but because it is an outcome of the domestic internal political competition to control and appropriate the national identity dynamic. Equally, it is not necessarily, though of course it may be, the result of statespersons' seeking ego gratification. From a practical point of view, the statesperson who succeeds in acquiring an increase in national prestige for her/his country will also tend to mobilise mass national public sentiment behind her/him.

High and low issues. This clarification, at a social–psychological level of analysis, of national interest and prestige points out that there exist two distinct levels of interstate activity. The first level is that which involves the national identity dynamic. The second is that which does not involve the national identity dynamic. The dividing line between the two levels is porous, as foreign policy issue areas move between a high and a low profile.

This differentiation has been clearly delineated, for example, in the workings and structure of the European Economic Community in which functionaries, civil servants and junior government ministers deal with the low issue areas, while prime and foreign ministers deal with the high issue areas. This occurs because all high issues can be appropriated by the domestic political competition to mobilise the national identity dynamic, whereas low issues are simply functional. A politician, of course, can change the status of a low issue providing that s/he manages to communicate about it in such a way that it becomes relevant in terms of national interest or prestige.[25]

All of this is to say that no government, or any political group seriously vying for power, can afford to put forward a policy that is outside the accepted rhetoric of national interest; i.e. no policies can be put forward which can be perceived as threatening or destabilising national identity. Politicians, therefore, have always to exercise great caution in order not to be associated with policies that can be interpreted, perceived or communicated about as being contrary to national interest. To do so is to risk being perceived as a threat to national identity and, therefore, to alienate mass national opinion.

MODERN MASS MEDIA AND NATIONAL AND INTERNATIONAL IMAGES

The practicalities of mass mobilisation have been profoundly facilitated, of course, by the nature of modern mass media. The importance of mass media rests on the fact that they are the major actors in the transmission of the communications which may effect and trigger the national identity dynamic. Images concerning symbols of national identity can be communicated to the whole nation at the same time.

In the past, communications concerning national identity were passed by proclamation, by pamphlet or from person to person. This, in turn, meant that (a) communications to the mass public took time, and (b) that it was less easy for any one source to possess a monopoly of communication as the modes of communication were *per se* decentralised. Contemporary mass media, however, provide the opportunity for virtually instantaneous mass communication and also for a monopoly of that communication. The possibility exists, there- fore, for a modern government to sustain a continuous manipulation of the national identity dynamic for political purposes. Thus, an immediate division can apparently be made between those mass media which are state controlled and those which are free and 'independent'.[26]

Such a division, however, is more apparent than real because a free press, like a controlled press, needs to satisfy the demands of its patrons – whether these demands are political or for financial profit. Ironically, this leads the press, in both open and closed societies, to manipulate international news in order to manipulate the national identity dynamic. Of course it is accepted, in times of international crisis and in situations concerned with national security, that a free press should function under much the same constraints as the most controlled totalitarian press, and that its truthfulness and freedom become 'the first casualty'.[27] But in times of peace, and free of govern- ment control, there is a clearly observable tendency within the media to dramatise and to play up international conflict. This is not simply due to the fact that very few journalists of international affairs have been academically trained in the discipline.[28] It is also due partly to the fact that there is no mass market for foreign policy analysis as such,[29] but most importantly it is due to the fact that national chauvinism is commercially successful.

In explaining this success, Nimmo and Combs have argued in *Mediated Political Realities* that a successful news story must be struc- tured on the classical elements of melodrama:

> Moral justice is at the heart of most melodrama – trials of the virtuous, calumny of the villainous, good rewarded, evil punished. Suspense is the key – from certain death to miraculous safety, disgrace to vindica- tion, paradise lost to paradise regained, vanquished to victor. *Anxiety is provoked*.
>
> These characteristics are more than qualities of melodrama, they are requirements. Related as they are to the elements and structure of dramatic logic, they define what an account must have to be melo- dramatic. They add up to a 'melodramatic imperative'.[30]

The main thrust of their thesis is to demonstrate how this imperative works in political news, with a section specifically devoted to foreign crises.[31] That this mode of presenting news should be attractive and influential makes intuitive sense; that the dramatic presentation of crisis should be entertaining is not extraordinary. What is extraordinary is that its emotive force is such that it can mobilise opinion in favour of war, and motivate those opinion-holders actually to go to war. Identification theory provides clear insight into the dynamics of this motivation.

In the media coverage of international politics, Nimmo and Combs's 'melodramatic imperative' manifests itself within a stylistic framework of 'them' and 'us'. Within this framework, the media can appropriate any international issue and use it to defend or enhance national identity. The murder of a fellow citizen overseas, for example, can either be reported noncommittally, or can become an issue that is projected as threatening national identity. The same is true of any foreign event which involves an entity which can be identified with national identity, e.g. 'Indonesian' tourist, 'Japanese' company, 'Tanzanian' minister, and so on. Symbolically, then, what happens to the tourist, the company or the minister, can be perceived, and experienced through shared identification, as happening to the total national group. In terms of the 'melodramatic imperative' of newsmaking, there is a consistent tendency to project international news as a function of an ongoing competition between the in-group/nation and the out-group/international environment. Insomuch as all of a state's foreign relations can be perceived as an interaction between symbols of national identity and outside actors, all international interactions are, of course, capable of being appropriated and projected as affecting national identity.

From the perspective of the free capitalist press, the nation-building which results from this mode of international news presentation is coincidental to sales success. It may be that the editorial policy of a newspaper is patriotic and that it is considered editorially appropriate always to support competitive national chauvinism, but it is also financially successful as the mobilisation of the mass public ensures high sales. National chauvinism can be as appealing as sexist pin-ups.

The sales dynamic that comes from chauvinistic international reporting became apparent, for example, in Britain in the late nineteenth century when increased educational possibilities and new technologies were making a mass media possible. During this time, narrow party political stances were dropped by papers contending for the mass audience and were replaced by patriotism and imperialism, and 'blustering chauvinism marked the treatment of foreign affairs'.[32] This

87

chauvinism was remarkably successful in increasing sales; during the Boer War, for example, the *Daily Mail*'s sales increased some three hundred thousand to over a million.[33] This concern with commercial success rather than responsible reportage and analysis predominates in the mass circulation popular press.

The unacceptable face of this struggle for commercial gain *par excellence* was seen in the well-known circulation war that took place in the late 1890s between the *New York Journal* and the *New York World*. The proprietor of the *New York Journal*, William Randolph Hearst, recognising the need for a good story to boost sales, sent an illustrator to Cuba to provide illustrations of the insurrection against the Spanish. The illustrator found no such war and cabled Hearst: 'Everything is quiet. There is no trouble here. There will be no war. I wish to return.' Hearst cabled back: 'Please remain. You furnish pictures. I will furnish war.' The subsequent blowing up of a United States battleship in Havana harbour provided Hearst with the opportunity to wind up public opinion and boost sales; and war duly ensued.[34]

The power of the mass media and public opinion brought a substantial new factor to foreign policy decision-making in the nineteenth century. As Hale comments, however rarefied the environment of diplomacy and state practice, the elite could now 'not free itself entirely from the prejudices, the attitudes, and the opinions of the mass electorate, and these elements had to be reckoned with in the determination and execution of policy'.[35] The reality of this new relationship between decision-maker and mass national public was crudely expressed by Lord Milner's categorical statement that 'what is needed is a serious and resolute propaganda. The ordinary man has to be convinced of the burden before his answer is required.'[36] This sentiment echoed Bismarck who had once said that 'if diplomatic dispatches were published his work would be doubled, because he would be forced to write one dispatch to accomplish his purpose and another for publication'.[37]

A two-tier system of communication about international affairs is, of course, precisely what does exist in all countries whether their societies are open or closed. There is one tier of information possessed by the security services and decision-making elites; there is another tier in the public domain. The restriction on complete disclosure is precisely to avoid the possible triggering of the national identity dynamic which would take decision-making out of the hands of the 'responsible' and informed few.[38]

All of this is to point out that the modern mass media have

powerfully augmented the role of the mass national public as a factor in foreign relations. Arguments about policies which promote the interest of the state in relation to its international environment no longer solely take place in the rarefied atmosphere of an interested elite; any issue may at any time trigger the national identity dynamic if it is taken up by the mass national press.

CLASSIFICATION

It is possible now to suggest a taxonomy or classification which may help clarify the types of relationship between the national identity dynamic and foreign policy decisions. Three basic patterns are discernible:

1 *National identity as a foreign policy resource*. Government evokes the national identity dynamic for the pursuit of strategic foreign policy goals.

2 *Foreign policy as a tool for nation-building*. Government uses foreign policy to evoke the national identity dynamic for the purposes of nation-building with the result that either

(a) the national identity dynamic remains under government control

or

(b) the national identity dynamic, once mobilised, influences government.

3 *National identity dynamic triggered by non-government actors influences foreign policy*. Other actors evoke the national identity dynamic and the mobilised national identity dynamic then influences the government's foreign policy decisions.

The use of a 'resolute propaganda' to mobilise the mass national public behind a foreign policy that has already been decided or implemented (1) is not the concern of this thesis.[39] My purpose here is to illuminate the dynamic interaction between the national identity dynamic and foreign policy decisions – 2 and 3. The following brief foreign policy studies provide illustrations of how identification theory can be usefully applied as a tool of analysis. The canvasses are large and the brush strokes are necessarily broad; in the final chapter I discuss the methodological criticisms that can be levelled at such an approach. I do wish to stress again, however, that this mode of analysis is not intended to subsume the strategic realities of the situations described. It is merely intended to hold a mass psychological focus as defined by the national identity dynamic.

UNITED STATES FOREIGN POLICY AND THE COLD WAR

It is possible to state in a somewhat crude fashion that since 1947, for an American President or Presidential contender to be perceived as being soft on the Soviets or on Communism is to commit political suicide. The Soviet Union has become inextricably involved in the domestic politics of the United States in so much as its image has become a semi-automatic trigger for mobilising the national identity dynamic.

Most analysis of the Cold War and of its origins has focused upon the *strategic* competition between the two superpowers.[40] This analysis is based on the view that the two superpowers are in a real situation of jockeying for power. Decision-makers, then, both in the United States and in the Soviet Union, have based their foreign policy decisions on a strategic assessment of the configurations of the conflict. Decision-makers' perceptions, for one reason or another, might have been dissonant with 'reality' but the general paradigm that there was United States/Soviet conflict was accurate. The major thrust of the analysis, then, was to understand how the two sides were viewing each other and to assess the value of their respective strategic policies. There is, however, a domestic factor based in the national identity dynamic which provides another perspective.

This dynamic can be seen as having been set fully in motion by McCarthyism.[41] A full analysis of McCarthyism and the anti-communist hysteria of the late forties and early fifties is beyond the scope of this thesis, but it is worth drawing out certain distinctive connections between domestic political realities and United States foreign policy.

McCarthyism emerged in the United States in the years immediately following her victory in the Second World War, and as United States foreign policy became internationally engaged. The victorious images of 1945 which enhanced national identity were, however, being tainted by several other events distinctly threatening to United States prestige and national identity: Mao Tse Tung defeated the United States-backed Chinese nationalists under Chiang Kai Shek; there was the continuing aggressive ignoring of wartime agreements by the Soviet Union in Eastern Europe and elsewhere; there was also the failure to achieve a unified non-communist Korea. Despite, therefore, the allied victory of 1945, the United States' engagement in world politics could be clearly perceived and interpreted as unsuccessful and threatening to United States national identity. Joseph McCarthy, using the mobilisation of the national identity dynamic as his trump card, played a crude political game.

Against this backdrop of United States failure on the international stage at the hands of communist opponents, and with the help of a non-discriminating media and opportunistic, frightened or genuinely rightist politicians, McCarthy mobilised a substantial portion of mass public opinion behind a witch-hunt for communists within the United States establishment. He stated that a communist conspiracy directed from Moscow was responsible for American failure; and the national identity dynamic was mobilised against this enemy, i.e. against Moscow and against communism, all of which was Moscow-controlled. Indeed, McCarthy's initial accusation in February 1950 was that there were covert communists in the State Department itself and it was they who were responsible for United States failure abroad. For two years McCarthy received widespread support as 'a dedicated patriot and guardian of genuine Americanism'[42] while he triggered and sustained the hysterical witch-hunt of domestic communists. Finally, after a farcical 36-day televised hearing of his charges of subversion against army officers and civilian officials, McCarthy began to be seen more generally as the irresponsible manipulator that he was and he was ejected from the United States political scene.

The dynamic, however, that he had set in motion was immensely powerful and was not so easily removed. In terms of emotive rhetoric bound to trigger the United States national identity dynamic, the Soviet Union became (at least until the time of writing) a permanent feature of United States political culture. This is to say that the rhetoric of national interest which frames United States foreign policy was inextricably based in implacable opposition to Soviet/Communist threats. It can be said that this was the result of the domestic manipulation of the national identity dynamic, and not the result of a reasoned strategic reaction to external realities. Whatever the genuine strategic threat posed by the Soviet Union, and whatever the genuine Marxist–Leninist ambition for international proletarian revolution and global communism, psychologically the Soviet Union and communism had been appropriated by the domestic political competition to mobilise and harness the American national identity dynamic.

Certainly, since 1950 no President has been able to conduct a foreign policy with Moscow free of this highly charged domestic atmosphere. And, of course, real Soviet actions have been easily open to interpretation in such a way that they fit these perceptions, thereby reinforcing the dynamic.[43]

It is possible, then, to interpret the major thrust of United States foreign policy towards the Soviet Union as just as much a function of internal political competition to appropriate the national identity dynamic as it is the result of rational strategic decision-making. It is possible to understand the national identity dynamic as a substantial variable influencing United States foreign policy towards the Soviets.

In a very real sense, then, United States foreign policy is caught in domestic mass social–psychological constraints which continually play on the themes of national interest, national prestige and the struggle with the Soviet/Communist adversary. This spills over into other issue areas of United States foreign policy as the structural dynamics of this situation tend (1) to define *all* enemies of the United States as Soviet inspired communists and (2) to define *all* the enemies of the Soviet Union and of communism as friends and allies of the United States in the struggle to preserve freedom and democracy.[44] One clearly observable spillover has been in its own continental foreign policy.

Since the enunciation of the Monroe Doctrine in 1823, the whole of the American continent has been straightforwardly designated as a sphere of United States interest in which Washington would brook no outside interference. Since the inception of the Cold War, however, United States foreign policy in Central and Southern America has been legitimated in the rhetoric of the Soviet/Communist threat. Beneath the rhetoric, the actuality may well still be that United States policy in Central and Southern America has been motivated by simple power political or economic interests; it has not, however, been justified in those terms. It has been justified in the language of a response to Communist threat. There is an obvious tendency, then, for United States foreign policy to be legitimated by recourse to the anti-Communist rhetoric that mobilises national identity. Insomuch as this rhetoric has become a fixed part of popular political culture, United States foreign policy is a prisoner to it.

This anti-Communist, anti-Soviet, Cold War rhetoric, released into the political environment in the early fifties, has thus taken on a clear domestic dynamic of its own in terms of its mobilising appeal to the United States mass public and the need for American politicians to kowtow to it. Its exact role in decision-making obviously varies from situation to situation, as it works in relationship with domestic political contingencies, international realities and how these events are communicated and perceived. It is, however, a clear structural dynamic in the foreign policy process.

Purely in terms of identification theory, this history can be interpreted thus:

A non-governmental actor mobilised the national identity dynamic. It was then appropriated by Government, but took on a momentum of its own which continues to influence Government.

It is interesting at this point just to mention the possible interpretation of the Cold War as a function of the ongoing need for political integration and nation-building in both the United States and the Soviet Union. According to this interpretation, both societies suffer severe internal contradictions, and successive governments have, therefore, played up the Cold War in order to mobilise national sentiment and ensure internal coherence. The accusation has been levelled by one side against the other[45] and the Soviet leaders, of course, have not been slow to recognise the need for symbols more potent than dialectical materialism in order to stimulate and mobilise the Russian people. The language of 'Russia the motherland' has intertwined with that of Marxism–Leninism. A full discussion of this tantalising issue is beyond my scope and perhaps, following *glasnost*, no longer immediately relevant.

THE FALKLANDS/MALVINAS CONFLICT

The national identity dynamic, once deliberately mobilised, can run out of control. Equally, when mobilised by non-governmental actors, it can be appropriated by government for its own narrow political purposes. The Falklands/Malvinas conflict of 1982 can be interpreted as illustrating both cases.[46]

In the years immediately preceding the Argentine invasion, the Buenos Aires military junta was facing severe domestic difficulties due to economic failure and social injustice. To mobilise the national identity dynamic and thus ensure popular support for its regime, the junta began to play up the issue of sovereignty of the islands. Britain, which in fact was an historical and economic ally, was now projected as an imperialist enemy who was holding on to islands that were part of Argentina's sovereign territory. The islands were projected as a part of Argentina's national heritage and thereby had a psychological share in the dynamics of national identity; the British were the threat to this identity. In this situation of perceived and carefully projected threat, the junta could be seen to share the same experience as the Argentine people, and all mobilisation of the national identity dynamic could be appropriated as political support by the junta.

The rhetoric of retrieving the islands from the colonialists, however, obviously demanded action, action that had previously seemed out of the question due to the British naval presence. At this time, however, the British government, and particularly the Foreign Office, were careless in how they communicated about British resolve to hold on to the islands. This created a situation in which the junta had no excuse for winding down the rhetoric for action, and any back-down by the junta would have been domestically extremely dangerous. The momentum created by the junta's early actions, helped especially by the apparent lack of British firmness over the issue, left no choice but invasion. The first foray into the Georgias induced no British reaction and so a full-scale invasion was unavoidable. Ultimately, of course, the Argentine defeat led to the complete collapse of the junta and the imprisonment of its leaders as popular support reversed to almost complete alienation from the government. The Argentine nation remained built, but the state had to undergo substantial political adaptation in order to remain in tune with its people.

The British government's behaviour during this episode can also be interpreted using identification theory to define the level of analysis and to put forward the national identity dynamic as a coherent foreign policy variable. Although there were certain strategic and economic reasons for Britain to stay in the Falklands, the Foreign Office had in fact been seeking an accommodation with the Argentines for some time. Had it not been for the British nationals on the islands and the pressure from absentee British landlords, it seems probable that the islands would have been abandoned long before. And in the event, the Argentine interference in South Georgia was responded to with little resolution.

As a result, however, of the main invasion, the House of Commons was called to an emergency session on the morning of Saturday 3 April 1982. The Prime Minister opened the debate with a statement which demonstrated concern, but which certainly did not resonate with any patriotic or nationalist fervour; this was hardly surprising considering the lack of firm response to the Argentines in the preceding months. The speakers that followed her in the House of Commons debate, however, set up a chorus of jingoism in which only one voice of moderation was heard.[47] 'As speaker after speaker rose, Thatcher, astonishingly, seemed in danger of being outflanked on the right. Labour's leader, Michael Foot, veteran of peace marches through the decades, employed unprecedented warrior rhetoric . . . hardly a word of caution crossed his lips.'[48]

Whatever the Prime Minister and her cabinet might have been considering as potential policy before the debate, the mood of the House, and the jingoism on both the government and the opposition

94

benches, determined the path that she had to take. All the symbolic phrases that would mobilise the national identity dynamic were being used. In this situation, any voice raised against a belligerent stance was a voice not truly British, was a voice unpatriotic and perhaps even treacherous.[49] Even if, following the debate, the government had been inclined towards moderation, the popular press had taken up the note of national chauvinism, further mobilising opinion.

Whether she appropriated this momentum as an act of self-conscious political artistry or whether she was simply an enthusiastic victim, Mrs Thatcher directed the tidal wave of mobilisation through a successful military operation.[50] Moreover, the momentum of the mobilised national identity dynamic, with which Mrs Thatcher as leader of the British people was fully identified, continued for several years. The momentum of this dynamic was so clearly observable to political commentators that it was actually named 'The Falklands Factor', and was deemed by many to have won the Tories the next election. Certainly any Conservative domestic failures, particularly in the field of economics and unemployment, were forgotten.

This whole episode, then, following identification theory, could be summed up:

> The Argentine government mobilised the national identity dynamic in order to nation-build, but the mobilised national identity dynamic then forced the government into adventurism. Finally perceived, after defeat, as *the* threat to Argentine national identity, the government fell.
>
> In Britain, non-government actors started the process of mobilising the national identity dynamic which was then successfully appropriated by Government.

UNILATERAL DISARMAMENT AND AMERICAN BASES IN THE UNITED KINGDOM

The debate in the 1960s and 1980s in the United Kingdom over nuclear disarmament and American bases on British territory also provides an interesting area in which identification theory can be applied.

The campaign for British unilateral disarmament achieved little popular or media support. On the other hand, the campaign of militant, pacifist, feminist women at the Greenham Common American military base against the use of British territory for launching American missiles, received much more coverage and popular sympathy. This support was evoked despite the fact that the women themselves had a group image quite alien to mainstream British culture.

According to identification theory, the mobilisation of popular support for unilateral disarmament can only come about if the arguments for such a policy are framed in such a way as to be seen to enhance national identity. Most of the campaign, however, was framed within the rhetoric of idealism and 'world peace'; there was not even any sustained attempt to build up a powerful propaganda, based in the enhancement of national identity, by blazing a path of moral rectitude.[51] The opponents of unilateralism, however, were able to argue the need for strength and deterrence in the face of external threat. Whatever the actual strategic rights and wrongs of such a policy, it is obvious that the 'cold warriors' possessed far more emotively effective symbols for harnessing the national identity dynamic. It seems safe to predict, therefore, at the time of writing (1987), that if the Labour Party leader is to have any success with a policy of unilateral disarmament it will be because (a) the issue is kept in low profile compared to other policy arguments, or (b) he propagandises it as an enhancement of British national identity through moral leadership of the world, or (c) he projects conventional defence in a way that enhances identity rather than as a soft option. (I once saw a unilateralist persuade a large drunken bully of the merits of unilateral nuclear disarmament by saying: 'If they invade, at least you can fight them properly.' I do not put this forward as meaningful academic evidence.)

The Greenham women demonstrators, on the other hand, despite their general protest on behalf of 'life on Earth', presented a case that was clearly framed in a 'them/us' mode that could evoke the national identity dynamic. In this case, the 'them' was the United States whose bases demeaned national prestige since they could be perceived as pieces of British territory colonised by the Americans and beyond sovereign British control. Demonstrations around these United States bases, rather than those against the British nuclear capability, received approbatory press coverage and much public support.[52] Identification theory suggests that this phenomenon was not to do with the logic or rationality of any of the arguments, but was based in the mobilisation of the national identity against an external actor. It would seem, for example, that it was precisely the same syndrome which took France out of the formal structure of the North Atlantic Treaty Organisation, while she still remained securely within the western alliance.[53]

It is interesting to contemplate the possibility that the Greenham movement, which finally lost political steam, would have had a more sustained and more morally effective result had it been focused against British nuclear establishments. The protest might not then have received the immediate popular support that it did, but its essential arguments would not have been transcended and appropriated by a superficial anti-Americanism.

According to the level of analysis defined by identification theory then, it is possible to summarise thus:

> Two non-governmental actors sought to affect British foreign policy concerning the crucial subject of defence. The Campaign for Nuclear Disarmament did nothing to evoke the national identity dynamic and received little popular support. The Greenham movement, however, did evoke the national identity dynamic and received a measure of public support.

GREECE, TURKEY AND THE CYPRUS CONFLICT

The conflict between Greece and Turkey over Cyprus, in terms of the national identity dynamic, displays clear elements of manipulation, appropriation and then loss of control of the national identity dynamic.[54]

The coup of April 1967 in Greece brought into power a military regime which possessed minimal popular support. Constraint and terror replaced democratic legitimation. In 1973 and 1974 the situation became increasingly unstable, manifesting itself in massive street demonstrations, increasingly bold protests by students, and the mutiny of the navy. In the face of this severe domestic instability, albeit funded perhaps by the United States, the right wing junta decided to accelerate the process of *enosis*, the union of Cyprus and Greece, thereby mobilising the people behind a common national goal and securing a huge popular victory for itself. The Greek soldiers, who were stationed in Cyprus and who formed the National Guard, were ordered to lead a coup against Archbishop Makarios and to install a right wing stooge, Nikos Samson. They obeyed their orders.

It was impossible for the regime in Turkey, which was also dealing with domestic instability, not to react. There was a long history of intense rivalry with Greece over Cyprus, which was exacerbated by a complex of other long-standing disputes in the Aegean. In fact, the Turkish government had several times previously threatened to invade Cyprus, but had been placated and held back by United Nations intervention. The actual military interference by Greece in

Cyprus was an act that directly threatened Turkish Cypriots and one to which the Turkish government had no choice but to respond. In terms of the national identity dynamic, the attack on Turkish Cypriots was a clear threat to Turkish national identity, and a lack of military response by the Turkish government would have led to its downfall. The lack of policy options available to the Turkish regime was, then, based in the domestic dynamics whereby any action that was seen to be soft on the Greeks would have discredited the regime at the widest possible level.

The efficient and successful operation of the Turks was in stark contrast to the bombastic ineptitude of the Greek military. Within two days, Turkish troops had taken over 40 per cent of the island. What popular domestic support there had been for the Greek regime collapsed completely as the temporary identification with the junta, as representative of national identity in a situation of national mobilisation, turned to alienation. The common enemy, which had been the Turks for threatening national identity, now became the junta. The national identity dynamic, which the junta itself had triggered in order to appropriate its support, became the very cause of mobilisation which created the opportunity and dynamics to topple it. The Turkish regime was strengthened.

Following identification theory, it can be summed up:

> In order to nation-build, the Greek junta embarked on an adventurist foreign policy to mobilise the national identity dynamic; the adventure failed, alienating the mobilised dynamic from the junta. With Turkish national identity threatened, the Turkish government replied successfully and appropriated mobilised mass public opinion.

THIRD WORLD FOREIGN POLICY

Identification theory also suggests a possible general interpretation of the way in which the national identity dynamic may affect the foreign policy process of developing countries. It is, of course, dangerous to analyse at this level of generality, but the constraints of economic development and of nation-building suggest certain general structural features.[55]

The socio-economic and psychological pressures to achieve economic growth are considerable. Unlike those nation-states which were formed and integrated prior to 1945, the post-1945 states exist in a global communications village. Images of industrialised bourgeois life are communicated to the very centres of poverty and distress. This means that group and individual identities are threatened by images of metropolitan peoples who, by virtue of the possession of wealth and technology, have *in reality* a greater control over the primordial forces of life themselves – food, clothing and transport. As Sukarno remarked wryly, but with a sense of its profound reality, 'A refrigerator is a revolutionary symbol in a hot country like mine.'[56]

Added to these pressures to modernise, there are, in many African and Asian states, the other extreme pressures of ethnic, tribal or religious cleavage created by the metropolitan imposition of borders resonant with imperial and not native interests. The straight lines of the cartographers of the Congress of Berlin had no concern for 'natural' tribal territories. In fact, within most of the new African states of the 1950s and 1960s the only unifying domestic element which cut across tribal divisions was the shared experience of this European imperialism. If there was a geographical identity beyond that of the tribe, it was that of being a black African who had been subject to, and was now liberated from, white dominion. And, in fact, this particular sense of identity was sufficiently strong for there to be, before the realities of domestic political tensions and international competition took hold, a substantial pan-African movement based in this common identity which looked forward to a United States of Africa.[57]

The pressure to nation-build and achieve political integration, however, went hand-in-hand with the pressure to achieve economic growth and industrialisation/modernisation. According to identification theory, nation-building can be achieved either through materialistic state beneficence or through the use of an external threat. If neither of these policies is adopted, or if adopted are unsuccessful, perhaps due to lack of resources, then internal force must be used to constrain political integration. This general situation gives rise to an interesting syndrome which can be observed in terms of nation-building, foreign policy and the two broad sweeps of policy available – *laissez-faire* or socialism – to achieve economic growth. The two different strategies towards growth, *laissez-faire* and socialism, have distinct implications for nation-building.

If a policy of *laissez-faire* is adopted, then capitalist success at the centre of the state 'trickles' out to the periphery. If a socialist policy of state intervention is adopted, then the 'trickle' is replaced by centrally directed redistribution. Both these approaches are, of course, aiming at the same goal which is to achieve the socio-economic conditions already 'enjoyed' by the first and second worlds.

A distinctive feature of these two policy options, however, is that nation-building based in state beneficence under capitalist policies will

99

take longer than nation-building under socialist policies. This is so because under capitalist policies, there is bound to be a substantial time-lag before the beneficent results of the creation of wealth at the centre by an entrepreneurial class is felt by the whole population. In some cases, one wonders if it will ever reach the total population. Social justice and economic redistribution are not the major priorities of a government dedicated to economic growth through *laissez-faire* capitalism. There is, therefore, a huge perceivable disparity between the economic conditions of the centre and the periphery. Also, in very practical terms, while the wealth is being created, there are neither the resources nor the political will to finance social welfare and general state intervention in order to bring about the kind of nation-building discussed in chapter 2. Moreover, general global economic conditions may not even allow any wealth creation at the centre of new states.

A developing state, however, which deliberately adopts socialist policies can touch peripheral groups very quickly. This is not simply based in the peripheral peoples being directly and materialistically touched by state beneficence, but can be profoundly affected by a political style in which the metropolitan decision-making elite projects a clearly perceivable image of equality with their people. The socialist state prioritises social justice and economic redistribution alongside economic growth and wealth creation. Policies of social welfare are introduced as high priorities, and even if the resources are slender there will be a tendency away from ostentatious displays of wealth by the metropolitan elite.

None of this is to argue the economic and more general political case between *laissez-faire* and socialism. It is, however, to posit that:

> In developing states, socialist economic policies will tend to evoke nation-building more quickly than policies of *laissez-faire*.

We can now take up two earlier propositions:
1 Successful nation-building is a prime power resource of effective foreign policy.
2 A state may resort to an aggressive foreign policy in order to evoke nation-building, *but* will not do so if there is a possibility of risking internal cleavage.

A general model of developing states' foreign policy now suggests itself:
    a Developing states that adopt socialist economic growth policies will achieve early national integration and, relying on the

national identity dynamic as a resource, may, therefore, adopt aggressive foreign policies.

b   Developing states which adopt capitalist economic growth policies, and which have internal cleavages based in ethnos, tribe or religion, will not be able to rely on the national identity dynamic and will tend not to adopt aggressive foreign policies. If they do adopt them, the likelihood of internal collapse is high.

c   States which use internal force to constrain political integration may adopt the rhetoric of aggressive foreign policy in order to justify internal repression; this rhetoric, however, may mobilise the national identity dynamic so effectively that the rhetoric may spill over into actual international conflict.

Risking again the criticism of using too wide brush strokes on too broad a canvas, the following brief examples are illustrative.

Nigeria. Nigeria presents an interesting example of a state with a low profile foreign policy. Despite the fact that she is the richest and most powerful black African state, her foreign policy is both regionally and globally passive.[58] She has kept a low profile in the major local issue of French influence and a low profile in the major continental issues of neo-colonialism and the white South African regime. This is resonant with the fact that Nigeria is pursuing an economic policy of *laissez-faire* capitalist growth from the centre, and has a history of severe internal cleavages of which the breakaway of Biafra was an extreme example.

Libya and Tanzania. In contrast to Nigeria, Libya and Tanzania, two African states with extremely high foreign policy profiles, are both states with domestic policies that are highly focused on government intervention, social welfare and national integration. Though varying greatly in terms of economic resources, both Libya and Tanzania have pursued policies in which the government has acted as a materialistic benefactor to the population as a whole, regardless of class or ethnic status. According to one set of figures, Libya has the highest level of general welfare expenditure of any country on the African continent, including South Africa.[59] Tanzania, on the other hand, although beset by ongoing economic difficulties, has pursued a consistent policy of communal and self-reliant socialism as laid out in the Arusha declaration of 1967. Despite its poverty, then, Tanzania has displayed remarkable internal stability and social cohesion.[60]

Libya's foreign policy has been dramatic in terms of its revolutionary nature, its attempts at integration within the Arab nation and its support of international terrorism. Tanzania's foreign policy has also been extremely independent in terms of its aggressive non-alignment,

101

its moral stance and its material support for other African states. In 1978, in particular, after an incursion of its borders by Ugandan troops, Tanzania's retaliation led to the occupation of the Ugandan capital and the downfall of President Amin.

Once again, this is not to deny or to attempt to belittle the crucial role played in all this by strategic and other political realities, particularly the personalities of Mohamir Ghaddafi and Julius Nyere. It is, however, to point out that both leaders could act with confidence because they possessed widespread popular support based in success-ful nation-building.[61]

Argentina and Chile. Those South American states with policies of internal constraint for political stability, and of giving low priority to social and economic justice, tend to demonstrate an aggressive foreign policy rhetoric but a low profile in reality, unless the rhetoric overspills into action as was the case with Argentina and the Malvinas. There is also a general tendency here to have a military that is used for internal order rather than external security, and to attempt to use minor border and territorial disputes to mobilise the national identity dynamic.[62]

Indonesia. Indonesia provides a clear example of how a change in economic growth strategies was reflected in a change in foreign policy orientation.

From the time of national liberation until his overthrow, President Sukarno conducted a domestic policy of socialist nation-building which, despite divisive class, religious and ethnic divisions, was successful in terms of building a single political community.[63] At the same time, Sukarno was adroit in focusing national attention upon foreign policy issues for which his government's position had over-whelming national support, particularly with regard to anti-imperial-ism and the recovery of West Irian.[64] Sukarno's foreign policy was aggressively non-aligned and independent.

His overthrow and replacement by Suharto ushered in a completely new form of domestic policy, one based purely in *laissez-faire*. National cohesion began to disintegrate and the government resorted to terror and constraint in order to maintain internal order.[65] Concomitantly, there was a substantial change in Indonesian foreign policy away from aggressive non-alignment to a clear and passive alignment with the United States.[66] Once again, this is not to suggest that strategic and economic motivations are to be ignored – especially the new *laissez-faire* society's economic dependence on United States capital. It is only to point out the suggestive relationship between internal factors, based in mobilisation of the national identity dynamic, and foreign policy. A

102

policy of socialist nation-building under Sukarno was accompanied by an aggressive foreign policy; under Suharto, the new capitalism was accompanied by a passive foreign policy.

Burma. An interesting counterpoint to the preceding examples is provided by Burma which, after the coup of 1962, turned from a policy of active international involvement, particularly in the non-aligned movement, to one of almost complete isolation. The new government of General Ne Wim was dedicated to a policy of national integration based in traditional Burmese values. According to the perception of Ne Wim and his colleagues, all international contact, especially with cosmopolitan bourgeois culture, was destructive to the cultural integration of Burmese society. On assuming power, the Revolutionary Council, for example, banned beauty contests, required civil servants to wear the traditional *longyi* and insisted that members of the military forces neither displayed wealth nor indulged in conspicuous consumption; communalistic policies for growth and government were introduced.[67] In the two years following the seizing of power, all forms of external contact were perceived to be forms of interference, insomuch as they provided images and stimuli that were domestically destabilising.

To avoid the effect of destabilising images of relative deprivation inherent in global village communications and to sustain national integration, the regime adopted an aggressive foreign policy of active disassociation. In this instance, an aggressive foreign policy, that of autarchy, was a sustained and overt instrument of political integration. Whether such a policy can endure depends a great deal on whether the external threat continues to be perceived to be real.

CONCLUSION

Identification theory provides a distinct level of analysis which draws into clear perspective a consistent structural variable of the foreign policy of decision-making process. Recognition of the *National Identity Dynamic* – the giving to the mass national public of a methodologically coherent status – does not, however, give us a mechanical model for precise prophesy. It merely makes explicit the dynamics which, to a lesser or a greater degree, are inherent in the situation and which, for holistic analysis, require acknowledgement.

At the micro level, identification theory can say little about how the individual decision-makers will behave. Certainly, a powerful public opinion and a mobilised national identity dynamic must affect the decision-maker, but the actual decisions will depend upon the decision-makers' own degree of identification, peer pressure, group mores, individual psycho-history and so on – a kaleidoscope of elements worthy of substantial research.

5 IDENTIFICATION AND INTERNATIONAL RELATIONS THEORY

INTRODUCTION

In chapter 3, identification theory provided a methodological tool for investigating nation-building. Then in chapter 4, via the national identity dynamic, it was of some use in giving the mass national public a certain theoretical coherence in relation to foreign policy analysis. This chapter is now concerned with examining whether identification theory provides any useful insights into International Relations theory generally.[1] The possibility that such an approach will be useful exists because identification theory:

1   Puts forward a distinct theory of mass human behaviour

and

2   Defines a discrete social–psychological level of analysis.

The method of approach in this chapter will be to apply identification theory to what I take to be the three major areas of argument within International Relations. These are:

1   Historians/classicists versus behaviouralists/scientists.
2   Realists versus idealists.
3   State-centrists versus structuralists/Marxists.

Although such a classification risks undue parsimony, it is actually imperative to attempt to classify International Relations; otherwise there exists the very real problem of never knowing where to start. This problem is due to the fact that, in one way or another, connections can be made between almost any form of human behaviour and issues in International Relations. All insights, pre-theories, theories and world-views – psychological, social, economic and political – can be applied to International Relations. This is obviously so because the subject of International Relations is global society itself, what Charles Manning called 'social cosmology',[2] whether it is the society of four billion souls or the society of one hundred and sixty states.[3] The scope of the subject is such that any analysis of social behaviour may be subsumed by International Relations and, conversely, any presumptions about social behaviour may be generalised and projected into International Relations theory. In fact, the three divisions which I identified above can be restated in the form of three major debates which run through social theory generally:

1 Whether human beings are subject or object to social systems.
2 Whether human beings are essentially savage or cooperative.
3 Whether human society's essential structure is socio-economic or more variegated.

This chapter, then, approaches each of these divisions in International Relations, first describing the basic features of the debate and then applying identification theory.

HISTORIANS/CLASSICISTS VERSUS BEHAVIOURALISTS/SCIENTISTS[4]

The essence of the debate between the historians and the scientists concerns whether or not an explicit and internally coherent methodology, i.e. a scientific method, can be used for analysing international relations and for predicting international phenomena.

The historians/classicists criticise as wasteful scholasticism any attempt to achieve such a methodology. The essential attitude of the classical or historical approach in International Relations is to be wary of any analysis which seeks predictability beyond what is blatantly obvious. For the classicist, it is in the very nature of international relations that scientific predictability should be unattainable because of the almost infinite number of variables that are involved. To arrange these variables methodically so as to have access to any form of precise forecast is impossible.[5] This is not, however, to say that there are no general patterns which are discernible, but these patterns are to do with 'types' of situation. It is through a thorough knowledge of history that one may gain an awareness of the various patterns of action which do indeed recur in certain types of situation – and this knowledge may then be applied analogously to contemporary situations. Predictability, then, is only possible because contemporary situations are analogous to past ones, and the chances are that a certain pattern or cluster of patterns may repeat. The 'balance of power' paradigm is just such a pattern, but even acknowledging that there is such a repeatable pattern does not allow for prediction – for there are always buccaneers, cowboys and wimps on the international stage to upset the theoretical apple cart. To work with the balance of power paradigm, for example, is useful because it provides a theoretical frame within which the various possible courses of action can be analysed.

The historian may thus point out what is possible and even probable in a situation, but there are certainly no guarantees of prediction or even an attempt at 'scientific analysis'. At the very least, the historian may promise few surprises.

The behaviouralists, on the other hand, state that without an explicit methodology there can be no worthwhile analysis, as the analysis will be based purely in the ideological predisposition, explicit or implicit, of the historian. The whole classical approach is, therefore, woolly, and does not even begin to make use of the tools made available by twentieth-century social theory. Analysis based in history may be rigorous in terms of uncovering the apparent facts of a situation, and rigorous in its attempt to present all the relevant facts. But the crucial issue concerns by what criteria these facts are chosen in the first place and, again, by what criteria these facts are then related to each other. The accusation made by the behaviouralist is that the historian has no explicit methodology, has no clearly differentiated levels of analysis and works with a method that is purely intuitive or idiosyncratic. The behaviouralist seeks to bring International Relations under the same kind of methodical rigour applied to other academies in the social sciences.[6]

This debate concerning a rigorous methodological approach holds within it, though, a hidden debate concerning the more substantial issue of the nature of the relationship between the individual and society. Implicit in the classicist's position is the notion that the individual human being is capable of dynamic, initiatory and creative acts – whatever the value of the acts themselves. Thus, the individual human is obviously a major creative actor in social systems, and social systems are, in the final analysis, subservient to the acts of individuals. This is not to deny that in one form or another many, perhaps most, people are subject to social systems. It is, however, to state that all systems are, in fact, human-made, are ephemeral and may be dismantled by human action. Even when social systems are constructed with an extremely high degree of internal constraint, one individual's willpower, eccentricity or sheer stupidity may yet transcend or disrupt it. This individual may be a 'Great Man' of history, or it may equally be the unknown individual who casts the first stone or fires the first bullet. The stance of the historian/classicist is essentially humanistic.

Implicit in the behaviouralist's approach, on the other hand, are the two ideas that (1) human behaviour is predictable and that (2) human beings are subject to society. This approach is based partly in a general Hobbesian notion of society as civilising the instinctively savage human, and partly in the insights of twentieth-century social theory,

107

from Durkheim and Weber through behavioural psychology to systems theory. These assumptions of the behaviouralist marry with a methodological approach that finds its paradigm in the natural sciences and Newtonian order. In terms of this world-view, social systems are functionally integrated entities with their own coherent, scientifically analysable structures, and the human being is, thus, essentially only a social being created and constrained by the social system. The scientific approach to International Relations, then, assumes that: (a) human behaviour is predictable; (b) human action is subservient to, and determined by, the system; (c) if the system is repeated so too will be the human actions; (d) international phenomena can be quantified and ordered in such a way that distinct patterns emerge which lead to predictability.[7]

The major features of the debate between the historians and the behaviouralists appear to remain unresolved.[8] The two world-views are apparently incompatible and mutually exclusive: a system of human free will versus a system of measurable social constraint. This divide is often further exacerbated by the different personal backgrounds of the scholars – many historians totally lack any background in the methods of contemporary social theory, and many behaviouralists lack background in the humanism yet rigour of historical research.

There do exist, however, areas of International Relations study where the usefulness of discrete levels of analysis have been fully accepted by the historians, and in which coherent social–psychological theory has been successfully integrated. This area is to do with decision-making and perception. The history of this development within International Relations is well rehearsed: Richard Snyder and colleagues first identified the significance of the actual foreign policy decision-makers, particularly with regard to their motivations.[9] Graham Alison subsequently pointed out that these individuals frequently argued on behalf of their bureaucratic power-bases, rather than rationally in the interests of the state as a whole.[10] Robert Jervis, drawing on Festinger's theories of cognitive dissonance, next placed on the agenda the insight that all decision-makers were subject to cognitive predispositions and misperceptions regarding incoming information about the international environment.[11] And, during this same period, attention was also focused on the way in which decision-makers tend to behave in groups and in times of crisis.[12]

Despite quite severe criticism of these analyses, particularly of Alison's bureaucratic politics model,[13] the approaches have, in fact, been thoroughly absorbed into general International Relations analysis. This is to say that it is universally recognised within the discipline that no analysis of inter-state politics is thorough unless it has encompassed a focus on the decision-makers involved, their processes and their perceptions. Methodologically, these insights have provided a distinct level of analysis (scientific even!) which has been generally adopted. Its success has been such that the approach is now generally applied by *all* students of International Relations – including historians and classicists – as a level of analysis for investigating certain structurally inherent psychological variables in world politics. In any analysis of the relations between states, there must at some point be a focus on the decision-makers and upon the psychological factors which affect their behaviour.

That such a behaviouralist approach could be absorbed by the historians/classicists is due to the fact that theories of decision-making and misperception define *tendencies* in human behaviour and do *not* delineate situation-defined *constraints*. The level of analysis and the theory do not posit the decision-maker as a mechanistically predictable social dupe. The decision-maker still exercises unique creativity based in his/her unique situation, character and history. There are indeed certain tendencies, but there is no inherent determining factor. The human actor at the decision-making level of analysis – albeit bureaucratically inspired or cognitively misperceiving or group hysterical – is yet free to make eccentric, idiosyncratic and unique decisions that are not determined either by the system or by the psychological framework. The decision-making level of analysis and the theories of misperception and groupthink point out consistent behavioural tendencies which are not determined by the specifics of environmental input, yet are structurally inherent and unavoidable in all inter-state relations. The theoretical structures remain consistent, thus satisfying a behaviouralist approach; yet the individuals are still theoretically free to take unique and creative actions, thus satisfying the humanist historian.

Furthermore, as well as defining discrete *units* of analysis – e.g. the individual, the decision-maker, the group of decision-makers – discrete levels of analysis are also delineated. These clearly defined levels of analysis introduce a degree of methodological rigour into the criteria by which historians select and string together their evidence and material. Evidence is not drawn together intuitively, or for a coherent narrative, or in an attempt to get the 'whole' picture. Evidence is selected and arranged which is specifically and logically relevant to the particular mode or level of analysis currently being utilised – in this context, the levels of analysis delineated by theories concerning perception and decision-making.

The successful integration of these approaches into general International Relations theory suggests that identification theory can be equally well integrated. Identification theory also provides a clear level of analysis, while not introducing any deterministic constraints on human action. The unit of analysis, however, is not the relatively small decision-making elites – although they themselves, of course, are equally subject to identification – but the mass national citizenry.

Identification theory outlines the structural dynamics of the psychological relationship between a people and their nation-state. It analyses how this relationship may be developed and the elements which may create and sustain it. It explicates how the national identity dynamic is mobilised and how it can overcome, be triggered by, appropriated by and manipulated by, the state.

If identification theory and its political corollaries are accepted as useful tools for analysis, then any investigation of foreign policy decision-making and the relations between states must include, at some point, a focus upon the national identity dynamic – if only, at the very least, to acknowledge that it is not relevant to the situation being studied. Identification theory makes possible a coherent analysis of the influence of the mass national public.

Insomuch as these levels of analysis – that of decision-making and that of the national identity dynamic – and their specific theoretical tools are acknowledged and integrated by historians/classicists, so historians/classicists can claim intellectual rigour and even a scientific approach.[14] The historian can, with theoretical justification, hold on to the notion that human beings, not systems, make history. And, as discussed in the previous chapter, even those terms used freely by the classicists such as 'national prestige', 'honour', 'interest' and 'identity' now possess methodological coherence.

Moreover, these particular levels of analysis, and their psychological theories, severely criticise the most extreme behaviouralist approaches to International Relations, particularly systems theory.[15] To vindicate the operationalisation of any systems approach – i.e. the notion that a particular kind of system determines behaviour according to a set pattern – clear methodical links have to be explicated that demonstrate the *causal* connection between the structure of the system and the actual human behaviour. These causal connections must be based on clear insights of coherent social and psychological theory; if this criterion is not met, then there is no bridging logic and a systems analyst is merely working at perceiving patterns. Coincidence of behaviour is insufficient evidence. No purpose other than the construction of taxonomy is fulfilled unless the systems analyst can first demonstrate, by the explication of coherent social or psychological theory, that any social system *determines* human behaviour. This connection has thus far eluded the major thinkers in social theory. This is not to deny the attractiveness of systems or the possibility of general patterns that repeat themselves; it is merely to question its internal logic.

If the covert debate between historians and scientists in International Relations regarding the freedom of creative human action is not acknowledged, or if both sides decide to remain firmly in their respective camps – free will versus measurable social determinism – then the divide cannot be bridged. If, however, theories of human behaviour are acknowledged which, while psychologically precise and methodologically coherent – such as identification theory or theories of misperception actually work out as social tendencies, then a merging of the two camps is possible. Scientific rigour squares with the circle of humanism.

In general, however, it is possible to say that identification theory goes some way towards vindicating the classical approach in International Relations by providing it with a further psychological level of analysis that respects the dynamic nature of human beings.

As if in parentheses, it seems to me worthwhile to mention here a certain elegance in the way in which the human element in state actions has, in the theory, historically expanded. Psychoanalysis provided a scientific mode for analysing the behaviour of 'Great Men'. The decision-making level of analysis – with the analytical tools of bureaucratic politics, misperception theory, groupthink and crisis behaviour – then provided a clear and coherent frame within which to analyse the behaviour of decision-makers. Before the development of the decision-making level of analysis, there was simply no method for organising all the historical information about decision-making groups. Identification theory now frees the mass national public for analysis. The 'Great Man' approach expanded to include decision-makers which now itself expands to include the mass national citizenry. This is to be expected given the long-term historical trend away from divine kingship and absolute individual rule to the more democratic conditions constrained by a world of evolving mass media and information technology.

111

REALISTS VERSUS IDEALISTS

A second major divide in International Relations is that which exists between the realists and the idealists.

The realist proposition is that human nature is essentially savage and competitive, and that this nature inevitably manifests itself in the behaviour of states.[16] This notion has a respectable intellectual heritage beginning, at least, in Machiavelli and Hobbes.[17] And from this basic proposition it follows that the only morality in international relations is the practical one of self-help, of preserving state security and of pursuing power enhancement. Any lapse from such an approach threatens both national security and international stability because the appearance of weak resolve will tempt and lead other states to pursue their own territorial and power enhancement. The pursuit of state power is, therefore, not only a domestic imperative, but also an international good – as, through systems of self-help, of balance of power and of mutual deterrence, international order is maintained.

Moreover, given that human nature is essentially savage and aggressive, international cooperation in the form of an overarching international authority or world government would risk despotism rather than beneficence in the absence of competing and balancing power centres.

The idealist has a more benign view of human nature which is seen as essentially benevolent and cooperative. From this perspective, humanity's essential goodness is led astray by political and social dynamics. What is required, therefore, is the dismantling and then the reconstruction of political structures in terms of both inherent ideologies and hierarchies of power.[18] A good and peaceful world is possible provided we cooperate and plan together.

The realists and the idealists can both draw upon substantial evidence for their respective cases. For the realist, history abounds with examples of expansionist and aggressive states seeking territory and power enhancement at the cost of weaker, less prepared and less resolute states. Moreover, at a micro level of analysis, human beings demonstrate a propensity to behave in cruel, sadistic and destructive ways, reality frequently outstripping fiction in its horror. The idealist, however, can point to the fact that every social and political system consists of people cooperating. Cooperation is indeed the *sine qua non* of any human grouping. Further, the idealist can point out that the overwhelming majority of these groupings do not indulge in savage behaviour, either internally or externally. Moreover, in close and family groups, men and women display a distinct tendency towards selfless, self-sacrificing, generous and loving behaviour.[19]

What is clear from both sets of propositions is the precarious evidential basis for any confident assertions concerning absolute or exclusive tendencies to either savage or benign behaviour. The fact is that human beings seem capable of almost any kind of action. There exists, however, a second line of defence for both realists and idealists when presented with evidence contradictory to their stance. Realists, presented with evidence of cooperation, may argue that this is not evidence of a cooperative human nature, but is evidence of a realistic human nature: it is within order, rather than within anarchy, that human beings can best gratify their primal instincts. The idealist, on the other hand, presented with images of human bestiality, blames not the innocent human, but warped social constructs which chain free men. The realists upon one side and the idealists upon the other take heavily normative stances which are mutually exclusive. And, within International Relations, this division is demonstrated in extremity by, on one side, those students concerned with strategic affairs and, on the other, those concerned with international interdependence and integration. The two differing frames lead to vastly different interpretations and policy prescriptions.

Given that there is no safe evidential basis for exclusively justifying either position, the choice of being either a realist or an idealist is not a choice based in a clear, intellectually rigorous rationale. It must be a choice based in political, ideological or temperamental predispositions.

Identification theory, however, provides an analysis of both aggressive and cooperative mass behaviour – an analysis which bridges their apparent mutual exclusivity.

Identification theory presents this possibility because the identification dynamic works, in a janus-faced manner, towards internal group integration and cooperativeness, as well as towards external group aggressiveness. It thus provides an insight into the psycho-social *motivation* which makes for both political integration and international conflict.

The drive to internalise the mores and behaviour patterns of significant others in order to achieve psychological security, works out societally as the most basic form of cooperation: people share similar attitudes and behaviour patterns; people share a political culture. Yet once the shared culture has been achieved, the identification dynamic also works to defend and enhance that shared identity. If a mass of people who share the same national identity perceive that identity to be threatened, or perceive the possibility of enhancing it, then they will mobilise so as to defend and enhance it. The ironical truth, according to a dynamic identification theory, is that the drive to protect and enhance identity is, in certain situations, more powerful even than the drive to live. It has to be recognised that men and women sing happily as they go into battle, and some even remember wartime as the best years of their life, so great is the psychological security and euphoria which is experienced when identity is enhanced.

This crucial nature of the national identity dynamic takes on an even clearer profile when applied to defensive wars. The fight against invasion and external interference is precisely based in the fact that one people with a shared national identity is profoundly psychologically threatened by the prospect of rule by an alien culture. The crucial issue is not the *physical* threat – peaceful surrender may be gracefully accepted. What is crucial is that one people with a shared national identity – a common culture – will be ruled by, and subject to, an alien culture. And the alien culture is the very antithesis of an identity-securing interpretive system. The point that emerges clearly here is that identity is as tangible a factor as territory or property in situations of conflict; in fact, it can well be argued that territory is only a blatant symbol of national identity.

It is necessary, however, to state clearly and carefully that a perception of external threat and the ensuing mobilisation are not spontaneous. There are many hundreds of thousands of people involved, and for mobilisation to occur, these people must be presented:

1 With *images* that demonstrate external threat or the possibility of enhancement.
2 With a clear strategy of action that defends or enhances identity.

This, in turn, requires of course that some entity or entities present these images and, equally, that some individual or individuals suggest the prescribed course of political action. It is to state the obvious, but nevertheless one must be absolutely explicit, that without the projection of the appropriate images, and without the communication of a strategy for action, there would be no mass national mobilisation. This is to say that the national identity dynamic requires the appropriate trigger in order to mobilise. It cannot mobilise without such a trigger. This is not to deny that, once triggered, the national identity dynamic may roll forward with uncontrollable fury. This fury is based in the need of each individual to preserve and enhance her/his own personal identity – but mass national mobilisation will not, and cannot, occur unless externally triggered. This is axiomatic.

Thus we can state that the national identity dynamic provides the fuel and psychological motivation for aggressive mobilisation, but it requires external stimuli. These stimuli are projected images and communicated strategies. It is worth examining the sources of these stimuli.

In the previous chapter, the dynamic relationship between internal political competition and the national identity dynamic was discussed. Transcending religious, ideological and parochial divisions, the mobilisation of national identity is the largest mobilisation possible within a state in which there has been successful nation-building; there is, therefore, domestic political competition to appropriate it. Whoever can successfully mobilise and appropriate the national identity dynamic has the greatest possible popular power base. Because of this, the protection and enhancement of national identity – national interest, national prestige and so on – are crucial *domestic* political issues. They are crucial issues regardless of external international realities. Put crudely, no political incumbent or competitor for political power can allow herself to be seen as 'soft' in her international posturing for fear of it being interpreted as denigrating or threatening national identity. Moreover, as also discussed in the previous chapter, international posturing can mobilise mass public support in otherwise unstable domestic situations.

There is, therefore, the continual, if not tendency, then at least temptation, to trigger the national identity dynamic for domestic political purposes. It seems safe to say, then, that it is in the nature of the internal political structure of any state for there to be competition to trigger and appropriate the national identity dynamic. This, of course, is further complicated in western-style democratic states where a free capitalist press may also seek to manipulate the national identity dynamic as a way of increasing sales.

To state the obvious, then, it is domestic political actors who present the images and strategies which mobilise the national identity dynamic. The ease, however, with which the national identity dynamic can be mobilised is not based simply in the aggregate of individual psychological drives to defend and enhance identity. It is based also in the credibility of images concerning a competitive and dangerous international environment. There is indeed a reality of international conflict, both historical and contemporary. Thus any claim made by a domestic political competitor that there is an international threat is made within a general cognitive framework which supports such a statement. The history and contemporary reality of conflict give licence to 'make up' such threats.

This, of course, is further complicated by the fact that there may indeed be a real strategic threat. Even then, however, the way this threat is perceived by the mass national public is mediated by domestic media and communicators. Any external action touching any sphere that can be interpreted as being 'national', can be communicated about as threatening national interest.

Following Waltz's discussion of whether the origins of war lie in Man, the State or the International System,[20] it is possible, using identification theory, to attempt some clarity:

1 *Human:* People do not have a proven instinctive drive for aggression. They do, however, have a drive to protect and enhance identity. The national identity dynamic, however, requires appropriate images and strategies in order to be mobilised.

2 *State:* The nature of domestic political structures is such that there is competition to trigger and appropriate the national identity dynamic. This is done by mediating and manipulating images of the international environment, and putting forward defensive and enhancing strategies. The mobilisation may: (a) remain contained; (b) overspill and force international aggression; (c) be deliberately channelled into international aggression.

3 *International system:* (1) The historical and contemporary reality of international conflict lends credibility to domestically projected images of external threat. (2) Actors in the international system may, of course, genuinely provide a threat.

There is, thus, an unfortunate dialectic between the imperative dynamics of identification and the nature of political competition, a dialectic which takes place against an historical and contemporary reality of international aggression. And the synthesis of this dialectic is itself international aggression.

This analysis puts severe pressure on both certain realist and certain idealist positions. Hans Morgenthau's statement, and the assumption underlying most of his influential writing, that international conflict is the result of the savage urges of the mass of people and that peace is the result of the wisdom and wiles of statesmen, is shown to be untrue.[21] The savage urge of the mass of people is, in fact, the drive of psychologically insecure human beings to defend and enhance their identity; and the drive is, in fact, mobilised into mass movements by the wisdom and wiles of competing politicians, some of whom may be those very same statesmen. And, of course, international conflict has historically been essentially a conflict between elites – between statesmen, be they monarchs or clerics – and the mass of people have hardly been involved. The military competition for control of a territory was frequently irrelevant to the mass of people as there was no shared culture between the mass of people and their rulers.[22]

Equally, the idealist position concerning the innocence of the mass of people is also severely strained. According to this approach, the mass of people are merely the manipulated dupes of self-seeking political forces.[23] Identification theory points out that although they may be duped by propaganda and by the manipulated images of political intrigue, the mass of people do in fact have a clear and rational motive for mobilising for aggression: they are mobilising to defend their identity. They are not innocent bystanders, and to argue that they are wrong to defend their identity, for example when faced with real invasion by an alien culture, is in fact to argue pacifism. I shall return to these issues in the final chapter.

At a level that is purely theoretical, identification theory should thus have gone some way towards bridging the gap between the realist and the idealist stance. If one accepts the integrating analysis of identification theory, then there is no longer a mutually exclusive choice between a realist stance which believes in a savage human nature and an idealist stance which believes in a cooperative human nature. For a student of International Relations, identification theory provides a norm-free level of analysis which takes full account of, indeed is based in, human nature. The purely theoretically inclined student is, therefore, provided with an analytical tool which allows her to avoid the realist–idealist clash.

At a level, however, that is more normative and prescriptive, the clash between idealist and realist may still continue. An analysis which integrates identification theory may indeed be accepted, but it can nevertheless still be used to prescribe for particular goals. The idealist, remaining an idealist, may wish to use the analysis to prescribe strategies for disarmament, international integration or other idealist goals. And the realist, equally remaining a realist, may exploit it to prescribe strategies for enhancing state power. Moreover, the realist may argue that although the analysis using identification theory is correct, it is not a level of analysis that she chooses to employ. She may choose to continue to work at a level of analysis which accepts international conflict as the norm.

The application of identification theory, however, presents the challenge to, and the chance for, both realists and idealists to be more carefully explicit about the intellectual basis of their relative positions.

117

Certainly, identification theory presents a level of analysis which is detached from normative arguments concerning human nature, and this allows students of International Relations to adopt realism or idealism as prescriptive strategies without attempting to invest them with the status of theoretical truth.

STATE-CENTRISTS VERSUS STRUCTURALISTS

The argument in International Relations between state-centrists and structuralists is perhaps the most difficult to resolve because their division is based in more subtle ideological predispositions than those which divide the historians from the scientists, and the realists from the idealists. Identification theory, however, suggests a level of analysis which might go some way towards resolving their mutual exclusivity.

State-centrism. The state-centric perspective is that the major actor and unit of analysis in international politics is the nation-state.[24] This focus, however, is not based purely in a perception of power realities, but possesses a powerful normative aspect whose source is eighteenth-century European political theory. In one form or another, this theory posits that people have voluntarily contracted into arranging their communities as states; that, either for the imposition of minimal order or for cooperative communal benefit, people have granted a central organ a monopoly of political authority and power.[25] The state-centric analysis, then, is implicitly and normatively legitimated by the idea of the active and voluntary opting into the state by the mass citizenry. This is not the place to analyse the sociology of Enlightenment political theories. One can, however, point out that there was indeed a growing eighteenth-century middle and intellectual class which was increasingly ambitious for authoritative involvement in state power and whose ambitions these theories reflect. Any idea of a mass opting into a social contract to create the state is mythical and not based in any historical realities. This is not to deny that the mass of people may come to identify with their state and form a national community harmonious with the state – that indeed has been the major theme of this thesis. It is only to make clear that it was *not* the people who willed the state, but that the state emerged from political contingencies in which one of several power resources may have been a national identity.

This western European political theory has been bolstered by the general success of nation-building in Europe. Whatever the historical background, contemporary European states are also nations.[26] Thus,

118

for Europe at least, its political arrangement into nation-states seems appropriate and normatively validated. This perspective is further substantiated by the other states which also appear to be integrated national communities. In fact, the state-centrist accepts this European reality as the norm for territorial political arrangements, and projects it on to the total international environment both as the major level of analysis and as the universally applicable goal for all territorial arrangements. The world is thus divided into nation-states, normatively validated – or moving towards being normatively validated – by the voluntary social contracts of their citizens. And the major global interactions are those between these states.

Structuralism. The structuralist perspective in International Relations, however, posits that the most useful and the most real unit of analysis is that of class.[27] Moreover, it posits that the nation-state arose in western Europe as a power political superstructure to protect and bolster feudal, and then bourgeois, class interests. A major thrust of the structuralist critique, then, is that the nation-state emerged as the result of changing socio-economic forces and that the ongoing changes of these forces may equally well take the state out of existence. The state is a temporary political arrangement manifested by the power needs of the ruling bourgeois class. From the structuralist perspective, therefore, any approach which accepts the state as the major unit of analysis is merely a superficial description of shallow realities beneath which determining class forces are actually at work.

It is implicit in state-centrism that the major and transcending allegiance and identification is with, and ought to be with, the nation-state. In a tautological fashion, this in itself legitimates the state system. To the structuralist, however, this identification with the nation-state is only a temporary form of political false consciousness until true class interests are recognised – and class interests are international and not territorially bound. Dangerously, this academic debate between state-centrism and structuralism is reflected in the opposing ideologies in the East–West conflict and increasingly in the North–South divide.

Identification theory provides the possibility for a detached psychological standpoint which can bring a new perspective to bear on the competing paradigms. In providing this perspective it may act as a form of theoretical diplomat, a third party mediator, which, although not perhaps defusing the conflict between statism and structuralism, may work towards some form of holistic theoretical accommodation.

119

The major question which identification theory can ask is somewhat crude:

With which entity do the mass of people identify – nation-state or class?

In political terms, this is a crucial question because where the identification has been made, there lies the power resource of mass mobilisation. Chapter 3 discussed the elements which work towards nation-building. Identification theory can also be used to analyse the dynamics that work towards identification with class.

Following the basic tenets of identification theory, individuals make an identification when it is psychologically beneficial so to do. For a group identification there must, of course, be common symbols with which the identification can be made. The nation-state has a large array of high profile informal, and formal, symbols and social rituals which work towards nation-building. The nation-state also has an immensely well-resourced structure of governance which provides day-to-day communicated experience of the reality of the nation-state, e.g. post-men, police, state broadcasting, education system, flag and so on. Class, however, by its very nature, is diffuse. In a certain way, a class exists only as the socio-economic concept of social and political theor-ists rather than as a social group with a clearly defined identity – an identity which is self-consciously acknowledged and known by its constituents in the same way that nationality is.

It is possible here to ask another unsubtle question:

What are the symbols of class which can be internalised?

We are not here referring to the symbols, rituals and mores that exist in every parochial culture. We are inquiring about symbols, rituals and mores which exist *internationally* – which can give reality, in terms of identification, to the notion of an international proletariat or an international bourgeoisie.

International working class. First, it is important to recall that, accord-ing to identification theory, identification occurs with either a benefi-cent actor/symbol or an actor/symbol which provides the appropriate behaviour in the face of threat.

Second, it is important to note that the working class is externally identifiable as a class which exists in a state of subservience or relative deprivation in contradistinction to that of the bourgeoisie. The middle class life style is *per se* materialistically superior. For proletarian identi-fication to take place, some form of symbol, some form of identity-securing interpretive system, must mediate between the individual and her/his life reality. The individual must somehow or other inter-pret the reality of relative deprivation in such a manner that it is

120

psychologically enhancing to internalise it. Moreover, for there to be such an entity as an *international* proletariat, in the terms of identification theory, the internalised identity-securing interpretive system must be a shared international one.

There are, of course, *parochial* identity-securing interpretive systems which work with just such a purpose. The Hindu caste system is such a system, creating a secure cosmological place for the deprived. A similar religious perspective is displayed in the notion of 'It is God's will and divinely intended'. Equally, that poverty is a form of spiritual purity is another system that meets the requirement. None of these systems, however, is internationally applicable. The one interpretive system which comes closest to international acceptance is the Marxist one. According to this system, deprivation is not the will of a deity, but a temporary historical situation which will be transcended as the proletariat free themselves to take control of their own labour, production and the fruits thereof.

Certainly, Marxism provides a clear international, or universal, interpretation and revolutionary prescription. It competes, however, with the local, frequently spiritual or religious, interpretive systems. Even in continuing situations of gross relative deprivation, where the ideologies of spiritual acceptance or historical passivity have been broken down and there exists no identity-securing interpretive system to mediate between the deprived and their existential situation, an ideology of revolutionary action may still not be adopted. This is because revolution is a dangerous affair at the best of times. Revolutionary Marxism is not a safe interpretive system to adopt, for it prescribes a course of action that involves struggle against ruling bourgeois class forces and physical danger. Therefore if the individual has not *already* internalised the identity of being Marxist, there is no psychological benefit in taking a Marxist stance.

Furthermore, the proletarian individual may have made a prior identification with the nation-state, and the Marxist system may well conflict with this national identity. In fact, working class patriotism and nationalism – proletarian identification with the nation-state – has been a major theoretical thorn in the side of Marxism.[28] A classical Marxist analysis would state that class interests are bought off by materialistic promises, but this does not explain wars in which the poor are mobilised for conflict with *no* expectation of materialistic gain. In this context, patriotism – or the mobilised national identity dynamic – not religion, is the opium of the people. The fact is that mobilised nationalism and patriotism provide a benefit in terms of enhanced identity that completely ignores class and simple materialistic interests. This is not, however, to deny that vested bourgeois interests may deliberately manipulate the national identity dynamic. This can appear highly ironical as the reality of class, through gross relative deprivation, may impinge far more directly on the actual daily life of the mass citizenry than their nationality does.

Moreover, revolution that is purely Marxist has none of the reinforcing rituals of mass national mobilisation which occur when a state goes to war. Revolutionary warfare requires a far greater psychological commitment than the organised patriotic euphoria which can be mobilised for international conflict.

Marxism also, of course, competes with local political ideologies which promise, via one form of economic growth or another, an end to this deprivation.

Certainly this theoretical appearance of the lack of a coherent international proletarian class identity is borne out by historical realities. The strength, for example, of national identity has been such that class revolution has not occurred in waves of international solidarity, but has, in fact, always been defined by nation-state boundaries.[29] The Socialist International broke down into national loyalties in 1914, and a few years later the Russian Revolution, despite the expectations of the Bolsheviks, was not the beginning of an international revolution. In fact, successful proletarian revolutions have been mainly based in, or have successfully harnessed, the triggering symbols of the national identity dynamic – proletarian revolution has moved in tight concert with domestic *national* liberation. Perhaps the most dramatic example of this harnessing of the national identity dynamic to class revolution was Mao Tse Tung's use of the Japanese incursions to mobilise popular Chinese support behind the Chinese Communist Party.[30] Furthermore, in power after revolution, proletarian socialist states have demonstrated no more solidarity with each other than bourgeois ruled states. This is obviously so, for example, in the relations between the Soviet Union and the People's Republic of China.

Although the socio-economic situation of relative deprivation is a structurally consistent feature across the world system, it consists in fact of geographically isolated groups of people. They may indeed, at the time of writing, make up the majority of the planet's population, but they do not make up a group that shares, according to identification theory, a common identity. This is not to deny that they share a common reality of deprivation – or that they might not in the future come to share a common identity. The careful manipulation of international mass media and political symbols could evoke a coherent international working class. It is possible that the 'South' in the North–

122

South conflict represents the seed of just such an awareness. If and when the international proletariat comes to share a common ideology and, therefore, is mobilisable as one unit – for example, in international strike action or concerted revolution – then the international working class will be identifiable as a major actor.

International middle class. By definition, a middle class life style is one of relative materialistic advantage over that of the working class. The middle class possesses objects which in a very real sense enhance the quality of life. In a very real way these objects bring physical security in terms of control of the environment – heating, food, dwellings, clothes, social influence and so on. These objects not only supply human creature comforts, but they also provide real life survival enhancement in a world environment of deadly human competition and of potential, and frequently realised, dearth and disaster. To act to achieve enhanced physical security is 'natural'.[31] In the struggle to achieve this enhanced physical security, however, social divisions appear, as certain individuals and groups do indeed succeed in enhancing their physical security whilst others do not.[32]

As with the international proletariat, we need now to examine whether there is any symbolic system which interprets this materialistic advantage with which the international middle class universally identifies.

The rationale for such relative materialistic advantage might simply be one of 'might equalling right', in which case the identity-securing interpretive system which explains class advantage is one which simply states that some men are stronger than others – and that is the existential reality. The problem with such a brutal ideology is that it *per se* justifies, if not actually invites, revolution and threat from any individual or group who wishes to overthrow the current holders of the materialistic advantage. Various other more subtle and more generally acceptable interpretive systems have, however, evolved. Historically, the major ideology justifying class advantage is some form of spiritual or metaphysical cosmology in which the 'better off' are in some way 'divinely chosen'. The monarch or chief, for example, is a direct representative of deity, or a microcosmic reflection of macrocosmic divine principles. In turn, the monarch's or the chief's clan, relatives or associates have shared in this divine beneficence. There is also the alter ego of that set of spiritual interpretive systems which explain relative deprivation as being a matter of incarnational karma or divine will. To be materialistically advantaged is equally a matter of God's will or of one's spiritual position in the caste hierarchy.

The rise of capitalism and the beginnings of industrialisation, however, brought the need for an interpretive system which accounted for the relatively huge numbers of people now entering the advantaged class. The Protestant Work Ethic surely provided just such an identity-securing interpretive system for western Europe: God wants you to work hard and if you work hard you will be rewarded with material benefits. Material benefits are a form of divine approval.[33] The rise of capitalism, however, also went hand-in-hand with an Enlightenment liberation from religious dogma and the beginning of a more secular and explicitly political interpretation of social realities. A Darwinian sense of progress and competitive evolution, and the phenomenal success of western capitalism, entwined to produce a more materialistically pragmatic ideology. Essentially, this middle class ideology states that everything is in the process of economic growth and general progress, the end result of which is that *everyone* will enjoy material advantages. Also inherent in this ideology is the notion that competition is healthy, normal and, moreover, the most efficient way of achieving rapid and sustained economic growth. Seen from the outside, this ideology is the whole western notion of modernisation. The Worldview is that economic growth is the macro reality and a personal *career* structure is the micro reality.

It is also possible to state that the higher up the class scale the individual rises, so, through higher education and international travel, she or he becomes increasingly socialised into a single high technology and *haute bourgeois* culture which transcends parochial national culture. To belong to the international middle class with its coherent ideology of material benefit, progress and economic growth is certainly identity enhancing.[34] This may not be obvious in the already industrialised areas of the globe, but it is clearly observable in developing areas where life style differences are extreme.

All this can be brought into clearer focus by asking the following question about members of a third world elite and bourgeoisie: Do they share a common identity with (a) their fellow nationals of all classes or (b) with an international middle class? There is a powerful tendency for members of a third world metropolitan elite with electricity, consumer goods, changes of clothing and vehicles, who are literate and, most of all, who have careers, to be culturally and socially at one with their class siblings across the globe; and to be culturally and socially alienated from their proletarian and peasant fellow countrypeople. The rhetoric of a third world elite may be nationalistic, but their norms, mores and general culture tend not to be parochial and indigenous, but international and bourgeois.

124

This identification with the international middle class is continuously reinforced, by ongoing contact with the visitors, long and short term, from first and second world countries, the vast majority of whom are middle class. These middle class visitors – diplomats and business people – moreover, display a life style that is particularly distinguished by high levels of disposable income. Visiting holidaymakers display the same disposable income and security enhancing control of their environment. This, in turn, is further reinforced by third world visitors to first world societies, where they experience a general life style which, compared to their own countries, appears to be thoroughly middle class for everyone. Deprivation and advantage are always relative.

It is possible, then, to state that, according to identification theory, an international middle class sharing a single culture does indeed exist. It possesses the same symbols, mores, behaviour patterns and ideology. It is interesting, then, to enquire how this shared class actually manifests itself in terms of action on the international stage. First, one should recall that those people who have made a general identification with the global middle class will seek to protect and enhance that identification. There will be, therefore, an unconscious psychological dynamic in middle class elites to adopt ideologies, strategies and cultural stances that enhance and defend middle class identity. This works, then, to create a dynamic in which bourgeois elite discourse and decision-making are determined by their international middle class identity rather than by their parochial national identity. This pattern is clearly discernible in the trading and commerce of international financiers, multinational executives and third world elites.

International trading, particularly as practised by third world elites, hardly begins to consider the interests of their mass of fellow citizens, or their local ecology; to do so would be to alienate themselves from the very culture which gives them security.[35] Their fellow citizens are fellows, then, purely in theory and not in the psychological fact of shared identity. In a very real sense then, the state may be used by third world elites simply as a tool for achieving their own materialistic interests, and as they have no sense of solidarity with their mass of countrypeople, their states are in no sense nation-states. Third world pockets of 'modernised' culture experience definite conflicting loyalties and interests in terms of nationality and class. This is not to say, however, that some, if not many, middle class third world citizens will not have a sense of national identity which overrides and transcends their international middle class identity.

125

To summarise:

International working class

1 There is only one identity-securing interpretive system for the international proletariat which approaches universality. This is Marxism.
2 Marxism competes, however, with:
   a Parochial spiritual/religious interpretations of deprivation.
   b The dangers of revolution.
   c National identity.
   d Political ideologies which promise a peaceful end to deprivation.
3 The working class acts as a single coherent culture only domestically and within national borders.

International middle class

1 There is one identity-securing interpretive system for the international middle class. This is an ideology of progress, competition and modernisation.
2 This ideology competes only with national identity.
3 The middle class acts as a single coherent culture both domestically and internationally.

This whole model is an attempt to produce an ideal construct and is flawed by the fact that the dividing line between the classes is not clear, particularly in the industrialised first and second worlds. Moreover, the classes within themselves are variegated.[36] Also, especially in the developed states where nation-building has been relatively successful, middle class individuals may change their loyalty from national to transnational middle class mores according to their instrumental needs. The model is, however, merely an attempt to produce an ideal type to aid analysis at the most general level.

Continuing at this general level, there are several other structural features which can be noted:

1 The majority of middle class (relatively advantaged) people live in the first and second industrialised worlds.
2 The majority of the proletariat (relatively deprived) live in the third industrialising world or the South.
3 Due to historical circumstances, nation-building tends to have been successful in the already industrialised, predominantly middle class states.

4   The middle class of the industrialised states, therefore, tends to have internalised symbols of national identity more than the middle class of developing states.

5   This means that middle class individuals of industrialised states may act according to an ideology that is either (a) of national identity or (b) of the international middle class.

6   This also means that middle class individuals of developing states will tend to act according to the culture of the international middle class rather than that of their nation.

7   There will, therefore, be a distinct tendency for middle class international decision-making to favour international middle class interests rather than national interests.[37]

Identification theory thus provides a distinct analytical perspective for studying international class. The state-centrist can use this form of analysis as a non-ideological mode for getting to grips with the notion of class and the impingement of class interests on international relations. Via this mode of analysis, it can be perceived that international class interests, rather than the interest of the nation or the mass national population, do indeed, in certain situations, govern state decisions. The purely state-centric mode of analysing international politics has to expand to include class factors, but in so doing does not need to resort to a Marxian form of analysis with its implicit socialist determinism.

Equally, the structuralist can use this form of analysis as a tool for coming to terms with the fact that, regardless of the existential reality of class interests, working and middle-class individuals invest their states with a legitimacy and a loyalty that transcends class identity. The structuralist can acknowledge this psychological legitimacy of the state without the acceptance of western democratic and capitalist norms.

6 CONCLUSION – APPRAISAL, PRESCRIPTIONS, PARADOXES

This final chapter assesses the analysis as a whole. It begins with a general appraisal of the original intentions of the analysis. It then addresses the various methodological criticisms that can be raised against it before proceeding to draw out some of the policy implications. It concludes with a few general and philosophical comments.

APPRAISAL

The purpose of this research is to make explicit a dynamic identification theory and then, using it as the analytical tool for aggregating from individual attitudes and behaviour to group attitude and behaviour, to give the mass national citizenry a methodologically coherent status in international political theory. In the introductory passage of the first chapter, I raised four questions that required satisfactory answers before such a status could be bestowed upon mass national publics. These were:

1 Is it possible to know the attitudes of individual citizens?
2 Even if one does know these attitudes, is it possible to predicate that these attitudes will dictate action?
3 Is it possible to aggregate or generalise from an individual citizen's attitude in a way that explicates the attitude of the total citizenry? Can there be an explicit theoretical link between individual attitudes and mass national attitudes?
4 Is there a method for explicating the relationship between these mass attitudes and actual foreign policy decisions?

These questions were echoed later in the first chapter when the general impasse in the political application of psychological theory was discussed. Two major difficulties were noted. The first, in Lipset's words, was 'that psychology itself has come to no agreement about how to characterise personality, or how to resolve differences concerning competing models'.[1] The second, as Smelser pointed out, was that 'we do not at present have the methodological capacity to argue causally from a mixture of aggregated states of individual members of a system to a global characteristic of the system'.[2] Or in Greenstein's equation:

Personality structures ≠ political belief ≠ individual political action ≠ aggregate political structures and processes.[3]

In terms of knowing overt individual attitudes, there is no great problem; opinion polls are precisely in the business of registering such attitudes. The uncovering of deeper psychological traits, however, is more problematical. The attitude with which this thesis is concerned, however, manifests itself overtly. It is the sentimental attachment and loyalty to the nation-state, an attitude seen at its most explicit when men and women are prepared to lay down their lives for it. The real problem, of course, has been in uncovering a theory which explains (1) the basic psychological motivation, and then (2) with methodological coherence, aggregates from the individual to the group.

Lipset stated the problem of having no consistent personality model. But this is precisely not the case when it comes to the structure of identity. As chapter 2 demonstrated, at the most profound theoretical levels, the two major contending psychological schools – the psychoanalytic and the behaviourist – are in agreement: There is a bio-psychological drive to internalise the behaviour of significant others in order to create identity. Furthermore, this is an ongoing adaptive process throughout life, concerned with fundamental aspects of psychological well-being.

Identification theory is a universal psychological dynamic which precisely explains, through identification and internalisation, the deep psychological nature of the relationship between the individual and his/her identity – for the sake of this thesis, national identity. Moreover, the power of the dynamic is based in that primitive but poignant ontology of the prolonged vulnerability of the human infant, and the continuing need throughout adolescence and adult life to achieve, maintain, protect and enhance identity. Identification theory provides the theoretical structure and dynamic which substantiates Renshon's insight: 'In the complex interchange between the child's biological needs, their frequency and the nature of their satisfaction, basic beliefs about the nature of the world are being developed. These basic beliefs are not in themselves political, but I would argue that they have important political implications.'[4]

The profound usefulness of identification theory lies in its ability to explain both political integration and national mobilisation. As an analytical tool, it is able to explain various modes of behaviour. It provides a coherent explanation for a spectrum of mass social behaviour, running from a low-key and agreeable sense of national solidarity through to actions of mass terrorism. Identification provides Durkheim's 'glue' of national solidarity and of a collective national 'conscience'. Identification when triggered, also provides the fuel for mobilisation, whether it manifests itself in the form of disciplined and orchestrated parades, in the form of informal bar songs and brawls, in the form of middle class elitism or in the form of full-scale international aggression.

Identification theory explains how the mass national public – via a shared identification – is evoked into being, and can then explain how that mass national public may then tend to behave. Politicians and statespeople sensitive to their constituents, whether for altruistic or self-seeking ends, must work with this mass social psychological dynamic.

Identification theory, then, provides 'the methodological capacity to argue from a mixture of aggregated states of individual members of a system to a global characteristic of the system'. This is because it is absolutely logical that if two or more individuals share the same identification and receive the same communications and experiences concerning that identity, they will then tend to behave together in the same mode. Greenstein's equation can thus be successfully completed:

Identification theory	*Greenstein's equation*
The identification dynamic leads, via nation-building, to individuals internalising national identity.	Personality structures
The nation-state is a 'good' thing: patriotism, nationalism.	Political belief
The individual may act to defend/ enhance national identity.	Individual political action
In the politically integrated (nation-built) state, the mass citizenry share the same identity and may, therefore, act together to defend/ enhance national identity: the *National Identity Dynamic*.	Aggregate political structures and processes

130

Thus, at a level of analysis defined by identification theory, it is possible to justify the new equation:

Personality structures based in identification = political beliefs = individual political action = aggregate political structures and processes.

Where the analysis apparently lacks a certain clarity is where it ignores degrees of attachment to the nation-state according, for example, to the classification drawn up by Kelman.[5] Certainly, there are different degrees of attachment according to the psychology and circumstances of each individual. Kelman's initial division into two types of attachment, the sentimental and the instrumental, is certainly useful. If, however, the attachment is not purely instrumental or pragmatic, then whatever the degree of sentimental attachment, its dynamic motivational source lies in the profound unconscious psychological mechanism of identification. The sense of attachment and the willingness to mobilise, to defend or to enhance national identity – no matter how easy or slow – is based in identification. Where other psychological explanations become important is in the analysis of the leadership – from that of the state through to that of the mob – which triggers the mobilisation.

Similarly, there has been no clear focus on the micro level of the pressures that may bear down on the individual and which finally mobilise him/her to act. The amount of disturbance to identity which is required to mobilise individuals will vary from individual to individual. For some individuals, because of their unique psychological histories, it may be sufficient only to perceive the possibility of threat from an archetypal enemy in order to mobilise to defend national identity. For others, it may be the euphoria experienced with mobilised peers which triggers their own mobilisation. For yet others, it may be the fear of ostracism by their social group, and thus the loss of their social identity, which is the mobilising factor. And, in other cases, it may be a real and actual experience of external threat which finally triggers reaction. Whichever the trigger, the mobilising dynamic is that of identification.

Chapter 3 discussed nation-building and described how a mass of people may come to share the same national identity; it delineated the political and socio-economic factors which evoke such an identification. Where nation-building has been successful, then, there will be a mass national identity and a *national identity dynamic* to defend and enhance that identity. Chapter 4 on *Foreign policy* explained how the national identity dynamic worked to influence, and be influenced by,

131

foreign policy decisions and perceptions of the external international environment. The logic of the influence of the national identity dynamic on foreign policy making was as follows:

1 The mass national public will mobilise if it perceives that there is a threat to, or the opportunity of enhancing, national identity.
2 The mobilisation of the mass national public is, by definition, the largest possible mobilisation within a nation-state.
3 It is a feature of domestic politics that there be competition to appropriate the national identity dynamic.
4 The national identity dynamic, if mobilised, necessarily influences government decisions.

The general pattern – that the state, in terms of its foreign policy decisions, may trigger, manipulate, appropriate or be manipulated by, the national identity dynamic – was then illustrated by various case histories. At a level of analysis rigorously defined by identification theory, the mass national public has a coherent methodological status and a theoretically integrated role as a foreign policy variable. There are certain criticisms, however, that still need to be addressed.

METHODOLOGICAL CRITICISMS

The use of identification theory as a major methodological tool in an analysis of political integration and mass political behaviour, is open to five specific criticisms which require assessing. These concern:

1 Psychological reductionism
2 Eurocentrism
3 Lack of internal consistency
4 Falsifiability
5 Evidence

1 Psychological reductionism: It may seem, in using identification theory as a major analytical tool for investigating nation-building, which in turn – via the national identity dynamic – is the basis for the mass social–psychological analysis of foreign policy, that one is being crudely reductionist. Political and socio-economic realities are too fundamental, too determining – particularly so in the extremely complex context of the modern state – to be relegated to being handmaidens of a psychological interpretation.[6]

Yet, psychological attachment to a polity is self-evidently not unique to the modern state. Although in the modern era, and particularly following the western model, it appears that economic realities and overt political structures are the essential components in defining and understanding the concordant relationship between a citizenry and its polity, the fact is that in other polities displaying this concord, economic and political factors have been relatively marginal. Myth, religion or kinship have proved the essential structural factors.[7]

Nor is it legitimate to suggest that the mass psychological attachment to the modern state is substantively different from the psychological attachment to a 'primitive', organic community. It is undeniable that modern industrial societies are hugely different from pre-literate or pre-industrial communities, and it may seem that no 'natural' sentimental attachment is possible, but that belies the evidence. National anthems and other national rituals, international competition and above all mobilisation for international aggression – all these display the same psychological dynamics as the association that the noble savage had for the 'primitive' community. (In fact, any student of International Relations has surely to recognise that we are all potential savages in a primitive community – sometimes more primitive even than in the past.)

This is to say that a social–psychological level of analysis is entirely appropriate for a function that manifests itself in all kinds of polity, regardless of socio-economic or political structure. In fact, without a social–psychological theory, no meaningful analysis of nation-building or mobilisation is possible. Certainly, a central argument presented here has been that identification is the major psychological mechanism involved in national integration, and this same mechanism is the motivating force for mass national mobilisation. For the accusation of psychological reductionism to be substantiated, it would be necessary to present other explanations for integration and mobilisation. What might these be? Passivity, personal interest and fear are strong contenders – but none of these explains the emotionalism and sentimentality of patriotism, and the enthusiasm for mass national rituals and mobilisation. A general accusation might also be that domestic power political and socio-economic constraints have been given insufficient attention, but the analysis has been concerned with the dynamics of *all* nation-states which, regardless of internal political culture, appear to demonstrate the same syndrome of national integration and mobilisation. This is not, however, to say, nor has it been posited, that the psychological dynamic of the identification imperative is the major *determining* factor. Identification requires environmental triggering. The identification dynamic, as a structural aspect of a political society, does not act as a crude determinant imposed upon the social, political and economic realities. On the contrary, it is necessarily triggered by

133

external experience and therefore always works in a dialectic with social, political and economic factors. Identification theory provides a psychological level of analysis that takes full account of political and socio-economic contingencies. But it also provides a new and distinct level of analysis for investigating those contingencies.

2 Eurocentrism: The second criticism that needs to be addressed is that it is not possible to generalise from the experience of mediaeval England and France to contemporary nation-building. If the analysis of nation-building is only appropriate for the western European experience, then the rest of the thesis which follows on logically from chapter 3 is severely flawed and limited in its international applicability. The dynamics of nation-building in early France and England may be correctly described, but they do not describe a set of dynamics which is universally applicable. African and Asian countries, for instance, have such substantially different experiences and cultures that the analysis is not transferable. The western European experience should not be exported as a piece of chauvinistic or academic imperialism.[8]

This criticism can be answered both sociologically and psychologically. Sociologically, it is axiomatic that the France and England used as paradigms were pre-industrial. The model, therefore, does not contain any of the structures of a capitalist or industrialised society that would be applicable from the sixteenth century onwards. This analysis of nation-building, therefore, does not contain any of the normative and ideological notions concerned with the progress of industrialised western society. It is not in that sense bound by those Eurocentric notions which were inherent in the modernisation theories of the sixties. The central feature of this psychological analysis – how a mass of individuals comes to identify with a national culture – stands free of the boundaries of a post-industrial mass communicating society.

It is also worth noting that mediaeval England and France, like contemporary third world nations, had recently been subject to waves of imperialist invasion.

Psychologically, the answer to the criticism of Eurocentrism is that the identification dynamic is not culture-specific. If identification theory is correct, it is correct as a general feature of human nature regardless of culture; identification is an anthropological constant. The whole analysis, therefore, is based in a psychological insight which provides a tool of investigation for human groups in general and not early western European peoples in particular; the approach is anthropologically, and not culturally, based. Of course, identification theory would flounder totally if it were shown that there are inherent, genetically based psychological differences between the races of the world. There is no evidence to suggest any such differences.

Where care needs to be exercised, however, is in the amount of time one assumes is involved in nation-building. Nation-building in contemporary Europe is, by and large, complete, and one might forget the lengthy history that has preceded it. One needs to be careful, therefore, about making any presumptions concerning the time needed for other countries to nation-build. Appropriate policy and the right circumstances might create the necessary evocative binding in one generation. Inappropriate policy and alienating circumstances might lead, however, to centuries without political and cultural integration.

Where, however, the analysis might be fairly criticised as being Eurocentric is in its apparent assumption that the nation-state itself is the right and proper mode for the political arrangement of humans on the globe – and, therefore, that nation-building as such is a good and necessary thing. I can only confess, in answer to this, that thus far my business has been analysis and not value judgement. If I am to judge, then my predilection is for a situation in which nations are disengaged from the political process and allowed, as Herder expressed it, to blossom as cultural flowers. My analysis of nation-building does not require ideological attachment to the modern state. I shall return to this in my conclusions.

3 Lack of internal consistency: A severe criticism regarding consistency can be usefully raised against my analysis. It concerns the ignoring, in the political analysis, of a specific aspect of identification theory.

The criticism is that the paradigm of nation-building suggested in the description of early English and French experiences ignores one of the basic propositions put forward in the earlier exegesis of identification theory; that identification takes place not only with individuals who provide a suitable model in the face of threat, but also with individuals *who are themselves actually threatening.* (In psychoanalytic theory, the resolution of the Oedipus complex is precisely the mechanism of internalising the attitudes and behaviour of the threatening parent.) Internalising the modes of, and behaving like, the threatening figure brings safety and survival. In the discussion of nation-building in France and England, there was mention only of the state as a materialistic benefactor, or of the state as sharing an experience of external threat with its people and providing the suitable identity-enhancing attitude. There was no mention in the discussion of the dynamics of a state which legitimates itself purely by the constraints of

135

force and terror. According to identification theory, this too should evoke identification.

The logic of identification with a terrorising oppressor is that the mores and behavioural patterns of a significant oppressor will be internalised in order to achieve psychological safety and security; i.e. the individual will come to behave like his/her terrorising oppressor and thus achieve psychological security. One of the most distressing examples of this kind of identification was described by Bruno Bettelheim in his account of how some Jewish prisoners in Nazi concentration camps took on fully the characteristics of their sadistic guards.[9] The crucial point here, however, is that those prisoners were *allowed* to behave like their guards. Self-evidently, in terms of nation-building, this means that an oppressive and terroristic state will only evoke the identification of its citizens if it *allows* those citizens to behave in the same way as the oppressive agents who symbolically represent the state. Otherwise, oppressive state behaviour will evoke only alienation – albeit passive and fearful.

To put it crudely, this is to say that a terrorist state will evoke identification and have a culturally integrated nation-state only if the citizens are also allowed to behave like terrorists. This raises very practical political problems of integration and stability which can be solved only by restricting the licence to act terroristically to a particular class or group, or by canalising the mass acts of terror so that they do not destabilise the existence of the state itself. In practice, if mass mobilisation into a mode of terror is allowed, and if the state is to survive, the victims of the terror must be either an internal enemy (Jews, Communists, foreigners) or an external foe.[10]

There are, of course, other situations in which a state's constraints of force are more subtle than simply terror. A certain kind of police state can evoke an identification in which members of the same family may spy upon each other. In a similar mode, the Chinese movements of Thought Reform and the Cultural Revolution evoked an identification in which centrally directed verbal violence against ideological impurity became also the behaviour pattern of its citizens in public rituals of criticism.[11]

As, however, no evidence presents itself of a terroristic state sustaining both itself and mass psychological support, except in situations of mass mobilisation for international conflict, it does not seem appropriate to classify this mode of political identification as a viable form of nation-building.

4 Falsifiability: It is fashionable amongst social scientists to apply Popperian notions of falsifiability to social theories. Can the theory be tested? Can it be falsified? If not, then the theory is not a theory but simply a statement of opinion, perhaps insightful, but without any intellectual credibility based in rigour and, therefore, not really useful. Before dealing specifically with whether the political application of identification theory is testable, there are three general points which I want to raise about applying the criterion of falsifiability to any social theory.

The first concerns the appropriateness in general of such a procedure. The framework in which Popper originally wrote about falsifiability was that of the physical sciences where testability by empirical measurement is possible.[12] Popper himself did not suggest its applicability to the social sciences. Indeed, the major conceptual thrust of his volumes *The Open Society and Its Enemies* and *The Poverty of Historicism*, is precisely a condemnation of predictive and deterministic social and political ideas. The only way to test such ideas is by actually putting them into effect via political policies and then awaiting results; such a method is not consistent with a respect for open society and human dignity.[13] Furthermore, and fairly obviously, with specific reference to International Relations theory, as Singer pointed out, from a practical point of view there is a severe difficulty in testing any macro theory; political and social systems are not laboratories in which scientifically constructed tests can be repeatedly – or even once – carried out.[14] There is, therefore, a certain irony in International Relations theorists referring to Popper in order to justify their own predilection to give their theory 'scientific' status.

This leads clearly into the second point that perhaps, like *philosophy*, social theory is not anyway in the business of setting up coherent and testable theories. Like philosophy, social theory may, in fact, be in the business of discourse and of finding ways of discussing social phenomena that are useful by virtue of being illuminating and insightful.[15] The value of philosophical discussion is never judged against a criterion of testability. It may be equally inappropriate to apply such a criterion to social theory. The concept of the 'ideal type' in social theory, for example, is precisely concerned with a dynamic general pattern which is theoretically useful but in actuality always in flux and, therefore, incapable of being tested; anyway its purpose is not to be testable but to give insight into analysis. The built nation, the result of successful nation-building, is just such an ideal type. The fully integrated nation-state which assumes mass psychological loyalty, or total mobilisation behind a particular foreign policy, is a dynamic image and a scientific analysis of its separate constituents would always show up levels and pockets of dissension and difference. These pockets of exception would not, however, undermine the general thrust of the analysis.

The academy of International Relations, as a whole, is not itself fully persuaded of the usefulness of scientific criteria anyway, and there has been a vigorous debate about the merits of a scientific approach and about the status of scientific theory. F.S. Northedge took the most aggressive anti-scientific stance when he accused American behaviouralists of giving doctorates to students for counting international phone calls, letters and parcels; and for coming to 'some perfectly obvious conclusions which could have been reached in a few minutes by common observation and reflection'.[16] Hedley Bull made a more reasoned but similar case in his paper 'International Theory: The Case for a Classical Approach'.[17] In a language more resonant with contemporary social theory, Avner Yaniv also made a significant contribution to this debate, part of which is worth quoting at length.

> The operationalization of a concept 'is its application to the materials of existence'. It calls for a series of operations which are unique for every concept. The failure to perform these operations reflects on the coherence of the concept to which they relate. As even such behaviorists as Kaplan and Rummel now admit, social phenomena are not easily given to operationalization in the strict or quantitative sense of the term. Any attempt to ignore that basic limitation leads to an overemphasis on rigor which may either paralyse research or lead to a belabored and excessive preoccupation with methodology, coupled by a paucity of substantive results. Hence operationalization of social and political concepts *should be imputed a more flexible meaning*. For example, operationalization could be defined as a logically constructed, systematic but essentially observative and imprecise application of a concept to the materials of experience. Such exercises are incapable of leading to results other than somewhat imprecise taxonomies. But as another recent study of foreign policy analysis has pointed out, 'rough measures are better than no measures'.[18]

This same point was made by Most and Starr in a paper that recognised that coherent theories concerning the making of foreign policy have to take account of the reality of substitutability, insomuch as the same configuration of variables could produce an outcome that could be substituted for another. As a result of this: 'Applications of the standard approaches for testing models and hypotheses are likely to produce misleading results and lead analysts to reject theories and models that are "good", "nice" and "useful", even if they are not general, or universally "true".'[19]

All of this said, however, my purpose is not to detach the political application of identification theory from scientific appraisal and to claim for it only a discursive value. It is simply to state that to expect the application of identification theory to meet the same nice exactness of enquiry as in the physical sciences is to apply an inappropriate criterion.

The political application of identification theory can, however, be judged with intellectual rigour in terms of the internal consistency of its logic. It can also be judged as to whether it meets scientific criteria in relation to the classical structure of *if . . . then . . .* propositions. The political application of identification theory does indeed put forward discrete propositions of such a nature. In terms of nation-building, it is conceptually exact about the circumstances that it predicts will evoke identification. Identification theory is also predictive as regards national mass mobilisation in relation to foreign policy. It clearly proposes that the trigger to such a mobilisation must be the perception of threat to, or the opportunity of enhancing, national identity. This, in turn, is falsifiable if evidence can be brought forward that demonstrates mass national mobilisation triggered by other factors.

But, given the nature of social and political reality, given the scale of the systems under analysis, and given the kaleidoscopic sets of variables that can be brought into play, it is unrealistic, impractical and not useful to expect the theory to satisfy quantifiable tests.

5 Evidence: Even though laboratory tests on a macro-political scale cannot be set up, the issue of evidence should not be avoided. There are two levels at which the question of evidence is crucial. The first concerns identification theory itself. The second concerns its political application for nation-building and for foreign policy analysis.

Is identification theory sound? Is there evidence for it being true? If not, then the whole analysis is falsely based. It was expounded in chapter 2 by way of an exegesis of Freud, Mead, Erikson, Parsons and Habermas. In each case, identification theory was a way of understanding phenomena already observed by the theorist. None of the five put forward the identification imperative as an *a priori* assumption, following which suitable evidence was garnered. (If there was any tendency towards this *a priori* error, it lay with Habermas who approached the subject from a more philosophical basis concerned with the Hegelian search for identity.) The evidence was already there as universally observable human phenomena made sense of by identification theory. The evidence is to be seen in every individual acting in culture and society, the deviant exceptions proving the rule. The die-hard logical positivist, however, will find acceptable evidence only when science produces a methodology capable of actually perceiving the physiological brain patterning that makes for the identification dynamic. I take the stance that, though more subtle, the identification imperative is a drive similar to that of sex or hunger. The fact that humans – infants to adults – seek to eat demonstrates hunger: no food, death. The fact that humans – infants to adults – seek to have an identity demonstrates the identification dynamic: no identity, breakdown.

If identification theory, however, were seen to be the exclusive preserve of the psychoanalytic school, then severe theoretical difficulties could be expected as psychoanalytic theory has been subject to severe methodological scrutiny. The most aggressive of these enquiries was conducted by Hans Eysenck, but the thrust of his attempt totally to undermine Freudian theory did not touch the issue of identification at all. Eysenck's one attack that did approach the issue of identification was in his dismissal of Freud's map of id, ego and super-ego, but even here he acknowledged the general acceptability of the notion of internalised social controls.[20]

An extremely careful study of the validity of psychoanalytic theory which specifically addressed the issue of identification was Paul Kline's *Fact and Fantasy in Freudian Theory*.[21] In it he concluded, 'There is relatively little support for the Freudian claim that loss of love or fear of aggression are the important variables. From this it follows that *other models than the parent will be important sources of identification* whereas in psychoanalytical theory this parental identification is of crucial importance.'[22] (My italics.) My thesis is not dismantled by his criticism, as my argument agrees fully that other models, apart from parents, are important sources. Kline makes no attempt – and it is not his brief – to clarify what motivates identification with non-parental figures, but acknowledges its occurrence.

The theoretical reality is that it is impossible to envisage a psychology that does not comprehend the internalisation of others' behaviour and mores. It is, as stated earlier, the coincidence of psychoanalytic and behaviourist theory with regard to the construction of the social personality which provides the epistemological basis to my use of identification theory.

In terms of demonstrating its group effect – that a group will seek to defend or enhance its group identity – there is also substantial universal evidence. Certainly, working from a base in cognitive theory, social psychologists have demonstrated, in laboratory conditions, collective behaviour in relation to group identity fully resonant with identification theory.[23] The real problem, however, is in substantiating that the identification dynamic is the motivating source both for integration and mobilisation. A contending theory, for example, might state: (1) socialisation and integration are functions of behaviourist imitation; (2) mobilisation is a function of an animal instinct for herd behaviour; and (3) group aggression is merely the function of an innate aggressive instinct finally given loose reign by authoritative social approval. Equally, the psychoanalytic school may claim that the motivation for aggressive mobilisation rests in a synthesis of Thanos, the Innate Death Wish, and Narcissism. In the first chapter, I showed that such interpretations had little internal consistency and less political usefulness.

Whether identification theory is correct or not is to be judged by the evidence generally available of which identification theory provides a coherent, logically consistent and insightful interpretation.

There is also the question of whether, in applying identification theory to foreign policy, it would have been more profitable to analyse in depth one single case rather than the many that I put forward. If so, what kind of evidence would have been accessible, acceptable and helpful? Such an approach might have led to a detailed analysis of the media and political communications about a particular international event, and then listed the various pieces of evidence for mass national reaction. It might then have analysed the reactions of decision-makers to the movements of the mass national public. However, at both the media/mass public level and the decision-maker level, the gathering of such information – if possible – would have led us, in Fred Northedge's words again, to 'some perfectly obvious conclusions which could have been reached in a few minutes by common observation and reflection'. These obvious conclusions are that people mobilise when their nation is threatened, and that foreign policy decision-makers take account of the mood of the mass public. The observable facts, in terms of consistent patterns of behaviour, are clearly there. What identification theory does is to provide a coherent way of interpreting them. The problem here is not the quality or quantity of the evidence, but whether the theory itself has brought to light some consistent patterns in the relationship between the national identity dynamic and foreign policy decisions. To demonstrate a consistent pattern necessarily requires the analysis of several histories rather than one in depth.

PRESCRIPTIONS

Identification theory has led to some very clear *if . . . then . . .* propositions. This, in turn, leads to certain clear policy prescriptions. I

141

shall look first at the implications for nation-building, then for international integration, and then for foreign policy and diplomacy.

POLICIES FOR NATION-BUILDING

Chapter 3 made explicit the basic thrusts of policy and circumstance required for successful nation-building. The first feature is that the community within the state should share a common experience with actors who symbolise the state; and, second, that this experience should either be one of state beneficence, or that the state should represent an appropriate attitude in a perceived situation of threat.

These policy prescriptions can be brought into more dramatic practical relief by taking a perspective that is purely politically defensive: i.e. how can the government *qua* state best prevent a political opponent from mobilising local territorial or ethnic support on the basis of parochial or ethnic identifications?[24] How can the government prevent the opposite of nation-building and political integration – territorial disintegration?

As was made clear in the discussion on nationalism, an ethnos, simply because it is an ethnos, does not as such seek political autonomy, equality or advantage. In reality, what happens is that certain political individuals and groups *decide* that an ethnos should have such aspirations and policies, and these individuals then attempt to mobilise the other members of that ethnos. This has been described by one writer as the 'decision-making' model of nationalism.[25] These local or nationalist leaders can successfully mobilise their territorial or ethnic groups if the centralising state can be presented as overtly or covertly *disadvantaging* the ethnos; thus the centralising state is perceived as not enhancing but devaluing and threatening identity. By communicating about this common experience of disadvantage, and by providing a suitable symbolic attitude, peripheral leaders create an identity-securing interpretive system based in ethnic or territorial community and culture which can mobilise the people or ethnos. Such an interpretive system is a nationalist ideology.

The success of nationalist leaders, however, depends upon a changing constellation of political, economic, social and cultural factors, and the ability successfully to manipulate what Rokkan and Urwun have called 'the politicization of peripheral predicaments'.[26] To achieve nation-building, the state, therefore, must successfully act to block parochial ethnic sentiment being appropriated by nationalist and ethnic leaders. This is a crucially practical objective in terms of power politics if the state is to sustain itself.

Nation-building and the Standardisation of Culture: It has been the policy of many governments, in order to nation-build and to control peripheral ethnic groups, deliberately to manipulate educational and religious structures in order to bring about cultural standardisation and a culturally homogeneous citizenry. Policies are, therefore, pursued which attempt to bring about the use of one language, the language of the power centre, the adoption of one religion and the adoption of the general norms of the metropolitan culture. The various programmes of pre- and post-revolutionary Russification; the Ottomans' Turkification; Slavification; the recent attempt to introduce Swahili as the common language for Tanzania, Uganda and Kenya – are all examples of this policy approach.[27]

According to identification theory, however, this manipulated creation of homogeneous culture will not have any immediate effect in terms of evoking identification with, and therefore loyalty to, the nation-state. The direct manipulation of culture, language or religion evokes alienation rather than identification because as a political activity, by its very nature, it *threatens* already made identifications. It devalues peripheral cultures by attempting to impose metropolitan culture upon them. Thus, central government action to homogenise culture, in fact provides a political hook for peripheral agitators to demonstrate the disadvantaging effects of the relationship with the central state and, therefore, to mobilise hostile peripheral mass opinion. Rokkan and Urwin have made a list of the types of leaders, and their strategies, who emerge in just such situations.[28] Moreover homogeneous culture itself is no guarantee of identification with, or loyalty to, any particular political centre. It merely provides a common mode of communication. What, in fact, is crucial, of course, is *what* is communicated about and the experiences which trigger that communication.

A programme of homogenisation might be beneficial to nation-building in the short term, providing that it is accompanied by the perception of a beneficent experience courtesy of the state. For example, if education for its own sake is deemed good, then the government's distribution of increased educational opportunities and enhanced educational facilities – regardless of the cultural, linguistic or political strings – will tend to evoke identification with the benefactor. This beneficent experience, however, must be more powerful than the sentimental mobilisation that can be triggered by a local leader communicating about the threat to local culture.

In the long term, such a programme may prove constructive for nation-building in that:

1 It facilitates communication about common experiences between fellow citizens. This function of facilitating communication, however, is only relevant if (a) a common experience is being communicated about, if (b) this experience evokes identification and if (c) this identification coincides with symbols of the state. A common mode of communication, in itself, guarantees an ability *just as much to argue* as to agree. Common experience and shared symbols of identification are the crucial factors, not the medium, of communication.

2 It removes, if thoroughly carried out, distinctive cultural features that can be manipulated by nationalist leaders. Insomuch as every existing state, as we have discussed, has had to nation-destroy in order to nation-build, such a policy can obviously be successful. But even in the 'old continuous nations' there is a distinct tendency for 'dead' cultures to resurrect. It seems that cultures go dormant rather than disappear; regionalism can arise after centuries of quiet if the political correlation of forces is appropriate. Unless peripheral cultures are the recipients of real benefits courtesy of the state, then their quiescence can only be bought by the state's monopoly of force; I am thinking here not simply of a monopoly of military force, but of a monopoly of economic and social power that also occurs when culture coincides with class as in all colonial situations and states with an internal tribal hegemony.

3 A programme of homogenisation also facilitates the upward social mobility of ambitious individuals from the periphery to the centre, rather than leaving them as disgruntled peripheral troublemakers. With regard to providing a channel for social mobility, there is obviously no doubt that a standard mode of communication is required, but frequently this does not necessitate the disappearance of other languages; often a two-tier system of languages happily operates. This two-tier system is made up of a base structure of local territorial dialects and languages, on top of which there is a single language used by those participating in any form of labour that requires intermediate, further or higher education.[29] Many post-colonial situations demonstrate this syndrome with the metropolitan language remaining as the upper tier language. Providing that there is open access to this 'educated culture' language, the existence of the two tiers is not counterproductive to nation-building. Respect and support from the centre for the peripheral cultures, rather than denigration and threat, are the key factors for evoking identification.

Generous central government policies for peripheral cultures can, in fact, cut the ground out from under ethnic leaders as they find themselves hoist on their own petards. The emergence, for example, of a Welsh nationalist movement in Great Britain in the 1970s and its demands for cultural autonomy were generously met by the Westminster government: official recognition was given to the Welsh language, as well as a new broadcasting frequency and funds for a Welsh-only television channel. These actions demonstrated a respect for cultural distinctiveness while at the same time enhancing citizenship of the United Kingdom. In this way, central government was able to associate itself symbolically with Welsh culture by acting beneficently; there was no symbolic alienation between Welsh culture and central government. Those left out in the cold were the Welsh nationalist leaders who, although responsible for setting in motion the process which led central government to recognise the peripheral culture, now had no symbols of disadvantage with which to mobilise their people.[30] None of this is to deny the motivation of cold political calculation by the central government at Westminster. Nor is it to disregard the fact that central government could afford financially to support such peripheral culture. It is, however, to focus on it through the lens of identification theory. Lack of financial resources and lack of political maturity would have led to other consequences.

Policies, then, which seek to create linguistic, religious and cultural homogeneity do not, as such, produce nation-building. If these policies are constrained by force, then they will positively alienate. *There is more to be gained by the practical encouragement of subsidiary cultures than by their persecution.*

Respect for peripheral cultural identities can be built into state and government structures in a way which also acts as a channel of social mobility for potential peripheral agitators. This can be seen in all systems of participative government based in geographical divisions – from the constituencies of Britain through to all federal structures. These structures can even be stacked in favour of territorial peripheries. In Britain, for example, the Scottish and Welsh have more seats proportionally in the House of Commons than the English; and in the Soviet Union, the Soviet of Nationalities, which is theoretically at the apex of government and power management, has thirty-two deputies from each union republic, eleven from each autonomous republic, five from each autonomous region and one from each national district – all of these figures irrespective of size.[31]

Political policies of cultural homogenisation are given theoretical justification in modern social theory by a major functionalist approach which posits education and the creation of a homogeneously educated culture as the central structural thrust in nation-building and national-

145

ism.[32] Central to this whole theory is the prime importance of upward social mobility. 'The political significance of social mobilisation is that it promotes the formation of consensus at the national level by encouraging nationalism and economic and social integration, strengthening, in the process, the hold of the national community over all of its citizens.'[33] This approach, however, confuses the educated class with the general citizenry, making national sentimental association the prerogative of the educated. Certainly, a certain level of education is a prerequisite for industrialisation and modernisation, but it is irrelevant to nation-building. It is, in fact, to the dismay of many that nationalism and fervent patriotism can be precisely a major mobiliser of a mass of people *uneducated* in the ways that would give them access to participation in the processes of modern society and the modern state. Democratic and educated political participation in contemporary society is no more necessary for nation-building that is the ability of twenty thousand emotionally involved football supporters to kick a football more accurately than this author. Social mobility from the periphery to the centre is important only insomuch as it syphons off agitators. Increased opportunities for social mobility do not, as such, work towards evoking national identity from the mass peoples and, therefore, at a purely psychological level of analysis do not aid nation-building. From a pragmatic political perspective, social mobility can be crucial in absorbing potential peripheral agitators.

The policy implications for nation-building are thus clear:

1 Government constraints to homogenise culture are counter-productive as they politicise peripheral interests. Homogenisation is anyway no guarantee of identification with, and therefore loyalty to, the state.

2 Education which is provided must be clearly presented as a public good given by a beneficent state; this should be clear whether the actual educational organisation is based in local or regional authorities.

3 There should be no attacks on local, cultural or religious symbols as this will evoke only alienation.

4 Where possible, state actors should be seen to be supportive of local cultures in a beneficent manner that undercuts any peripheral leader's communications about peripheral disadvantage.

Economic and social welfare: In the advanced economies of the world, despite extreme levels of uneven development, the obvious disadvantaging of peripheral or ethnic groups is mitigated by the various welfare systems. State welfare policies not only act to remedy blatant disadvantages that could be used as mobilising symbols by peripheral leaders, but they also act to evoke identification with the state as the common benefactor. Whatever the peripheral politicians' utterances about relative disadvantage, central government is still seen to be providing essential welfare. In a very real sense, welfarism is the bottom line of nation-building in the modern industrialised state.[34] It is not simply that the silence of the disadvantaged is cheaply bought, but that the state plays a parental role in meeting minimal needs and thus evoking identification. It must, however, be clearly acknowledged that notions of disadvantage and relative deprivation are culture bound.

Beyond the industrialised nations, there is a problem of social and political culture conflicting with social and political reality. The political culture might posit materialistic egalitarianism as a norm, but the norm is thwarted by gross differences between the materialistic life styles of the centre and of the periphery. If the local culture approved of such a display of hierarchical differentiation – for mystic or religious reasons, for example – then there is no intrinsic political problem;[35] but if there is no such identity-securing interpretive system for such hierarchical differentiation, political instability will be endemic. Nation to nation, and culture to culture, the criteria for what is acceptable does, of course, vary. I cannot, however, think of a contemporary area where a differential between famine and a satisfied appetite is overtly culturally acceptable.[36] It is also difficult to think of a region where there is not an expectation of rising standards of living.[37]

If it is accepted that nation-building is essentially a psychological dynamic evoked by political action and not a coincidental function of modernisation, then the effects of economic policies for nation-building in developing states take on some clarity. If nation-building has high political priority, then gross economic differentials between the centre and the peripheral areas *should not be perceivable*. It is, however, a virtually unavoidable fact that the trickle-down model of economic growth – i.e. that the efforts of individual capitalist entrepreneurs in a free market will increase wealth so that it trickles down to the rest of the national society – although arguably presenting the best chances for long term growth, inherently creates extreme forms of relative deprivation and is, therefore, counterproductive to nation-building in the short term. Moreover, in many developing states, there is an internal tribal hegemony which limits the opportunities of members of other ethnic groupings, thereby exacerbating the situation.

In order to nation-build, government economic policy must be to distribute public goods which materialistically benefit the peripheral masses. This is to say that in order to nation-build in situations of high profile relative deprivation, welfarism has to be introduced immediately. (In this context, by welfarism I mean the distribution of social justice as well as more materialistic public goods.) There is only one alternative to this – that those citizens operating at the centre affect an image that is culturally close to those citizens at the periphery. The other practical alternative, which does not of itself evoke mass national identification, is to ensure that there are clear channels of social mobility from the periphery to the centre.[38]

In developing economies with socialist economic policies, welfarism and egalitarianism are essential ideological features. Nevertheless, disparities in standards of living are still inevitable between the state centre and rural periphery. It has, therefore, in fact, become a distinctive feature of developing economies with a base in socialist policies for their leaders deliberately to eschew any signs of prestige. This model was given its highest profile in the personal culture of Mao Tse Tung and then spread throughout post-revolutionary Chinese society generally in the enforced adoption by everyone, for example, of the simple 'Mao suits'. One does not rely on a political culture whose norm is a materialistic hierarchy. The image of the leader and leading elite says: 'We are all in the same boat and we approach the situation together.' Not only, then, do the leaders wear simple clothing, but they might also live simply and be publicised doing the same kind of things as their peripheral citizenry might do. Presidents Nyerere of Tanzania, Castro of Cuba and Ghaddafi of Libya have displayed just such approaches.

Charisma and political religion: There is a further pattern in relation to nation-building, not directly related to policy prescription but important for detached analysis, which can be usefully noted. This concerns situations where a society is in a state of crisis which threatens the identities of the mass of the citizens. This phenomenon was widespread, for example, in the years after the Second World War when imperial colonies passed rapidly into post-colonial independence. In transitional social crisis situations such as these, people generally will actively seek to make a new identification which will give them psychological security – to find an identity-securing interpretive system for the new political experiences and realities.

This security may be found in an identification with a single person who is in tune with the group culture and who displays the appropriate attitude for dealing with the crisis. In this situation, that one individual alone supplies the appropriate symbolic behaviour and, in a

148

very real sense, is appropriated by the aggregate need for that satisfactory identity-securing interpretive system. It may be that the leader has much political talent and oratorical artistry, but her charismatic power comes from the emotional investment made in her by the people and not from any intrinsic magnetism or transcendent qualities.[39] The emergence of charismatic leaders in times of transitional social crisis is, therefore, as much to be expected as it is in times of warfare. In both situations, a mass psychological need is appropriately met by a leader who is indeed close to Freud's notion of the safe parental figure with whom to identify in times of threat. The charismatic leader, then, can serve a very necessary purpose in times of threat and transition, despite the dangers and manipulations inherent in any personality cult.

Equally, simplistic ideology may also meet the needs of transition crises. The manner in which the mass population may adhere to this new ideology may be reminiscent of religious attachments, but again this is to miss the psychological function of ideology in times of change.[40] As with the charismatic leader, the new ideology – usually one of nationalist or socialist symbols in recently created states – provides a way of psychologically coming to terms with the experiences and perceptions of the new political realities. It may be that the social rituals for communicating with each other about this shared identification are reminiscent of their religious rituals, but this does not alter the social–psychological nature of the ideology. In the West, for example, there is a distinct similarity between the sermon from the pulpit and the speech from the platform; equally, in Africa, the songs and dances surrounding political meetings may resemble animist religious ceremonies. The point is that the similarity of style does not mean that the content is religious rather than political.

Moreover, at least since the industrial revolution, all societies have been in a state of continuous change and can, therefore, be described as passing through crises of transition. In the contemporary world, there is, thus, always the possibility of the deliberate political manipulation of symbols of crisis in order to create a situation that welcomes a charismatic leader.[41] It is beyond the remit of thesis to pursue this line of thought, but it is in many ways the meat of domestic political competition.

International threat: Finally, one needs to mention that the appropriation and manipulation of images of the international environment can be used for nation-building. As was fully discussed in chapter 4, the presentation of an external threat evokes group cohesion.

Nation-building failure: This analysis clearly suggests that there will be a failure in nation-building if the general policy prescriptions described above are not followed. Ian Lustick's *State-Building Failure in British Ireland and French Algeria* is the history of just two such failures.[42] His study is an examination of the factors that prevented the integration of Ireland into Britain and Algeria into France.

Lustick compares English behaviour and the policies of Westminster towards Ireland with its behaviour and policies towards Scotland and Wales. In a similar manner, he compares French actions in Algeria with its actions in Sardinia. The central thrust of his argument, applicable to both English action in Ireland and French action in Algeria, is that integration was blocked by the existence of metropolitan settlers who, over many centuries, held themselves culturally apart from, and who maintained an elite economic status over, the local inhabitants. Phrased within the identification theory paradigm, this is to say that these settlers mediated all perceptions and experiences of the metropolitan centre; the indigenous populations, therefore, never experienced any materialistic beneficence from the central state, nor did they have the opportunity for a communal experience against a common external threat. In fact, the settlers themselves presented an ongoing external threat to the indigenous population.

One can say, in fact, that in the most general way, anti-imperialist movements demonstrate *par excellence* the failure of nation-building policies.

SUMMARY OF POLICIES FOR NATION-BUILDING

The preceding discussion can be summed up:

1 Welfarism
2 External threat
3 Egalitarian images
4 Social justice   evoke mass national identity
5 Respect for peripheral culture   and nation-build
6 Social crisis + charismatic
    leader or simplistic ideology

1 Social mobility
2 Modern communications   do not evoke mass national
    system   identity, do not nation-build
3 Enforced homogeonisation of
    culture

150

INTERNATIONAL INTEGRATION

Identification theory can be similarly applied to deduce the policy requirements for international integration whose object is to achieve transnational loyalty. ('Supranation-building'?)

Following identification theory, the requirements are straightforward:

1 There should be a clearly recognisable symbolic form with which identification takes place.
2 That symbolic form should evoke identification by:
   (a) Being protective in the face of external threat.
   (b) Being materialistically beneficent.

To repeat the same point made several times earlier with reference to nationalism and nation-building: that international integration is good or sensible or rewarding, no matter how much trumpeted by visionaries and media, is insufficient to evoke mass identification and loyalty. A transfer of loyalty, an identification with a new polity, will not occur unless a clearly identifiable symbolic form *evokes* that identification.

It is an essential necessity, therefore, that there should first of all be a symbol or set of symbols which are clearly representative of the supranational polity and with which identification can take place. The symbols must then mediate, and be associated with, those types of experience that evoke identification (i.e. materialistic beneficence or appropriate attitude in the face of external threat); equally importantly, of course, these experiences must be the subject of communication in formal and informal social rituals.

The European Community, for example, lacks just such a set of symbols, although for a certain intellectual class 'European culture' has fulfilled that function;[43] similarly in Africa, the notion of 'negritude' also once fulfilled that role.[44]

The first task of any entity, therefore, seeking supranational identification, must be one of careful propaganda, publicity and public relations. The polity must be clearly perceivable, must have symbols which can be internalised and it must be experienced and communicated about. The track record of international integration is, of course, unremarkable. Most academic studies posit the European Economic Community as the most successful example, but even here there has been no mass identification with the new organisation; concern over national sovereignty and national identity have not declined in potency.[45] Thus far, mobilisation of the parochial national identity dynamic has ensured a general blocking of any form of integration that

151

impinges upon images of national sovereignty. Crucially, of course, even though it has a high profile and is generally known, the European Economic Community is not perceived to be materialistically benefi-cent to its European constituents; in fact, state by state, domestic arguments continue about the economic cost or benefit of membership of the Community. Where, however, the Community does perhaps take on some experiential psychological meaningfulness is in its image of providing a secure community in the face of United States and Japanese economic threat. Some experiential meaningfulness may also be found in the political rituals which surround the Community; these occur regularly at the times of the elections to the European Parlia-ment, and in the form of predictable arguments that are associated with payments into, and subsidies from, the Community. As symbols of the European Community emerge, take on a higher profile and begin to have some meaning for the mass of people; as actions of the European Community impinge directly upon the mass of people and are perceived and communicated about as being to the general good; as the European Community increasingly becomes an identifiable block in contradistinction to the international environment; as politicians begin to trigger, manipulate and appropriate a European identity dynamic, and so on. As all these factors work together, over time it is possible that allegiance will be transferred from the individual nation-states to the supranational community, and thus real integration will occur.

Theoretically, the organisation which might best be able to evoke a general supranational identification is the United Nations. Through its various activities, both in its central and subsidiary organs, it has the potential to present a clear image of an organisation working for the materialistic benefit of the mass citizenry of the planet. But, although the United Nations has initiated many issue-specific practical and propaganda campaigns, there has not been a consistent and integrated campaign for the United Nations itself. The actual functions of the United Nations lend themselves perfectly to evoking identification: peace-keeping, international law, care for children, health, education, human rights, food and so on. High profile media and political focus on the United Nations, however, has been mainly concerned with interstate conflicts for which the United Nations bodies and Assembly provide a setting; mass media has not focused upon the functioning of its welfare aspects. Even when there has been focus upon its welfare aspects, it has been upon campaigns to study and to solve existing problems rather than upon those areas where the organisation has functioned harmoniously, successfully and to the general benefit.[46]

From the perspective of identification theory, mass identification with the United Nations will only occur if all these functions are perceived and communicated about. It is easy to imagine a propaganda campaign on behalf of the United Nations which lists its successes and benefits, and which identifies the United Nations with the very highest human ideals – as opposed to the current image of an idealistic organisation manipulated by partisan interests and perceived to be continually failing.

The role of local politicians is also crucial. In relation to supranationalism, national politicians behave like peripheral agitators. This is because it is inherent in contemporary mass politics that supranational integration will only become a proposition pushed by national politicians when it might possibly carry mass support. This is to say that domestic politicians, seeking power, will only attempt to mobilise support behind a supranational polity when the circumstances are favourable for a generalised identification with that supranational polity – for only then can national politicians trust that there will be mass mobilisation behind the supranational polity, and that they can then appropriate that dynamic for their own power base.

NATIONAL CHARACTERISTICS, DIPLOMACY AND THIRD PARTIES

As discussed in chapters 1 and 4, there is no observable correlation between national characteristics and foreign policy behaviour or international conflict. It is certainly true that national cultures have particular, idiosyncratic characteristics which, through socialisation and identification, are passed down from generation to generation. But unless a particular culture possesses a norm of organised and state approved group violence which spills over beyond the state's borders, there is no methodologically coherent reason why differences in culture, as such, lead to international friction. Conflict between different national masses of people arises only if the peoples are presented with images which threaten, or which provide the possible enhancement of, national identity. Whether that happens or not is a matter of media and political decision-making.

The fact that there is no correspondence between national characteristics and international conflict can obviously be seen in the rapid changes of attitude which can take place on the international scene. After 1945, for instance, it did not take long for the Germans to become allies of the British and the Americans and for the Russians to become enemies. Equally, the rehabilitation of the Chinese in western eyes was miraculously fast after a few ping-pong matches and the visit of the United States President. International friction is politically, and not culturally, inspired.

Where national characteristics may directly impinge upon international relations is when diplomats and statesmen have not transcended the perceptual and communication limitations of their own parochial national culture. It is, in fact, precisely the job of diplomats to be able to communicate with each other regardless of background and cultural mode. 'The diplomat finds himself operating between cultures, and sometimes in the midst of several simultaneously . . . He interprets and appraises for his client situations and developments in foreign cultural contexts . . . Cross-cultural interpretation is therefore the basic professional function of the diplomat.'[47]

Of course, the purpose of diplomacy is not simply effective interpersonal communication. Its purpose is to allow states to communicate and to negotiate with each other in a dimension free of the constraints and pressures of domestic politics. Stated within the identification theory paradigm, the purpose of diplomacy is to create interstate communication which cannot be appropriated by local politicians and communicators in order to mobilise the national identity dynamic. Issues raised in diplomacy are to be open to negotiation and not to be appropriated by domestic politicians in order to mobilise national identity on behalf of their own vested interests. In the contemporary world, of course, unless negotiations are kept secret, there is little possibility of avoiding this domestic political dynamic. This modern situation structurally resembles the courts of warrior kings: for the king to survive he must act according to the mores of the warrior class; for the modern government to survive, it too must show no signs of weakness lest internal opponents mobilise the national identity dynamic. Historically, the need for diplomatic communications transcending warrior mores led to ambassadors and diplomats having a status that transcended, and was other than, the warrior culture. For the diplomat to be effective he had to have a certain metaphysical quality; he was the enemy's representative who was not eaten or thrown to the lions. Further, as diplomacy evolved, it actually took on forms of more ritualised communication and protocol which not only transcended warrior mores but also transcended parochial/national cultural differences. These rituals can be seen, for example, in the way in which the seating is arranged at a conference table and the order of precedence for ambassadors when visiting a Head of State.[48] In a very real sense, the diplomat, although representing national interest, belongs then to a transnational culture and is *detached* from any possibility of mobilising the national identity dynamic. It was, for example, precisely this ability to detach from national culture and to relate culturally in the widest possible way that gave Henry Kissinger such an ethos of success.[49] The 'sacred' communication and ritual of diplomats, therefore, not only avoids culturo-centric communication, but also sidesteps appropriation by domestic political dynamics.

The disastrous effect of diplomacy conducted in the full glare of open publicity can be seen in the progress of the East–West arms negotiations. Technically, strategically and politically, these talks hold the possibility of line by line disagreement. And each one of these disagreements can be appropriated by domestic politicians for use in the domestic political game. Every hint of disagreement, or any nuance of weakness, can be appropriated by the domestic media and by competing domestic politicians and used to trigger the national identity dynamic. Identification theory thus suggests that a major difficulty in East–West negotiations does not lie in overt strategic and ideological conflicts, but in the domestic dynamic of how these talks are perceived and communicated about.

Carefully stage-managed diplomacy, then, if possible to arrange, gives states who are in conflict an opportunity to adjust their original demands and positions, and to back down, without loss of prestige, without any threat to, or denigration of, symbols of national identity. It is in this sense that the United Nations, or any mediation by a symbolically detached third party, is constructive and helpful. The aid from third party mediation in international conflict comes not so much from any ability to present the cases of the two antagonists in any novel or uniquely shrewd light; nor is it based in the ability of the arbitrator to seduce the opponents into common sense and mutually agreeable positions – though both, of course, are useful.[50] The aid comes from the fact that submission to, and arbitration by, the United Nations, or any other transcendent mediator, can be perceived as *not* being a threat to national identity. It allows room for backdown and the redefinition of positions without risking domestic instability due to the mobilisation of the national identity dynamic. It provides a forum for communication between hostile parties when other communication environments would imply weakness. The image of the United Nations as a primitive medicine man dressed in leopard skins and drawing an imaginary line of peace between savage antagonists, and thus allowing the antagonists to cool down without losing face, has a substantial reality when understood from the perspective of the national identity dynamic.[51] It would be to everyone's benefit to invest the United Nations or other

155

third party arbitration with the highest form of ethical prestige that attracts mass political support. Only then could governments surrender to international arbitration without jeopardising their domestic power base by being prey to competition for the national identity dynamic.

FOREIGN POLICY AND DECISION-MAKERS

In terms of the successful consummation of foreign policy, there is little to add to what has already been said in chapter 4. Given that the ability to mass mobilise a politically integrated national citizenry is a primary power resource in effective foreign policy, identification theory has clearly pointed out how to achieve such a situation. First, there must be successful nation-building. Second, the mass national public must have foreign policy presented to it in such a way that that foreign policy is perceived to be protecting or enhancing national identity in the face of external threat. The question that does remain to be discussed concerns notions of political responsibility and ethics. It concerns how people in the mass media, politicians and decision-makers behave in relation to international images and to the national identity dynamic. It concerns the responsible and irresponsible behaviour of media figures, politicians and decision-makers in terms of triggering or calming the national identity dynamic; and could be the subject of further research.

PEACE AND PARADOXES

What becomes clear from an analysis based in identification theory is the very real and crucial psychological dimension of international relations – a dimension which includes not only leaders and decision-makers, but also the mass national peoples. In recognising clearly and explicitly the types of communication which may trigger the mobilisation of the mass national citizenry, one can equally clearly prescribe concerning the types of communication which are conducive to international peace. The point which has first of all to be accepted is the fallacy of the notion that 'sticks and stones may break our bones, but words will never hurt us'. This is untrue. Actions and utterances, overt or covert, that can be interpreted as threatening symbols of national identity, do hurt. They threaten the sense of identity and disturb feelings of psychological security. Communications which threaten identity always provide the possibility for setting in motion domestic political processes which can overspill into international conflict.

It is unrealistic to expect human nature to change, to expect humanity – overnight, over millennia, ever – to mature and transcend what appears to be one of our most basic bio-sociological drives. Not satisfying hunger or lust would obviously mean the disappearance of humanity. Equally, not satisfying the identification imperative would also mean no humanity, at least as we know it. Since it would be impossible to alter the essential nature of the animal, our prescriptions, based in identification theory, for a better ordered, more peaceful global society must then be concerned with: (a) the communications which affect national identity; or (b) the political dynamics entwined with national identity.

The communications: Morgenthau made the cavalier and fallacious suggestion that international conflict was the result of the savage urges of the mass of people, and that peace was the result of the wisdom and wiles of statesmen.[52] Lord knows how much damage that idiotic statement has done to young (and old) minds reading international politics, but its crass stupidity is demonstrated, for example, by thinking back to times before the mass public was involved in international relations, when international conflict was mainly, in fact, the *preserve* of an elite and privileged few. Historically, the mass of people has mainly not been involved in international conflict. The age of total war is a recent phenomenon, arguably dating from the Thirty Years War. Identification theory explicates how the mass public can indeed be mobilised for war, but the causal factor is not an innate urge-to-destroy for its own sake, but a behavioural imperative to defend and enhance identity in the face of an external threat.

The crucial and fundamental question then arises: *Who communicates about the threat and for what purposes?* The answer is extremely simple. It is domestic politicians who communicate about the threat in order to mobilise public support for their own policy and power base. It is also the mass media who communicate about it in order to mobilise an increased audience.

In terms of effective foreign policy, identification theory has told us that in order to mobilise mass public support behind a particular foreign policy initiative, that initiative must be associated with the defence or enhancement of symbols of national identity. This is merely the theoretical explication of a practical, well-rehearsed political art. Conversely, if one seeks peaceful coexistence, the prescription is blatantly obvious: Politicians and mass media communicators should not *play* upon the national identity dynamic in their utterances. It is too dangerous a dynamic to be used in the cut and thrust of domestic political competition or as a tool for achieving successful sales or viewing figures.

157

Peaceful coexistence is not, then, simply a matter of controlling intentions, communications and propaganda to *other* states.[53] It is also a matter of self-control by domestic actors in their communication with their *own* constituents. This is a call for an intelligent and responsible sensitivity to the way in which information concerning international relations can affect the national identity dynamic and, like the sorcerer's apprentice, unleash forces that get out of control. Is this call for maturity amongst our politicians and communicators naive? Are the partisan political and commercial benefits of playing the national identity dynamic too great to allow for the consideration of such a sense of responsibility? I would hope that the lack of responsibility displayed thus far is due, at least in part, to ignorance concerning the structure and dynamics of mobilising national identity.

In a perilous nuclear world, it is surely possible for leaders and communicators to appreciate that the benefits which come from manipulating the national identity dynamic are short-term and short-sighted. The world is quite simply too dangerous for careless emotive communication. In the face of nuclear holocaust, not to mention the horrors of contemporary non-nuclear war, it is imperative that a new maturity be achieved in domestic and international communications. It is simply too stupid and too dangerous to continue playing the national identity dynamic game in domestic politics.

Equally, the constituents, the mass national citizens themselves, could also display a new maturity in terms of what they actually expect of their leaders and communicators – and what they are prepared to believe. Hope always lies in education and in enlightenment – why else are we in this educational business? The basic propositions of this analysis are not too complex to be stated in simple non-esoteric language: 'For psychological safety we have a behavioural imperative to identify. Having then made an identification, there is a dynamic which works towards defending and enhancing it. There are various social dynamics which lead us to internalise a national identity which we will then, if appropriately stimulated, seek to enhance or defend. We must, therefore, be *self-consciously* careful about how we allow ourselves to be motivated by this drive.' To propose such self-control is surely not naive. It is not safe to overindulge any instinct and, just as the more overt appetites can be controlled for self-interest, so the identity dynamic can also be controlled. First, however, we need the education and insight to acknowledge it, and then the self-discipline to bring it under intelligent control.

Paradox 1: This, however, leads to the first paradox which must be acknowledged. The discussion has progressed on the basis that it is mainly the mass national citizenry which is subject to national identification and that the leaders and communicators are somehow separate and above such an identification. It has been implied that politicians and communicators are self-consciously manipulating the national identity dynamic for their private purposes whilst being themselves separate from the dynamic. Unfortunately, this is not quite the case. While some politicians and communicators may identify themselves with some transnational culture, many of them are great patriots. The political competition to appear more patriotic than one's competitors is not necessarily a public performance aimed simply at mobilising political support, but is also a manifestation of a genuine identification with the nation-state by the politician. Unscientifically, it is not difficult to identify those leaders of contemporary states who genuinely experience patriotism. These patriotic leaders accept as real, true and good their stances on national interest and their perceptions of external threat. Indeed, in order to enhance their own sense of national identity and for other psychological reasons (beyond the remit of this thesis) these leaders may build, encourage and even whip up mass national feeling because they think that such a national feeling is a public good in itself.[54] Their attitude displays no psychological insight into either themselves or their constituents, and displays no practical political insight into the genuine dangers for the international political system of such sentiments. They serve a domestic psycho–political game which spills over into a spiral of images of the international system in which competition and conflict is necessarily accepted as the norm.

This patriotism amongst political leaders is but a hint of the patriotism that exists professionally in the armed services. There is a whole industrial complex and mass of people who are professionally involved in serving national identity and what is interpreted as national interest. Within this psychological gestalt it is axiomatic that the world is divided into competing warrior-states – for, if it were not, these people would have no purpose. Within the academy of International Relations, this world-view is accepted and reinforced by students and teachers of Strategy.

Let us be clear, though, that a mature attitude to communications about national identity and international threat is possible. In Scandinavia, after centuries of conflict, Swedish and Norwegian leaders deliberately chose to seek a path of friendship and cooperation – and disciplined their communications consistently.[55] This is perfectly normal where an alliance is agreed and considered necessary. Western Europe since 1945 displays generally such a maturity in its interstate communications. It may be that such a maturity has been achieved in

159

the face of a perceived common threat from the East, but the nature of the motivation should not detract from the fact that western European states have been capable of so ordering their affairs. Equally, when it was deemed appropriate for the United States to have friendly communications with the People's Republic of China, a new mature form of communication was employed. Similarly after Sadat's visit to Israel, there was care in the communications between Egypt and Israel. All this is to say that it is not idealistic to ask for such a maturity.

The problem lies in extending this maturity, based in self-interest, from specific international relationships to *all* international relationships.

One needs to be clear, though, that as there will always be renegade states, this is not a call for a passive and duped universal foreign policy. It is a call for discretion towards the international environment and for an end to appropriating apparent conflicts with stereotyped enemies for the domestic political game. This appropriation is essentially dishonest and can have dire consequences. This is a call for a more mature leadership, a more mature media and a more mature constituency. This requires also a mature democracy in which open discussion concerning the illusory quality of external threat is accepted as a normal aspect of everyday political discourse – and not as potential treachery subject to threats and constraints.

Political structure: What has also become clear from the analysis based in identification theory are the profound dangers which come from joining the nation with the state. Once a cultural, therefore psychological, community becomes concordant with a political system, that political system takes a quantum leap from being a purely functional power entity into being a psycho–political entity. The state in which there has been successful nation-building can draw on that most basic of its power resources, the psychological attachment of its people. Certainly, from a viewpoint based purely in analysing domestic state interests, this is a good and necessary thing. Perceived from a paradigm beyond that of domestic interest, it has created a dangerous and volatile entity – dangerous and volatile because that mass psychological attachment, based in identification, is prey to all the manipulation and propaganda of irresponsible domestic political competition and media interests.

In the previous section, I called for a maturity amongst politicians and communicators, but why call for that maturity when, possibly, a different form of political arrangement could remove the dangerous toy from the children's hands in the first place? What is being suggested here is the disengagement of national culture from polity. One is looking to the dismantling of the ideology that each nation should have its state and all the implicit political prescriptions.

A bundle of paradoxes: But here arises a bundle of paradoxes which takes us into the very essence of political philosophy. These paradoxes concern political legitimacy and what is the natural psychological way for human beings to associate and order their affairs.

People naturally, as part of the historical process, move into self-identifying groups. Even if their original motivation for associating together is purely instrumental, over time, with shared communications about common experiences and in contradistinction to the external environment, they come to share a common culture. It is one of the natural riches of human life to enjoy the psychological security of shared culture, but people belong simultaneously to many overlapping cultural and social groups – from nuclear family, through age set, leisure interests, profession and so forth, to planetary citizenship. Thus, in suggesting that culture be disengaged from polity, one may be asking for the impossible; over time, it is surely inevitable that people endow their associations with culture. This is the very essence of human social life. We may seek to disengage culture from polity for the common good, but there is an anthropological dynamic to endow polity with culture, to endow any social system with an appropriate identity-securing interpretive system.

The reason that one comes to think, in the first place, of disengaging national culture from polity is because of the terrible history of mass mobilisation for conflict. It is precisely the shared culture, the shared identity, which provides the psychological dynamism of mobilisation. But need this be so? People are not prepared to mobilise and die for *all* the different cultures in their lives with which they have made an identification.

Our problem may lie, therefore, not so much in the fact that culture coincides with polity, but in the fact that the actual culture of national citizenship legitimates, and presents as a norm, mass national mobilisation for international conflict as a good and proper thing. Built into the ideological notions of nationality and good citizenship is that extraordinary concept that it is a good and noble thing to die for one's country. One's country, but not one's tennis club. One's country, but not one's village.

It is logical, therefore, that the *noble death* ethic should be exorcised from the culture of national citizenship. On reflection it is not quite so obvious. This is so because there are occasions in history – contrary to

161

the philosophy of pacifism – when the struggle for one's nation is also inextricably involved with personal freedom. One thinks of the struggles of national liberation from alien cultures and one thinks of the conflicts against totalitarianism. These perhaps are not occasions when the mass national citizenry is duped either by its own emotionalism or by the manipulations of domestic leaders. In fact, these appear to be occasions when there is a distinct nobility in being prepared to die for one's country. How one judges these situations, though, will depend upon one's own political perceptions and psychological predispositions.

Perhaps, however, the paradox of whether the mobilised mass nation is duped or being noble, can be resolved by examining the reality of the threat. Are physical constraints involved in forcing people to change their culture, to change their identity? If so, then a basic human freedom is threatened and justifies mobilisation. One moves now into philosophical arguments of natural justice. I almost begin to yearn nostalgically for ancient days when international conflict was between elites and when a change of elite meant little to the masses of people. The warfare could progress at a certain warrior caste social level while the rest of life, with all its varied cultural pockets, continued as normal. To a degree this, too, is romantic as one looks to the history of religious persecution. Certainly, industrialisation, modernisation, mass media, massive state bureaucracies – have changed everything. The ideology of the modern state affects everyone within the state. Mass media and massive economic/industrial planning leave no one untouched. If Washington's system was imposed on Moscow – or vice versa – it would be felt right through to all strata of the population. That this is an age of total war is not simply the result of the function of modern weapons, but also of the psycho–social involvement of total populations in the state and in the culture of the nation-state.

Decentralisation and the breaking down of monolithic state-inspired national cultures now surfaces as a possible prescription for a more peaceful global society. What then is the future of the state? Is it possible to envisage it as a purely instrumental and functional entity? Is it possible to imagine it not being endowed with an identity-securing interpretive system and not to have it legitimated by a concordant culture? These are questions beyond my remit.

Socialisation into national citizenship – the internalising of national identity – carries with it powerful and true images of a history of terrible international conflict. That it be a norm of national citizenship to mobilise for conflict is given rich justification by the realities of history and contemporary conflict. This syndrome is then manipulated and played upon by domestic political competition. The leaders, as well as the led, believe that what they are doing is real and good. There is a destructive false consciousness here which creates a self-perpetuating political psycho-drama. The drama has to change. The histrionic arias of nationalism and patriotism played on the stage of domestic political competition must, quite simply, be banned from the repertoire. The audience should refuse to listen, the musicians refuse to accompany and the singers refuse to sing.

The notion that it is a glorious thing to die for one's country is a dangerous and terrible idea. It is not to be dealt with flippantly, stupidly or self-seekingly. Anthropologically we are all of the same species and it is only chance that causes our birth in this or in that particular country. It is through the identification imperative that we then become psychologically linked with that country. There is a poignant and awful innocence here – for what begins as a blind psychological action, in which insecure human beings seek a necessary psychological security, becomes in the tornado of political realities the fuel for mass mobilisation and total war.

What can we ask for that is in the realms of possibility and reality? We can ask for a more profound understanding of human psychology and that, on the basis of this understanding, we – citizens, teachers, communicators, leaders – then act and communicate with greater sensitivity and greater responsibility.

NOTES

PREFACE
1 Edward Glover, *The Dangers of Being Human*, Allen and Unwin, 1936; Glover, *War, Sadism and Pacifism*, Allen and Unwin, 1937.

1 PROBLEM AND REVIEW
1 For a discussion of the behavioural upheaval in International Relations and its effects, see James E. Dougherty and Robert L. Pfaltzgraff, *Contending Theories of International Relations*, Harper and Row, 1981, pp. 35–8; also all the essays in Steve Smith (ed.), *International Relations: British and American Perspectives*, Basil Blackwell/BISA, 1985.

2 F.S. Northedge, 'Transnationalism: The American Illusion', *Millennium*, V, 1, Spring 1976, p. 22; Hedley Bull, 'International Theory: The Case for a Classical Approach', *World Politics*, XVIII, April 1966.

3 All this is discussed fully below in chapter 4.

4 The one major exception to this is Hans J. Morgenthau who perceived the masses, fuelled by nationalism, to be a force ever seeking international conflict. I shall deal with this notion fully in my final chapter. I do not involve Morgenthau in these preliminary remarks as his seminal *Politics Among Nations*, Knopf, 1948, was published before the behavioural upheaval.

5 This is discussed fully in chapter 3.

6 See chapter 3.

7 Again, see chapter 3.

8 Gabriel A. Almond, 'Political Theory and Political Science', in Ithiel de Sola Pool (ed.), *Contemporary Political Science: Toward Empirical Theory*, McGraw Hill, 1967, p. 5.

9 See, for example, Graeme Duncan, 'Political Theory and Human Nature', in Ian Forbes and Steve Smith (eds.), *Politics and Human Nature*, Frances Pinter, 1983, pp. 5–20; Peter A. Corning, 'Introduction', in J.R. Pennock and J.W. Chapman (eds.), *Human Nature in Politics*, New York University Press, 1977, pp. 1–16; also David Apter's three chapters on political philosophy, 'The Classical Tradition', 'The Enlightenment Tradition', 'The Radical Tradition', in his *Introduction to Political Analysis*, Winthrop, 1977, pp. 47–136; William F. Stone, *The Psychology of Politics*, Free Press, 1974, chapter 2, 'Approaches to the Study of Political Psychology', pp. 21–44.

10 More recently, there has also been an attempt to justify this Hobbesian view by recourse to biological argument; see Konrad Lorenz, *On Aggression*, Bantam, 1967; Robert Ardrey, *The Territorial Imperative*, Atheneum, 1966; also Desmond Morris, *The Naked Ape*, Jonathan Cape, 1967. For a more general discussion of theories of human needs in relation to politics, see chapters 1 and 2, 'You Can't Change Human Nature' and 'Social and Individual Nature', in James C. Davies, *Human Nature in Politics*, John Wiley, 1963.

11 John Chapman in Pennock and Chapman (eds.), *Human Nature*, pp. 295–6.

12 *Ibid.*, p. 297.

13 Brian Redhead in his 'Introduction', British Broadcasting Corporation, *Political Thought from Plato to Nato*, Ariel Books/BBC, 1984, p. 9.

14 R. Thomson, *The Pelican History of Psychology*, Penguin, 1968; E.G. Boring, *A History of Experimental Psychology*, Appleton, 1950; R.I. Watson, *The Great Psychologists: From Aristotle to Freud*, Harper and Row, 1978.

15 Graham Wallas, *Human Nature in Politics*, Constable, 1908.

16 *Ibid.*, p. 45.

17 Stone, *The Psychology of Politics*, chapter 2, 'Approaches to the Study of Political Psychology', p. 21.

18 Sigmund Freud, 'Thoughts for the Times on War and Death' (1915) in *Collected Papers*, IV, Hogarth Press, 1949, pp. 288–317; *Civilisation and Its Discontents*, Hogarth Press, 1930; 'Why War?' (1932) in *Collected Papers*, V, Hogarth Press, 1950, pp. 272–87. See also P. Roazen, *Freud: Political and Social Thought*, Knopf, 1968.

19 Edward Glover, *War, Sadism and Pacifism*, Allen and Unwin, 1933; Alix Strachey, *The Unconscious Motives of War*, Allen and Unwin, 1957; William Brown, *Essays in War and Peace*, Adam and Black, 1939. For helpful essays on this topic, see James E. Dougherty and Robert L. Pfaltzgraff, *Contending Theories of International Relations*, Harper and Row, 1981, chapter 7, 'Microcosmic Theories of Violent Conflict', pp. 251–300; see also Steve Smith, 'War and Human Nature', in Forbes and Smith (eds.), *Politics and Human Nature*, pp. 164–79.

20 Sigmund Freud, *Beyond the Pleasure Principle* (1920), vol. XVIII of the *Standard Edition of the Complete Works of Sigmund Freud*, Hogarth Press, 1957, p. 93.

21 Glover, *War, Sadism*, p. 27.

22 Strachey, *The Unconscious Motives of War*, p. 202.

23 Harold D. Lasswell, *Power and Personality*, Viking, 1948; *Psychopathology and Politics*, Viking, 1960.

24 S. Freud and W.C. Bullitt, *Thomas Woodrow Wilson: A Psychological Study*, Houghton Mifflin, 1967; Alexander L. George and Juliette L. George, *Woodrow Wilson and Colonel House: A Personality Study*, Dover, 1964; B.A. Brodie, 'A Psychoanalytic Interpretation of Woodrow Wilson', *World Politics*, 9, 1957, pp. 413–22; L.P. Clark, *Lincoln: A Psycho–Biography*, Scribner, 1933.

25 See, for example, George Malcom Stratton, *Social Psychology of International Conflict*, D. Appleton, 1929. This unpleasant book contains a psychologism

almost every line and its style can be exemplified by the titles of its first two chapters, 'The Minds of the Backward Races' and 'The Advanced Races'. See also his *International Delusions*, Peace Book Club, 1938.

26 Leon J. Kamin, *The Science and Politics of IQ*, Penguin, 1977, quoting from C.C. Bingham, *A Study of American Intelligence*, Princeton University Press, 1923.

27 I shall return to this subject in more detail in my discussion of nationalism in chapter 3.

28 See 'Behaviourism' and 'Behaviouralism', Allan Bullock and Oliver Stallybrass, *The Fontana Dictionary of Modern Thought*, 1977, pp. 57–6.

29 Richard Jensen, 'History and the Political Scientist', in Seymour Martin Lipset (ed.), *Politics and the Social Sciences*, Oxford University Press, 1969, p. 5. For the most useful survey of the history and state of political psychology, see Jeanne N. Knutson (ed.), *Handbook of Political Psychology*, Jossey-Bass, 1973, particularly the essays by James Chowning Davies, Jeanne N. Knutson, M. Brewster Smith and Fred J. Greenstein. For important overviews and bibliographies see also Fred I. Greenstein and S. Tarrow, *A Source Book for the Study of Personality and Politics*, Markham, 1971; R.W. Goehlert, *Political Psychology – A Bibliography*, Monticello, 1981.

30 B.F. Skinner, *Walden Two*, Macmillan, 1948; for a purely behaviourist approach see also H.J. Eysenk, *The Psychology of Politics*, Routledge Kegan Paul, 1954.

31 Walter Lippmann, *Public Opinion*, Harcourt, 1922; V.O. Key Jnr, *Public Opinion and American Democracy*, Knopf, 1961. See also, for example, James N. Rosenau, *Public Opinion and Foreign Policy*, Random House, 1961; G. Almond, *The American People and Foreign Policy*, Harcourt, 1950. Warren Miller, for example, has pointed out 'the chaotic nature of the connection between public opinion on foreign policy and the electoral behavior of the same public' in his essay 'Voting and Foreign Policy' in Rosenau (ed.), *Domestic Sources of Foreign Policy*, Free Press, 1967, p. 213. For the relationship between individual attitudes and foreign policy, see: B. Christiansen, *Attitudes towards Foreign Policy as a Function of Personality*, Oslo Press, 1959; T.W. Adorno *et al.*, *The Authoritarian Personality*, Harper, 1950; D.J. Levinson, 'Authoritarian Personality and Foreign Policy', *Journal of Conflict Resolution*, 1, 1957, pp. 37–47; M.B. Smith *et al.*, *Opinions and Personality*, Wiley, 1956; Herbert McClosky, 'Personality and Attitude Correlates of Foreign Policy Orientation', in Rosenau (ed.), *Domestic Sources*, pp. 51–109.

32 Joseph B. Perry Jr and Meredith David Pugh, *Collective Behavior – Response to Social Stress*, West Publishing, 1978, p. 25. This book also contains a useful digest of psychological theories, 'Theoretical Perspectives', pp. 25–45.

33 For a useful digest of these theories, see Charles Tilly, *From Mobilization to Revolution*, Addison-Wesley, 1978, especially chapter 2, 'Theories and Descriptions of Collective Action', pp. 12–53. See also J.P. Nettl, *Political Mobilization – A Sociological Analysis of Methods and Concepts*, Faber, 1967.

34 Gustav Le Bon, *The Crowd – A Study of the Popular Mind*, Unwin, 1903. See also Robert A. Nye, *The Origins of Crowd Psychology: Gustav Le Bon and the Crisis of Mass Democracy in the Third Republic*, Sage, 1975.

35 Wilfred Trotter, *Instincts of the Herd in Peace and War*, Oxford University Press, 1953.

36 Herbert Blumer, 'Collective Behaviour', in Alfred McCluny Lee (ed.), *Principles of Sociology*, Barnes and Noble, 1951, pp. 167–222; Blumer, 'Outline of Collective Behavior', in Robert E. Evans (ed.), *Readings in Collective Behavior*, Rand McNally, 1975, pp. 22–45. The idea of 'circular reaction' was derived from Floyd Allport, *Social Psychology*, Houghton, 1924.

37 Ralph Turner and Lewis M. Killian (eds.), *Collective Behavior*, Prentice Hall, 1972; Ralph Turner, 'Collective Behavior', in R.E.L. Faris (ed.), *Handbook on Modern Sociology*, Rand McNally, 1964, pp. 382–425.

38 T. Parsons and E.A. Shils (eds.), *Towards a General Theory of Action*, Harper, 1951.

39 Neil J. Smelser, *Theory of Collective Behavior*, Routledge Kegan Paul, 1962.

40 Richard Berk, *Collective Behavior*, Richard C. Brown, 1974.

41 Seymour Martin Lipset, 'Introduction', in Lipset (ed.), *Politics and the Social Sciences*, p. xvii.

42 Smelser, 'Personality and the Explanation of Political Phenomena at the Social System Level: A Methodological Statement', *Journal of Social Issues*, XXIV, 3, 1968, p. 123.

43 Fred I. Greenstein, *Personality and Politics – Problems of Evidence, Inference and Conceptualisation*, Norton, 1975, p. 123.

44 To which he nicely adds, 'Political scientists are probably less naive than psychologists about this.' M. Brewster Smith, 'Political Attitudes', in Knutson (ed.), *Handbook of Political Psychology*, p. 77; the map appears on p. 76; M.B. Smith, J. Bruner and R. White, *Opinions and Personality*, Wiley, 1956.

45 M. Brewster Smith, 'Political Attitudes', in Knutson (ed.), *Handbook of Political Psychology*, p. 75.

46 Emile Durkheim, *The Division of Labour in Society* (trans. George Simpson), Free Press, 1964, pp. 79–80.

47 *Ibid.*, p. 196.

48 Irvin L. Child, 'Socialization', in Gardner Lindzey (ed.), *Handbook of Social Psychology*, Vol. II, Addison Wesley, 1954, p. 655.

49 Kurt Danziger, *Socialization*, Penguin, 1971, p. 29.

50 See, for example, J.L. Gewirtz, 'Mechanisms of Social Learning', in D.A. Goslin (ed.), *Handbook of Socialization Theory and Research*, Rand McNally, 1969.

51 Justin Aronfeed, 'The Concept of Internalization', in Goslin (ed.), *Handbook of Socialization*, p. 263.

52 See, for example, Erik H. Erikson, *Childhood and Society*, Norton, 1950.

53 Child, 'Socialization', in Lindzey (ed.), *Handbook of Social Psychology*, Vol. II, pp. 656–7.

54 Kenneth P. Langton, *Political Socialization*, Oxford University Press, 1969, p. 4.

55 Herbert H. Hyman, *Political Socialization: A Study in the Psychology of Political Behavior*, Free Press, 1959.

56 For a helpful history and assessment of political socialisation in contemporary political theory, see Richard G. Niemi, 'Political Socialization', in Knutson (ed.), *Handbook of Political Psychology*, pp. 117–38.

57 David C. Schwartz and Sandra Kenyon Schwartz (eds.), *New Directions in Political Socialization*, Free Press, 1975, in their 'Introduction', p. 9. The same point was, of course, implicit in the whole thrust of Fred Greenstein's work, especially his seminal *Personality and Politics*; see also Daniel J. Levinson, 'The Relevance of Personality for Political Participation', in Gordon J. Di Renzo (ed.), *Personality and Politics*, Doubleday, 1974, pp. 445–55.

58 Stanley Allen Renshon, 'The Role of Personality Development in Political Socialization', in Schwartz and Schwartz (eds.), *New Directions in Political Socialization*, pp. 29–68; Renshon, *Psychological Needs and Political Behavior*, Free Press, 1974.

59 Abraham Maslow, *Motivation and Personality*, Harper and Row, 1954, p. 84.

60 Renshon, 'The Role of Personality Development in Political Socialization', in Schwartz and Schwartz (eds.), *New Directions in Political Socialization*, p. 37.

61 *Ibid.*, pp. 43–7.

62 *Ibid.*, p. 44. He refers to M. Wolfenstein and M. Mead (eds.), *Child-Rearing in Six Cultures*, University of Chicago Press, 1966.

63 *Ibid.*, pp. 44–5.

64 *Ibid.*, p. 46.

65 H.C.J. Duijker and N.H. Frijda, *National Character and National Stereotypes*, North Holland Publishing Company, 1960; R.F. Benedict, *Patterns of Culture*, Houghton Mifflin, 1934; R.F. Benedict, *The Chrysanthemum and the Sword: Patterns of Japanese Culture*, Houghton Mifflin, 1946. Alex Inkeles and Daniel J. Levinson, 'National Character: the study of modal personality and sociocultural systems', in Lindzey (ed.), *Handbook of Social Psychology*; Erich Reigrotski and Nels Anderson, 'National Stereotypes and Foreign Contacts', in Louis Kriesberg (ed.), *Social Processes in International Relations*, John Wiley, 1968, pp. 65–80; for the most recent review of the literature, see Pat McGowan and Helen E. Purkitt, *Demystifying 'National Character' in Black Africa: A Comparative Study of Culture and Foreign Policy Behavior*, Monograph Series in World Affairs, University of Denver, 1979, chapter 3, 'Previous Research on Culture and Foreign Policy', pp. 13–17.

66 Joseph Frankel, *International Relations in a Changing World*, Oxford University Press, 1979, pp. 92–4; Frankel, *The Making of Foreign Policy*, Oxford University Press, 1963, pp. 111–47; Nathan Leites, *The Operational Code of the Politburo*, Rand/McGraw Hill, 1951. Leites' work was made particularly relevant by George. See Alexander L. George, 'The "Operational Code": a neglected approach to the study of political leaders and decision-making', *International Studies Quarterly*, XIII, June 1969, pp. 190–222.

67 Otto Klineberg, *The Human Dimension in International Relations*, Holt, Rinehart and Winston, 1964, p. 54.

68 This is reflected, for example, in the fact that at the time of writing, there is not a single university course in the United Kingdom dealing specifically

with this subject. F.S. Northedge, and Charles Manning before him, ran a one term unit at the London School of Economics.

69 Klineberg, *The Human Dimension*; see also his *Tensions Affecting Human Understanding*, Social Science Research Council, 1950.

70 Herbert C. Kelman and Alfred H. Bloom, 'Assumptive Frameworks in International Politics', in Knutson (ed.), *Handbook of Political Psychology*, pp. 261–95; Kelman, 'Social–Psychological Approaches to the Study of International Relations: Definition of Scope' and 'Social–Psychological Approaches to the Study of International Relations – The Question of Relevance', in Kelman (ed.), *International Behavior – A Social–Psychological Analysis*, Holt, Rinehart and Winston, 1965, pp. 3–39 and 565–607; Jerome D. Frank, *Sanity and Survival in the Nuclear Age*, Random House, 1967, 1982; Ralph K. White (ed.), *Psychology and the Prevention of Nuclear War*, New York University Press, 1986; Joseph H. de Rivera, *The Psychological Dimensions of Foreign Policy*, Charles E. Merrill, 1968; for a more recent essay, see A.N. Oppenheim, 'Psychological Processes in World Society', in Michael Banks (ed.), *Conflict in World Society*, Wheatsheaf/Harvester, 1985; C.R. Mitchell, *The Structure of International Conflict*, Macmillan, 1981, pp. 71–98.

71 Kelman and Bloom, 'Assumptive Frameworks in International Politics', in Knutson (ed.), *Handbook of Political Psychology*, pp. 278–84; Kelman, 'Patterns of Personal Involvement in the National System: A Social–Psychological Analysis of Political Legitimacy', in J.N. Rosenau (ed.), *International Politics and Foreign Policy*, Free Press, 1969.

72 Kelman and Bloom, 'Assumptive Frameworks in International Politics', in Knutson (ed.), *Handbook of Political Psychology*, pp. 278–9.

73 *Ibid.*, pp. 280–1, referring to Johan Galtung, 'Foreign Policy as a Function of Social Position', in Rosenau (ed.), *Domestic Sources of Foreign Policy*.

74 Daniel Katz, 'Nationalism and International Conflict Resolution', in Kelman (ed.), *International Behavior*, pp. 356–92.

75 J. David Singer, 'Man and World Politics: The Psycho-Cultural Interface', *Journal of Social Issues*, XXIV, 3, 1968, pp. 127–56.

76 *Ibid.*, p. 140.

77 *Ibid.*, pp. 143–4.

78 Richard C. Snyder, H.W. Bruck and Burton Sapin, *Foreign Policy Decision-Making*, Free Press, 1963.

79 Robert Jervis, *Perception and Misperception in International Politics*, Princeton University Press, 1976; see also his *The Logic of Images in International Relations*, Princeton, 1970; Leon Festinger, *A Theory of Cognitive Dissonance*, Stanford University Press, 1957. For perception affecting negotiating, see Daniel Druckman, *Human Factors in International Negotiations: Social–Psychological Aspects of International Conflict*, Sage, 1973; Gerald Sperrazzo (ed.), *Psychology and International Relations*, Georgetown University Press, 1965. It did not, however, require the behavioural approach to uncover the existence of perception and misperception. Walter Lippmann in *Public Opinion*, had already written about the importance of the 'pictures in our heads' and Kenneth Boulding had written his important essay, 'The Image',

University of Michigan, 1956. See also G. Matthew Bonham and Michael J. Shapiro (eds.), *Thought and Action in Foreign Policy – Proceedings of the London Conference on Cognitive Process Models of Foreign Policy, March 1973*, Birkhauser, 1977; and more recently, Christer Jonsson (ed.), *Cognitive Dynamics and International Politics*, Frances Pinter, 1982.

80 For an interesting preliminary discussion of this issue, see Glen H. Fisher, *Public Diplomacy and the Behavioral Sciences*, Indiana University Press, 1972.

81 Graham T. Allison, *Essence of Decision*, Little Brown, 1971.

82 Irving Janis, *Victims of Groupthink*, Houghton Mifflin, 1972; Charles F. Hermann (ed.), *International Crises: Insights from Behavioral Research*, Free Press, 1972; Michael Brecher, *The Foreign Policy System of Israel: Setting, Images, Process*, Yale University Press, 1972.

83 K.J. Holsti, 'Role Conceptions in the Study of Foreign Policy', *International Studies Quarterly*, XIV, 3, 1970, pp. 233–309; and Carl W. Backman, 'Role Theory and International Relations: A Commentary and Extension', *International Studies Quarterly*, XIV, 3, 1970, pp. 310–19.

2 IDENTIFICATION THEORY

1 Ian Craib, *Modern Social Theory – From Parsons to Habermas*, Wheatsheaf, 1984.

2 Sigmund Freud, *On Narcissism* (1914), Vol. XIV of the *Standard Edition of the Complete Works*, Hogarth Press, 1957, p. 93. All further references to Freud are taken from the *Standard Edition* published by Hogarth Press.

3 *Ibid.*, pp. 95–6.

4 Freud, *Mourning and Melancholia* (1915), Vol. XIV.

5 Freud, *Group Psychology and the Analysis of the Ego* (1921), Vol. XVIII, pp. 107–8.

6 *Ibid.*

7 Uri Bronfenbrenner, 'Freudian Theories of Identification and Derivatives', *Child Development*, 31, 1960, pp. 15–40.

8 Freud, *New Introductory Lectures*, Vol. XXII, p. 63.

9 *Ibid.*, p. 67.

10 *Ibid.*

11 Quoted above.

12 Andrew J. Reck (ed.), *George Herbert Mead – Selected Writings*, 'Editor's Introduction', p. xxiv, Indiana University Press, 1964.

13 *Ibid.*, p. xxv, quoting from 'Cooley's Contribution to American Social Thought', *The American Journal of Sociology*, XXXV, 1930, p. 700.

14 George Herbert Mead, *Mind, Self and Society*, University of Chicago Press, 1934, p. 136.

15 *Ibid.*, p. 138.

16 *Ibid.*, p. 151.

17 *Ibid.*, p. 158.

18 *Ibid.*, p. 211.

19 *Ibid.*, p. 210. This point is repeated on p. 255.

20 There is, of course, a third perspective which would belong to a strict behavioural school of psychology. For the behaviourist, 'identification' would be simply an overcomplex notion to describe a deeply imbedded imitation that had been conditioned by certain positive reinforcers. See, for example, B.F. Skinner, *Beyond Freedom and Dignity*, Jonathan Cape, 1972, chapters 6 and 7. Following Mead, and more recently Chomsky, I reject the strict behavioural paradigm.

If, however, one *were* to accept the behavioural perspective on identification, Robert Sears effectively restates Freud's theory of sympathetic identification in the language of learning theory; see Robert Sears, 'Identification as a Form of Behavioral Development', in Dale B. Harris (ed.), *The Concept of Development*, University of Minnesota Press, 1957, pp. 154–5; also Bronfenbrenner, 'Freudian Theories', p. 28.

21 This is returned to in the following pages.

22 Freud, *Inhibitions, Symptoms and Anxiety* (1926), Vol. XX, 'Editor's Introduction', p. 78.

23 Since at least the early 1930s, psychoanalytic theory has explicitly incorporated the notion of adaptability as a major psychic mechanism. See Heinz Hartmann, *Ego Psychology and the Process of Adaptation*, Indiana University Press, 1958.

24 Erik H. Erikson, *Identity and the Life Cycle*, Psychological Issues, I, Indiana University Press, 1959. The few theoretical, rather than descriptive, passages in this, his major work, are more concerned with a topology of the phenomenon than an investigation of the drive itself.

25 *Ibid.*, p. 147.

26 Erikson, *Identity – Youth and Crisis*, Faber, 1968, p. 41.

27 Erikson, *Identity and the Life Cycle*, p. 116.

28 Erikson, *Identity – Youth and Crisis*, p. 94.

29 Erikson, *Identity and the Life Cycle*, pp. 112–13.

30 *Ibid.*

31 *Ibid.*, p. 23.

32 *Ibid.*, p. 89.

33 *Ibid.*, p. 118.

34 *Ibid.*, pp. 122–47.

35 *Ibid.*, p. 153.

36 Erikson, *Identity – Youth and Crisis*, p. 81.

37 *Ibid.*, p. 133.

38 Erikson, *Identity and the Life Cycle*, p. 142.

39 *Ibid.*, p. 157.

40 Sources for this review of Parsons' identification and psychological theory are: Talcott Parsons and Edward Shils, *Toward A General Theory of Action*, Harvard University Press, 1962; Parsons, 'The Position of Identity in the General Theory of Action', in Chad Gordon and K.J. Gergen (eds.), *The Self in Social Interaction*, John Wiley, 1968; Parsons, 'The Superego and the Theory of Social Systems', *Psychiatry*, XV, 1, February 1952; Parsons, 'Social Structure and the Development of Personality', *Psychiatry*, XXI, 4, November 1958; the two preceding papers are also published in Parsons,

Social Structure and Personality, Free Press, 1964; Parsons, *Family, Socialization and Interaction Process*, Free Press, 1955.

41 Parsons, *Social Structure*, pp. 321–40.

42 Robert Bocock, *Freud and Modern Society*, Nelson, 1978, p. 54; also Bronfenbrenner in Max Black (ed.), *The Social Theories of Talcott Parsons*, Prentice Hall, 1961.

43 See Parsons' description of Suckling in *Social Structure*, p. 85.

44 Parsons, 'The Position of Identity', p. 15.

45 Anthony Giddens, *Central Problems in Social Theory*, Macmillan, 1979, p. 52.

46 Parsons and Shils, *Toward a General Theory*, p. 115.

47 *Ibid.*, p. 114.

48 *Ibid.*, p. 121.

49 Parsons, *Family, Socialization*, p. 170.

50 *Ibid.*, p. 149.

51 *Ibid.*, pp. 217–19.

52 Jurgen Habermas, 'On Social Identity', *Telos*, 19, Spring 1974, p. 91.

53 Peter Berger, *The Sacred Canopy*, New York, 1967, quoted in Habermas, *Legitimation Crisis*, Heinemann, 1976, p. 118.

54 Habermas, *Legitimation Crisis*, p. 4.

55 This can be found in Habermas, 'On Social Identity', *Legitimation Crisis*, and Habermas, *Communication and the Evolution of Society*, Heinemann, 1979.

56 Habermas, *Legitimation Crisis*, p. 8.

57 Habermas, 'On Social Identity', p. 91.

58 *Ibid.*, p. 92.

59 Habermas, *Communication and the Evolution of Society*, pp. 183–4.

60 *Ibid.*, p. 180.

61 David Held in John B. Thompson and David Held (eds.), *Habermas: Critical Debates*, Macmillan, 1982, pp. 187–8.

3 NATION-BUILDING

1 Karl Deutsch and William Foltz (eds.), *Nation-Building*, Atherton Press, 1963.

2 Wendell Bell and Walter E. Freeman (eds.), *Ethnicity and Nation-Building – Comparative International and Historical Perspectives*, Sage, 1974, 'Introduction', p. 11.

3 For the most helpful bibliography, see Stein Rokkan, Kirsti Saelen and Joan Warmbrunn, 'Building States and Nations: A Selective Bibliography of the Research Literature by Theme and by Country', in S.N. Eisenstadt and Stein Rokkan (eds.), *Building States and Nations – Volume I*, Sage, 1973, pp. 277–397.

4 See Benedict Anderson, *Imagined Communities*, Verso/New Left Books, 1983.

5 Ferdinand Toennies (trans. and ed. C.P. Loomis), *Community and Society*, Routledge, 1955.

6 Ian Lustick, *State-Building Failure in British Ireland and French Algeria*, Institute of International Studies, Berkeley University Press, 1985, p. 3.

7 Walker Connor, 'Nation-Building or Nation-Destroying', *World Politics*, XXIV, April 1972, p. 336.

8 Rupert Emerson, *From Empire to Nation*, Harvard University Press, 1962, p. 97.

9 Lucian W. Pye, *Personality and Nation Building: Burma's Search for Identity*, Yale University Press, 1962, p. 52.

10 Claude Ake, *A Theory of Political Integration*, Dorsey Press, Illinois, 1967, p. 1.

11 For a helpful introduction, see Ake, *ibid.*, chapter 3, 'Political Integration and Social Theory', pp. 36–50.

12 For an early but cogent appraisal, see J.P. Nettl, 'The Study of Political Development', in Colin Leys (ed.), *Politics and Change in Developing Countries*, Cambridge University Press, 1969, pp. 13–34. For criticism of the Eurocentrism of these approaches, see Ernest Gellner, *Thought and Change*, Weidenfeld, 1969, p. 139.

13 Immanuel Wallerstein on the television programme 'Voices', Channel 4, United Kingdom, 25 April 1986.

The progress of the study of nation-building can be seen in the works of its major exponent Stein Rokkan. There is a clearly discernible trend away from a focus on issues of development and modernisation in the sixties to a more central concern with the Marxian issue of centre–periphery relations. See the Bibliography in Per Torsvik (ed.), *Mobilization, Center–Periphery Structures and Nation-Building*, University of Bergen, 1981, pp. 525–53.

14 Uma O. Eleazu, *Federalism and Nation-Building: The Nigerian Experience 1954–64*, Arthur H. Stockwell, 1977.

15 Deutsch and Foltz (eds.), *Nation-Building*, pp. 4–8.

16 See Bibliography in Torsvik (ed.), *Mobilization*.

17 Clifford Geertz, 'The Integrative Revolution', in Geertz (ed.), *Old Societies and New States*, Free Press, 1963, p. 111.

18 For a modern analysis, see Anthony Smith, *The Ethnic Revival*, Cambridge University Press, 1981.

19 This phrase comes from a toast given by Stephen Decatur in Norfolk, Virginia, in approximately 1816. 'Our country! In her intercourse with foreign nations, may she always be in the right; but our country, right or wrong!' J.M. and M.J. Cohen (eds.), *Penguin Dictionary of Quotations*, Penguin, 1960, p. 130, para. 13.

20 For working definitions, I take nationalism to be that ideology which posits that a nation should have its own state; and I take a nation to be any group of people that decide that it is a nation. For a more extended and particularly helpful analysis, see A.D. Smith, *Theories of Nationalism*, Duckworth, 1983.

21 Hugh Seton-Watson, *Nations and States*, Methuen, 1977, chapter 2.

22 Johann Gottfried von Herder, *Reflections on the Philosophy of the History of Mankind*, J. Johnson, 1880; F.M. Barnard, *Herder's Social and Political Thought*, Clarendon Press, 1965; G.W.F. Hegel, *Lectures on The Philosophy of World History*, Cambridge University Press, 1975; Johann Gottlieb Fichte, *The*

Destination of Man, Chapman, 1846.
23 Rudolph Steiner, *World History in the Light of Anthroposophy*, Adams, George and Adams, 1972; Alice A. Bailey, *The Destiny of the Nations*, Lucis Press, 1968; C.G. Jung, *Man and His Symbols*, Bell, 1968; Jung, *Psyche and Symbols*, Doubleday, 1958.
24 Marvin Harris, *Cannibals and Kings*, Collins, 1978.
25 A particularly good example is *The Times Atlas of World History*, Times Books, 1978.
26 Lord Acton, 'Nationality', in *The History of Freedom and Other Essays*, Macmillan, 1909, p. 292. For a more recent approach of the same line see Ely Kedourie, *Nationalism*, Hutchinson, 1960.
27 See Charles Tilly, 'Reflections on the History of European State-Making', in Tilly (ed.), *The Formation of National States in Western Europe*, Princeton University Press, 1975, pp. 3–83; John Breuilly, *Nationalism and the State*, Manchester University Press, 1982, pp. 28–34.
28 Raymond Aron, *Peace and War*, Krieger, 1981, p. 6.
29 See Maurice Edelman, *The Symbolic Uses of Politics*, University of Illinois, 1964; Charles D. Elder and Roger W. Cobb, *The Political Uses of Symbols*, Longman, 1983.
30 See, for example, Rachel Stillwell and Christopher Spencer, 'Children's Early Preferences for Other Nations and their Subsequent Acquisition of Knowledge about those Nations', *European Journal of Social Psychology*, III, 3, 1973, pp. 345–9; G. Jahoda, 'Development of Scottish Children's Ideas and Attitudes about Other Countries', *Journal of Social Psychology*, 58, 1962, pp. 91–102; Edwin D. Lawson, 'Development of Patriotism in Children – A Second Look', *Journal of Psychology*, 55, 1963, pp. 279–86; G. Jahoda, 'The Development of Children's Ideas About Country and Nationality. Part I: The Conceptual Framework', *British Journal of Educational Psychology*, 1963a, 33, pp. 47–60; Jahoda, 'The Development of Children's Ideas About Country and Nationality. Part II: National Symbols and Themes', *British Journal of Educational Psychology*, 1963b, 33, pp. 143–53; W.E. Lambert and Otto Klineberg, *Children's Views of Foreign Peoples: A Cross-National Study*, Appleton-Century, 1967.
31 Quoted in G.G. Coulton, 'Nationalism in the Middle Ages', *Cambridge Journal of History*, V, 1, 1935, p. 19.
32 *Ibid*.
33 F.F. Urquart, 'Christendom', in *The Catholic Encyclopaedia*, Vol. III, quoted in Coulton, 'Nationalism'.
34 Coulton, 'Nationalism', p. 19.
35 This is to avoid for the moment the very real problem that elites may have a greater identification with their transnational elite fellows than with the nation at the top of whose power hierarchy they are situated. Their interests, both purely materialistic and psychological, are tied to their class rather than to their national culture. This is hardly surprising as power politics and dynastic marriages mean the transplantation of foreign princes and rulers. I shall, however, return to this problem when discussing a structuralist analysis of international relations, see below chapter 4. I found

very useful G. Poggi, *The Development of the Modern State: a sociological introduction*, Stanford University Press, 1978; J. Strayer, *On the Mediaeval Origins of the Modern State*, Princeton University Press, 1970; Norbert Elias, *State Formation and Civilisation*, Basil Blackwell, 1982.

36 G.M. Trevelyan, *History of England*, Longmans, 1943, p. 232.

37 See G. Grosjean, *Le Sentiment National dans la Guerre de Cent Ans*, Bossard, 1927. M. Handelsman, 'Le Rôle de la Nationalité dans l'histoire du Moyen Age', *Bulletin of the International Committee of Historical Sciences*, 2, 1929, pp. 235–46.

38 M.J. Hewitt, 'The Organisation of War', in K. Fowler (ed.), *The Hundred Years War*, Macmillan, 1971, pp. 75–95.

39 Samuel Finer in Tilly (ed.), *The Formation of National States*, p. 92. No doubt, however, Thatcherism, à l'outrance, would approve.

40 *Ibid.*, pp. 92ff.

41 C.J. Allmand, 'War and the Non-Combatant', in Fowler (ed.), *The Hundred Years War*, pp. 163–83.

42 Trevelyan, *History of England*, p. 227.

43 *Ibid.*, p. 253.

44 Edward Miller, 'Introduction', 'The Economic Policies of Governments', *Economic Organisation and Policies in the Middle Ages*, Cambridge Economic History of Europe, III, Cambridge University Press, 1963, p. 285.

45 Thomas Aquinas, *De Regime Judaeorum*, Rome edit., XIX, p. 622, quoted in Elias, *State Formation*, p. 202. 'Constituti sunt reditus terrarum, ut ex illis viventes a spoliatone subditorum abstineant.'

46 J.F.C. Harrison, *The Common People*, Fontana, 1984, p. 88. For a more detailed discussion of taxation during this period, see Rudolph Braun, 'Taxation, Sociopolitical Structure and State-Building', in Tilly (ed.), *The Formation of National States*, pp. 243–326.

47 G.J. Hand and D.J. Bentley (eds.), *Radcliffe and Cross: The English Legal System*, Butterworths, 5th Edition, 1977, p. 35.

48 *Ibid.*, p. 43.

49 Trevelyan, *History of England*, p. 161. For a digest of the innovations in the English legal system during the Middle Ages, see *ibid.*, pp. 157–62.

50 *Cambridge Economic History of Europe*, III, p. 306.

51 *Ibid.*, p. 304 and p. 308.

52 *Ibid.*, p. 314. This is early evidence of the exact coincidence of the emergence of the new proto-capitalist world economy and the international system of nation-states which Wallerstein has made explicit. Immanuel Wallerstein, *The Modern World System*, Academic Press, 1974.

53 *Cambridge Economic History of Europe*, III, p. 321.

54 Jacques Le Goff, 'The Town as an Agent of Civilisation', in Carlo M. Cipolla (ed.), *The Middle Ages*, Fontana, 1981, p. 89.

55 *Ibid.*, p. 338.

56 *Ibid.*, p. 310 and p. 329.

57 See Kenneth E. Boulding, 'National Images and International Systems', *Journal of Conflict Resolution*, III, June 1959, pp. 120–31; Robert A. Levine, 'Socialization, Social Structure and Inter-Societal Images', in Herbert Kel-

175

man (ed.), *International Behavior – A Social–Psychological Analysis*, Holt, Rinehart and Winston, 1965, pp. 45–69; Robert Jervis, *The Logic of Images in International Relations*, Princeton University Press, 1970. None of this is to deny that there exist other sets of international images.

4 FOREIGN POLICY

1 Christopher Hill, 'Public Opinion and British Foreign Policy since 1945: Research in Progress', *Millennium: Journal of International Studies*, XX, 1, Spring 1981, p. 53.

2 See Neil J. Smelser, *Theory of Collective Behavior*, Routledge Kegan Paul, 1962.

3 See William D. Coplin and Charles W. Kingley (eds.), *Analysing International Relations – A Multidimensional Introduction*, Praeger, 1975, Table Two, pp. 18–19.

4 See 'The Human Elements – Quantitative and Qualitative', in Roy Macridis (ed.), *Foreign Policy in World Politics*, Prentice Hall, 1972.

5 Francis Bacon, *Of the True Greatness of Kingdoms and Estates* quoted in Frederick H. Hartmann, *The Relations of Nations*, Macmillan, 1978, p. 43.

6 Hans J. Morgenthau, *Politics Among Nations*, Knopf, 1960, p. 568.

7 *Ibid.*, p. 146. In my concluding chapter I shall discuss how Morgenthau arrives at his conclusion concerning the savage nature of the mass public.

8 Kenneth Younger, 'Public Opinion and Foreign Policy', *British Journal of Sociology*, 6 June 1955, p. 169.

9 Kurt London, *The Making of Foreign Policy – East and West*, Lippincott, 1965, p. 61.

10 K.J. Holsti, *International Politics – A Framework for Analysis*, Prentice Hall, 1977, p. 392. See also W. Phillips Davison, 'Mass Communication and Diplomacy', in James N. Rosenau *et al.* (eds.), *World Politics – An Introduction*, Free Press, 1976, p. 403.

11 See, for example, Bernard C. Cohen, *The Public's Impact on Foreign Policy*, Little Brown, 1973.

12 James N. Rosenau (ed.), *Public Opinion and Foreign Policy*, Random House, 1961.

13 Warren E. Miller, 'Voting and Foreign Policy', in James N. Rosenau, *Domestic Sources of Foreign Policy*, Free Press, 1969, p. 215.

14 Rosenau, *Public Opinion*.

15 *Ibid.*, p. 37, quoting from Gabriel A. Almond, *Public Opinion and National Security Policy*, pp. 376–7.

16 Almond, *The American People and Foreign Policy*, Harcourt Brace Jovanovich, 1950, p. 136.

17 See, for instance, Quincy Wright, *A Study of War*, University of Chicago Press, 1965, p. 140.

18 There are many discussions of the domestic images with which politicians work, but in the International Relations Academy Joseph Frankel has given it particular, albeit methodologically incoherent, attention; see, for exam-

ple, Joseph Frankel, *The National Interest*, Pall Mall Press, 1970, pp. 110–18; also his *The Making of Foreign Policy: an Analysis of Decision-Making*, Oxford University Press, 1963, pp. 105–10.

19 See John B. Owen, *The Eighteenth Century 1714–1815*, Nelson, 1974, pp. 51–2; W.T. Selley, *England in the Eighteenth Century*, A. and C. Black, 1962, p. 55.

20 See 'The Crimean War', in *The New Cambridge Modern History Volume X*, Cambridge University Press, 1967, pp. 468–92, especially p. 477.

21 See W.G. Beasley, *The Modern History of Japan*, Weidenfeld, 1981, chapter 9, 'Nationalism and Foreign Affairs 1890–1905', pp. 155–73; also Delmer M. Brown, *Nationalism in Japan*, University of California, 1955, chapter 6, 'Preservation of Japanese National Essence', pp. 112–30.

22 For discussions of the concept of national interest, see James N. Rosenau, *The Scientific Study of Foreign Policy*, Free Press, 1971, pp. 239–49; also, Steven M. Smith, *Foreign Policy Adaptation*, Gower Publishing, 1981, pp. 7–11; also Joseph Frankel, *International Relations in a Changing World*, Oxford University Press, 1979, pp. 85ff.

23 Edgar S. Furniss and Richard C. Snyder, *An Introduction to American Foreign Policy*, Holt, Rinehart and Winston, 1955, p. 17.

24 See, for example, Frankel, *The National Interest*, p. 116 and Morgenthau, *Politics Among Nations*, pp. 67ff.

25 For a history that illustrates the dialectic of high and low issues, see Paul Taylor, *The Limits of European Integration*, Croom Helm, 1983.

26 See Stuart Hall, 'Culture, the Media and the Ideological Effect', in James Curran *et al.* (eds.), *Mass Communication and Society*, Edward Arnold, 1977, pp. 315–48.

27 Philip Knightley, *The First Casualty*, Harcourt Brace Janovich, 1975. My italics.

28 See Bernard C. Cohen, 'Mass Communications and Foreign Policy', in Rosenau (ed.), *Domestic Sources of Foreign Policy*, p. 197.

29 See Alfred O. Hero, *Mass Media and World Affairs*, World Peace Foundation, Boston, 1959, pp. 80–1.

30 Dan Nimmo and James E. Combs, *Mediated Political Realities*, Longman, 1983, p. 16 (my italics). There is also the further point that newspapers, as the major form of communication in a large community, anyway fulfil social and psychological functions more often than intellectual and intelligence functions; see Bernard C. Cohen, *The Press and Foreign Policy*, Princeton University Press, 1963. For a further discussion of the media and foreign policy, see Andrew Arno and Wiman Dissanayake (eds.), *The News Media in National and International Conflict*, Westview, 1984; also David L. Paletz and Robert M. Entman, *Media Power Politics*, Free Press, 1981, especially chapter 13, pp. 213–33.

31 Nimmo and Combs, *Mediated Political Realities*, pp. 29–37.

32 Oron James Hale, *Publicity and Diplomacy – with Special Reference to England and Germany 1890–1914*, Peter Smith, 1964, p. 16.

33 Ibid., p. 15.

34 Knightley, *The First Casualty*, pp. 55–6.

35 Hale, *Publicity and Diplomacy*, p. 6.

36 *Ibid.*, p. vii.

37 *Ibid.*, p. 6.

38 Interestingly, many societies, both open and closed, also operate a third tier. Western democracies, for instance, publish the informed comment of the quality papers such as the *Washington Post*, *The Times* or *Le Monde*, which may nevertheless be chauvinistic. Equally, a closed society such as Communist China publishes a weeky analysis of international relations purely for Party members. See Jorg M. Rudolph, *Media Coverage on Taiwan in the People's Republic of China*, Occasional Papers/Reprint series in Contemporary Asian Studies, Maryland University, 3, 1983 (56).

39 See, for example, Z.A.B. Zemen, *Nazi Propaganda*, Oxford University Press, 1973; Harold D. Lasswell, *Propaganda Techniques in World War*, Smith, 1927; Daniel Lerner, *Sykewar*, Stewart, 1949.

40 See, for example, Paul Seaburg, 'Cold War Origins I', and Brian Thomas, 'Cold War Origins II' in *Journal of Contemporary History*, III, 1, January 1968, pp. 169–98; also, John Laloy *et al.*, 'Origins of the Post-War Crisis', *Journal of Contemporary History*, III, 2, April 1968, pp. 217–52.

41 See William F. Buckley and J. Brent Bozell, *McCarthy and His Enemies*, Regnery, 1954, chapters 3 and 4; Townsend Hoopes, *The Devil and John Foster Dulles*, Little Brown, 1973, pp. 151–8; Athan Theoharis, 'Truman and the Red Scare', in T.C. Reeves (ed.), *McCarthyism*, Krieger, 1978, pp. 75–85.

42 *Encyclopaedia Britannica, Micropaedia VI*, 1974, p. 432.

43 See, for example, Karl W. Deutsch and Richard L. Merritt, 'Effects of Events on National and International Images', in Herbert C. Kelman (ed.), *International Behavior – A Social–Psychological Analysis*, Holt, Rinehart and Winston, 1965, pp. 132–87.

44 This is not to deny a genuine struggle between capitalism and socialism; it is merely to interpret consistently at this level of analysis.

45 See Urie Bronfenbrenner, 'Allowing for Soviet Perceptions and Motives', in Gerald Sperrazzo (ed.), *Psychology and International Relations*, Georgetown University Press, 1965, pp. 20–36; Ralph K. White, 'Images in the Context of International Conflict – Soviet Perceptions of the US and USSR', in Kelman (ed.), *International Behavior*, pp. 238–76.

46 See Alejandro Dabat, *Argentina – The Malvinas and the End of Military Rule*, Verso, 1982.

47 See '3rd April 1982', *Hansard Parliamentary Debates*, Sixth Series, XXI, HMSO, 1982, pp. 634–67. See also Tam Dalyell, *One Man's Falklands*, Cecil Woolf, 1982, chapter 6, 'Emergency Debate, 3rd April', pp. 50–60.

48 Sunday Times Insight Team, *The Falklands War*, André Deutsch, 1982, p. 98.

49 In a very real way the House of Commons demonstrated on a large scale the hysteria that accompanies foreign policy decisions that Janis describes. See Irving Janis, *Victims of Groupthink – a psychological study of foreign policy decisions and fiascos*, Boston, 1972.

50 For a discussion of the role of the media in mobilising public opinion and the government's manipulation of it, see Liz Curtis, *Falklands/Malvinas – Whose Crisis?*, Latin American Bureau, 1982; Susan Greenberg and Graham Smith, *Rejoice! Media Freedom and the Falklands*, Campaign for Press and

Broadcasting Freedom, 1982; Robert Harris, *Gotcha – Media, Government and the Falklands Crisis*, Faber, 1983.

51 A.J.R. Groom, *British Thinking about Nuclear Weapons*, Frances Pinter, 1974, pp. 326–465.

52 Caroline Blackwood, *On the Perimeter*, Heinemann, 1984; Barbara Hanford and Sarah Hopkins (eds.), *Women at the Wire*, Women's Press, 1984.

53 See Michael M. Harrison, *The Reluctant Ally – France and Atlantic Security*, John Hopkins, 1981.

54 My main sources for this discussion are Jonathan Alford (ed.), *Greece and Turkey: adversity in alliance*, Gower for the Institute of Strategic Studies, 1984; Andrew Borowiec, *The Mediterranean Feud*, Praeger, 1983; Polyvios G. Polyviou, *Cyprus – Conflict and Negotiation 1960–80*, Duckworth, 1980.

55 For a general discussion of these problems, see Christopher Clapham (ed.), *Foreign Policy Making in Developing States*, Saxon House, 1977; and Clapham, *Third World Politics*, Croom Helm, 1985.

56 Harold D. Lasswell, Daniel Lerner and Hans Spier (eds.), *Propaganda and Communication in World History*, University Press of Hawaii, 1980, p. 389 quoting from Marshall McLuhan, *The Medium is the Message*, Allen Lane, Penguin Press, 1967.

57 See Immanuel Wallerstein, *Africa: The Politics of Independence*, Vintage Books, 1961, pp. 121–35; also, C. Legum, *Pan-Africanism: A Short Political Guide*, Praeger, 1962.

58 T.M. Shaw and Olazide Aluko, *Nigerian Foreign Policy – Alternative Perceptions and Projections*, Macmillan, 1983; for helpful background, see Uma D. Eleazu, *Federalism and Nation Building – The Nigerian Experience 1954–1964*, Arthur H. Stockwell, 1977.

59 Ruth Leger Sivard, *World Military and Social Expenditures 1983*, World Priorities, 1983; David Blundy and Andrew Lycett, *Qaddaffi and the Libyan Revolution*, Weidenfeld, 1987, chapter 13.

60 See Roger Yeager, *Tanzania – An African Experiment*, Westview Press, 1982; Okwudiba Nnoli, *Self-Reliance and Foreign Policy in Tanzania*, NOK Pubs, 1977.

61 For an interesting and ambitious attempt to build a total framework for the analysis of foreign policy in African states which includes cultural and state-building variables, see the inappropriately titled Pat McGowan and Helen E. Purkitt, *Demystifying 'National Character' in Black Africa: A Comparative Study of Culture and Foreign Policy Behavior*, Monograph Series in World Affairs, XVII, Book 1, University of Denver, 1979.

62 See, for example, Phillip O'Brien and Paul Cammack (eds.), *Generals in Retreat*, Manchester University Press, 1985, chapter 6.

63 See R. William Liddle, *Ethnicity, Party and National Integration – An Indonesian Case Study*, Yale University Press, 1970, particularly p. 216.

64 See Herbert Feith, 'Dynamics of Guided Democracy', in Ruth McVey (ed.), *Indonesia*, Yale University Press, 1967.

65 See Julie Southwood and Patrick Flanagan, *Indonesia – Law, Propaganda and Terror*, Zed Press, Australia, 1983.

66 Michael Leifer does not seem to find this change in direction particularly

meaningful. Michael Leifer, *Indonesia's Foreign Policy*, Allen and Unwin, 1983.

67 See K.J. Holsti, 'From Diversification to Isolation: Burma 1973–7', in Holsti (ed.), *Why Nations Realign*, Allen and Unwin, 1982. Useful background is provided by Lucian Pye, *Politics, Personality and Nation-Building – Burma's Search for Identity*, Yale University Press, 1962.

5 INTERNATIONAL RELATIONS THEORY

1 As this chapter works at the most general level with International Relations theory, almost all the literature in the field could be used in one way or another to illustrate the argument. This could lead to a bibliography or set of footnotes that might purely be an exercise in scholasticism – as I try to remember every relevant book I have read and looked at over the last years. I have chosen, then, only to list those books which particularly illustrate the discussion.

2 Charles Manning, *The Nature of International Society*, Bell/London School of Economics, 1962, pp. 1–10.

3 There are several texts concerned purely with summarising the different approaches to International Relations; see particularly James E. Dougherty and Robert L. Pfaltzgraff, *Contending Theories of International Relations*, Harper and Row, 1981.

4 For a clear illustration of the historical approach see, for example, Hedley Bull and Adam Watson (eds.), *The Expansion of International Society*, Oxford University Press, 1984; Adda B. Bozeman, *Politics and Culture in International History*, Princeton University Press, 1960; F.S. Northedge and M.J. Grieve, *A Hundred Years of International Relations*, Duckworth, 1971. For the scientific approach, see, for example, J. David Singer (ed.), *Human Behavior and International Politics*, Rand McNally, 1965. For insight into the debate, see Hedley Bull, 'International Theory: The Case for a Classical Approach', *World Politics*, XVIII, April 1966; and Morton Kaplan's rejoinder to this paper, Morton A. Kaplan, 'The New Great Debate: Traditionalism vs. Science in International Relations', *World Politics*, XIX, October 1966.

5 Classicists, of course, do have a predisposition to arrange the four billion souls in nation-states. I return to this issue below in the third section of this chapter, 'State-centrists versus structuralists'.

6 The whole issue of level of analysis in International Relations is a particularly contentious one. It has received its highest profile in the debate between Kenneth Waltz and Morton Kaplan. I find Kaplan's approach logical and helpful for methodological rigour; see Morton Kaplan, *Towards Professionalism in International Theory*, Free Press/Collier Macmillan, 1979; see also J. David Singer, 'The Level of Analysis Problem in International Relations', in Klauss Knorr and Sydney Verba (eds.), *The International System: Theoretical Essays*, Princeton University Press, 1961.

7 Singer (ed.), *Human Behavior*, demonstrated a major attempt to define the field in which this line of investigation was being attempted; its promise

180

was not fulfilled. For another definition of the field see James N. Rosenau, *Scientific Study of Foreign Policy*, Frances Pinter, 1980.

8 This is not to ignore those from an historical background who have accepted the need for greater rigour in defining scope and level of analysis. See, for example, the discussions in Steve Smith (ed.), *International Relations: British and American Perspectives*, Basil Blackwell BISA, 1985. Michael Nicholson also makes the point that a behaviouralist approach does not necessarily exclude individual freedom for choices; see Michael Nicholson, *The Scientific Analysis of Social Behaviour*, Frances Pinter, 1983, p. 167.

9 'Decision-Making as an Approach to the Study of International Politics', in Richard C. Snyder, H.W. Bruck and Burton Sapin (eds.), *Foreign Policy Decision-Making*, Free Press, 1963. See also Sidney Verba, 'Assumptions of Rationality and Nonrationality in Models of the International System', in James N. Rosenau (ed.), *International Politics and Foreign Policy*, Free Press, 1969. For a digest concerning the introduction of decision-making theories, see Dougherty and Pfaltzgraff, *Contending Theories of International Relations*, pp. 468–510.

10 Graham T. Allison, *Essence of Decision: Explaining the Cuban Missile Crisis*, Little Brown, 1971.

11 Robert Jervis, *Perception and Misperception in International Politics*, Princeton, 1976.

12 See Irving Janis, *Victims of Groupthink*, Houghton Mifflin, 1972; Charles F. Hermann (ed.), *International Crises: Insights from Behavioral Research*, Free Press, 1972; Michael Brecher, *The Foreign Policy System of Israel: Setting, Images, Process*, Yale University Press, 1972.

13 Steve Smith, 'Allison and the Cuban Missile Crisis: A Review of the Bureaucratic Politics Model of Foreign Policy Decision-Making', *Millennium – Journal of International Studies*, IX, 1, Spring 1980, pp. 21–40.

14 I acknowledge, though, the stiff resistance in western and first world International Relations students to taking on board any Marxian levels of analysis. Again, I pursue this topic in the third section of this chapter 'State-centrists versus structuralists'.

15 This may seem self-contradictory as in Footnote 6 of this chapter I clearly implied support for Kaplan in the Kaplan/Waltz debate. My support, however, was for the intellectual and analytic rigour that Kaplan demands in defining one's level of analysis. That he thinks systems are useful is another matter. It seemed to me that Waltz only argued with him about the usefulness of systems and never properly addressed Kaplan's criticism of lack of professionalism in terms of methodology.

16 The leading post-Second World War exponent of this approach is, of course, Hans Morgenthau; see Hans J. Morgenthau, *Politics Among Nations*, Knopf, 1968; for a classic analysis of the realist–idealist debate, see E.H. Carr, *The Twenty Years Crisis, 1919–1939: An Introduction to the Study of International Relations*, Macmillan, 1939. For a critique of the methodology of the realist approach, see John A. Vasquez, *The Power of Power Politics*, Frances Pinter, 1983.

17 See, for example, John Vincent, 'The Hobbesian Tradition in Twentieth-

Century International Thought', *Millennium – Journal of International Studies*, X, 2, Summer 1981, pp. 91–101; also Cornelia Navari, 'Hobbes and the "Hobbesian Tradition" in International Thought', *Millennium – Journal of International Studies*, XI, 3, Autumn 1982, pp. 203–22.

18 Compared to Morgenthau's position in relation to the realist approach, it is difficult to pinpoint a single writer who represents in toto the idealist position; see, however, Norman Angell, *The Great Illusion*, Putnam, 1933; David Mitrany, *A Working Peace System*, RIIA, 1943; J.W. Burton, *International Relations – A General Theory*, Cambridge University Press, 1967.

19 For a helpful introduction to how these two opposing views work out in terms of social theory, see Percy S. Cohen, *Modern Social Theory*, Heinemann, 1968, chapter 1.

20 See, for example, Kenneth Waltz, *Man, the State and War*, Columbia University Press, 1959.

21 Morgenthau, *Politics Among Nations*, p. 14.

22 Of course, it might be the case that the invaders have a reputation for greater cruelty or heavier taxes than the current regime; in that case, the people will fight and the shared experience with their regime will work towards nation-building.

23 For a clear example of this attitude, see Chadwick F. Alger, 'Effective Participation in World Society: Some Implications of the Columbus Study', in Michael Banks (ed.), *Conflict in World Society*, Wheatsheaf Books, 1984, pp. 131–45.

24 See, for example, Michael Donelan (ed.), *Reason of State*, Allen and Unwin, 1978.

25 See A. Passerin D'Entreves, *The Notion of the State*, Oxford University Press, 1967; also Kenneth H.F. Dyson, *The State Tradition in Western Europe: a study of an idea and an institution*, Martin Robertson, 1980.

26 This is not to deny the peripheral nationalities that, of course, exist in all European states. Yugoslavia is also a notable exception, but even without Tito her federal structure and respect for subnationalities gives the impression of political integration. It is probable that the nation-building dynamic here has been supplied by the ongoing external threat of the Soviet Union and the Warsaw Pact; only time will tell.

27 See, for example, Immanuel Wallerstein, *The Modern World System*, vols. I and II, Academic Press, 1974 and 1980, and *The Capitalist World Economy*, Cambridge University Press, 1979; Samir Amin *et al.*, *Dynamics of Global Crisis*, Macmillan, 1982; Samir Amin, *Class and Nation – Historically and in the Current Crisis*, Heinemann, 1980; Ralph Pettman, *State and Class – A Sociology of International Affairs*, Croom Helm, 1979; Johan Galtung, *The True Worlds*, Free Press, 1980.

28 See, for example, V.I. Lenin, *Critical Remarks on the National Question*, Moscow, 1951 (1913).

29 For an interesting discussion, see Melvin Lasky, *Utopia and Revolution*, Macmillan, 1977, pp. 92–3. There are also the power political realities of centralised state power; state power tends to contain any revolutionary movement within its borders and to exclude foreign influences. Also, in

simple practice, a revolutionary movement seeking power must take it from the state; all this also tends to define any working class movement according to the state in which it occurs.

30 Kuang-Sheng Liao, *Anti-Foreignism and Modernization in China 1860–1980*, Chinese University Press, 1984; Lloyd Eastwood, *Seeds of Destruction: Nationalist China in War and Revolution*, Stanford University Press, 1984.

31 Maslow's hierarchy of human needs nicely illustrates this. See Abraham Maslow, *Motivation and Personality*, Harper, 1959.

32 For an illuminating discussion of the ecological forces at work in social and international history, see Paul Colinvaux, *The Fate of Nations*, Penguin, 1983.

33 This, of course, is in blatant contradistinction to many spiritual approaches in which, for example, 'it is easier for a camel to pass through an eye of a needle than for a rich man to enter the kingdom of heaven'. In many religious systems, ownership demonstrates a lack of spirituality.

34 See, for example, Celso Furtado, *Accumulation and Development: the logic of industrial civilization*, Martin Robertson, 1983, chapter 4, 'From the Ideology of Progress to the Ideology of Development', pp. 71–81.

35 At a level of analysis purely using identification theory, Johan Galtung's theory of structural imperialism is given added theoretical support. Johan Galtung, 'A Structural Theory of Imperialism', *Journal of Peace Research*, VIII, 1971, pp. 81–117. See also Peter L. Berger, *Pyramids of Sacrifice: Political Ethics and Social Change*, Doubleday, 1976; Vicky Randall and Robin Theobald, *Political Change and Underdevelopment: a critical introduction to third world politics*, Macmillan, 1985.

36 See, for example, Anthony Giddens, *The Class Structure of Advanced Societies*, Hutchinson, 1982.

37 In the developing countries, true national interest will be a discursive framework free from the constraints of western notions of modernisation – though it may, of course, integrate these notions as a necessary part of domestic strategy. Decisions, however, will be made with a sincere regard for the interests of all national citizens, and not just middle class citizens. There is a very large development literature. For introductions, see K.M. McCord, *Paths to Progress – Bread and Freedom in Developing Societies*, Norton, 1986; Amiya Kumar Bagchi, *The Political Economy of Underdevelopment*, Cambridge University Press, 1984; R.H. Chilcote, *Theories of Development and Under-Development*, Westview, 1984.

6 CONCLUSION

1 Seymour Martin Lipset, Lipset (ed.), *Politics and the Social Sciences*, 'Introduction', Oxford University Press, 1969, p. xvii.

2 Neil J. Smelser, 'Personality and the Explanation of Political Phenomena at the Social System Level: A Methodological Statement', *Journal of Social Issues*, XXIV, 3, 1968, p. 123.

3 Fred J. Greenstein, *Personality and Politics – Problems of Evidence, Inference and Conceptualisation*, Norton, 1975, p. 123.

4 Stanley Allen Renshon, *Psychological Needs and Political Behavior*, Free Press, 1974, p. 46.

5 Herbert C. Kelman, 'Patterns of Personal Involvement in the National System: A Social–Psychological Analysis of Political Legitimacy', in J.N. Rosenau (ed.), *International Politics and Foreign Policy*, Free Press, 1969.

6 For a useful criticism of psychological reductionism in this field, see John Breuilly, *Nationalism and the State*, Manchester University Press, 1982, pp. 28–35.

7 See Lucy Mair, *Primitive Government*, Penguin, 1964; M. Fortes and E.E. Evans-Pritchard, *African Political Systems*, Oxford University Press, 1940; John Middleton and David Tait (eds.), *Tribes Without Rulers*, Routledge and Kegan Paul, 1958; also, Roger D. Masters, 'World Politics as a Primitive Political System', *World Politics*, XVI, 4, July 1964.

8 The title of K.S. Nandy's paper expresses this well: 'Is Modernization Westernization? What about Easternization and Traditionalization?' Paper presented to World Congress of Sociology, Evian, 4–11 September 1966.

9 Bruno Bettelheim, 'Individual and Mass Behavior in Extreme Situations', in his *Surviving and Other Essays*, Knopf, 1979, pp. 48–54.

10 For a discussion of this in European history, see Norman Cohn, *Europe's Inner Demons*, Heinemann, 1975.

11 See, for example, Tung Chi-Ping and Humphrey Evans, *The Thought Revolution*, Leslie Frewin, 1967.

12 Karl Popper, *Conjectures and Refutations: the growth of scientific knowledge*, Routledge and Kegan Paul, 1969.

13 Karl Popper, *The Open Society and Its Enemies*, Routledge and Kegan Paul, 1962; Popper, *The Poverty of Historicism*, Routledge and Kegan Paul, 1960.

14 J. David Singer in Singer (ed.), *Human Behavior and International Politics*, Rand McNally, 1965, pp. 8–9.

15 This point is made clearly in R.J. Anderson *et al.*, *The Sociology Game – An Introduction to Sociological Reasoning*, Longman, 1985, chapter 2, 'Sociology and Philosophy', pp. 27–50.

16 F.S. Northedge, 'Transnationalism: The American Illusion', *Millennium*, V, 1, Spring 1976, p. 22.

17 Hedley Bull, 'International Theory: The Case for a Classical Approach', *World Politics*, XIX, 1, October 1966, pp. 1–20.

18 Avner Yaniv, 'Domestic Structure and External Flexibility: A Systematic Restatement of a Neglected Theme', *Millennium*, VIII, 1, Spring 1979, pp. 33–4, my italics.

19 Benjamin A. Most and Harvey Starr, 'International Relations Theory, Foreign Policy Substitutability and "Nice" Laws', *World Politics*, XXXVI, 3, April 1984, p. 383.

20 Hans Eysenk, *The Decline and Fall of Freudian Theory*, Viking, 1985, p. 35 and p. 169; see also Hans Eysenk and Glen D. Wilson (eds.), *The Experimental Study of Freudian Theories*, Methuen, 1973.

21 Paul Kline, *Fact and Fantasy in Freudian Theory*, Methuen, 1972, pp. 138–49.

22 *Ibid.*, p. 149.

23 H. Tajfel (ed.), *Social Identity and Intergroup Relations*, Cambridge University Press, 1982; H. Tajfel, *Differentiation between Social Groups*, Academic Press, 1978; H. Tajfel, 'Social Psychology of Intergroup Relations', *Annual Review of*

Psychology, 33, 1982, pp. 1–39; H. Tajfel and J.C. Turner, 'An Integrative Theory of Intergroup Conflict', in W.G. Austin and S. Worchel (eds.), *The Social Psychology of Intergroup Relations*, Brooks/Cole, 1979; J.C. Turner and Howard Giles (eds.), *Intergroup Behavior*, Blackwell, 1981; 'Special Issue – Intergroup Processes', in *British Journal of Social Psychology*, XXIII, 4, November 1984.

24 For contemporary relevance, see A.D. Smith, *The Ethnic Revival*, Cambridge University Press, 1981; Cynthia H. Enloe, *Ethnic Conflict and Political Development*, Little Brown, 1973; Abdul A. Said and Louis R. Simmons (eds.), *Ethnicity in an International Context: The Politics of Disassociation*, Transaction Books, 1976.

25 See Wendell Bell, 'Ethnicity, Decisions of Nationhood and Images of the Future', in Bell and Walter E. Freeman (eds.), *Ethnicity and Nation-Building*, Sage, 1974, p. 283; and Wendell Bell, 'New States in the Caribbean: a general theoretical account', in S.N. Eisenstadt and Stein Rokkan, *Building States and Nations – Vol. II*, Sage, 1973, pp. 177–209. This is also the analytical stance of John Breuilly, *Nationalism and the State*, Manchester University Press, 1982.

26 Stein Rokkan and Derek W. Urwin, *Economy, Territory, Identity*, Sage, 1983. 'The Politicization of Peripheral Predicaments' is the title of chapter 4. For the most concise description of the variables that can affect and evoke nationalist movements, see Riccardo Petrella, 'Nationalist and Regionalist Movements in Western Europe', in Charles R. Foster, *Nations Without a State*, Praeger, 1980, pp. 8–28. I also found particularly useful: A.D. Smith, *The Ethnic Revival in the Modern World*, Cambridge University Press, 1981; Bell and Freeman, *Ethnicity*; and Robert B. Goldman and A. Jeyaratnam Wilson (eds.), *From Independence to Statehood – Managing Ethnic Conflict in Five African and Asian States*, Frances Pinter, 1984.

27 For general discussion, see A. Dankwart Rustow, 'Language, Modernization and Nationhood – An Attempt at Typology', in Joshua A. Fishman *et al.* (eds.), *Language Problems of Developing Nations*, John Wiley, 1968; Otto Jespersen, *Mankind, Nation and Individual from a Linguistic Point of View*, Harvard University Press, 1925.

28 Rokkan and Urwin, *Economy*, p. 133.

29 See Frank A. Rice (ed.), *Study of the Role of Second Languages in Asia, Africa and Latin America*, Centre for the Applied Linguistics of the Modern Language Association of America, 1962.

30 Neil C. Sandberg, *Identity and Assimilation: The Welsh–English Dichotomy*, University Press of America, 1981; Cledwyn Hughes, *The Referendum – The End of an Era*, 14 pp, University of Wales Press, 1981; for a general discussion, see Tom Nairn, *The Break-Up of Britain*, New Left Books, 1977.

31 For a discussion of the factors which successfully hold Scotland within the United Kingdom, see W.J.M. Mackenzie, 'Peripheries and Nation-Building: The Case of Scotland', in Per Torsvik (ed.), *Mobilization, Centre–Periphery Structures and Nation-Building*, Universitetsforlaget, Norway, 1981.

32 Its most learned exponent is Ernest Gellner; see Gellner, 'Scale and Nation', *Philosophy of the Social Sciences*, 3, 1973, pp. 1–17; and Gellner, *Nations and*

Nationalism, Blackwell, 1983.

33 C.E. Black, *The Dynamics of Modernisation*, Harper and Row, 1967.

34 This argument is best constructed in Jurgen Habermas, *Legitimation Crisis*, Heinemann, 1976.

35 The British mass public, however, seems to have an affectionate regard for the materialistic ostentation of its royal family.

36 While famine is not an acceptable condition domestically, it is acceptable in interstate culture.

37 At the time of writing (1987), however, Khoumeni's Iran has adopted an ideology in which materialistic benefits have been downgraded in favour of spiritual returns.

38 However, even when all conditions are satisfied – i.e. (1) there are clear channels for social mobility, (2) citizens at the centre are careful about their image and (3) substantial public goods are distributed to the periphery – there are still dangers intrinsic in any developing economy; and in a very real sense, given the latest revolutions in electronic technology, all economies are developing. Class and peripheral disadvantages can still be appropriated by regional leaders who cannot be bought off by social mobility towards the centre; this mode of analysis has, for example, been fully applied to the Welsh and Scottish nationalist movements of the 1970s. See Nairn, *The Break-Up of Britain*.

39 Max Weber, *The Theory of Social and Economic Organization*, Free Press, 1957, pp. 358–92; Edward Shils, 'Charisma, Order and Status', *American Sociological Review*, 30, 1965, pp. 199–213; R.J. Bradley, *Charisma and Social Structure*, Paragon, 1986.

40 For the most well-known exposition on this subject, see David E. Apter, 'Political Religion in the New Nations', in Clifford Geertz (ed.), *Old Societies and New States*, Free Press, 1963, pp. 57–104.

41 Charles D. Elder and Roger W. Cobb, *The Political Uses of Symbols*, Longman, 1983; Maurice Edelman, *The Symbolic Uses of Politics*, University of Illinois Press, 1964.

42 Ian Lustick, *State-Building Failure in British Ireland and French Algeria*, IIS, Berkeley University Press, 1985.

43 See, for example, H.M. Gladwin, *The European Idea*, Weidenfeld, 1966; Norbert Guterman, *The Idea of Europe*, Collier-Macmillan, 1966.

44 See, for example, I.L. Markowitz, *Leopold Senghor and the Politics of Negritude*, Heinemann, 1969.

45 See, for example, Amitai Etzioni, *Political Unification*, Holt, Rinehart and Winston, 1965; Charles Pentland, *International Theory and European Integration*, Faber, 1973.

46 Alexander Szalai, *The United Nations and News Media: a survey of public information on the UN by the world press, radio and television*, UNITAR, 1972; for an American view, Wilbur Edel, *The State Department, The Public and the UN*, Vantage Press, 1979.

47 Robert Rossow, 'The Professionalism of the New Diplomacy', in *World Politics*, XIV, 4, 1962, pp. 561–75, quoted in Luc Reychler, *Patterns of Diplomatic Thinking: A Cross-National Study of Structural and Social–Psychologi-*

cal Determinants, Praeger, 1979; for an interesting volume on varying negotiating styles, see R.P. Annand (ed.), *Cultural Factors in International Relations*, Abhinav, New Delhi/East–West Centre, Hawaii, 1981.

48 Harold Nicolson, *Diplomacy*, Oxford University Press, 1950.

49 Kissinger, in fact, made a point of knowing the personal backgrounds of each of the major international figures with whom he had to enter into negotiation, precisely so that he could find a mode of communication which was other than that of interstate interests. See his two volumes of autobiography, *The White House Years*, Weidenfeld/Michael Joseph, 1979; *Years of Upheaval*, Weidenfeld/Michael Joseph, 1982.

50 See John W. Burton, *Conflict and Communication: The Use of Controlled Communication in International Relations*, Macmillan, 1969; Burton, 'The Resolution of Conflict', *International Studies Quarterly*, 16, 1, March, pp. 5–29.

51 See Connor Cruise O'Brien, *Sacred Drama*, Hutchinson, 1968.

52 Hans J. Morgenthau, *Politics Among Nations*, Knopf, 1960, p. 146.

53 See B.S. Murty, *Propaganda and World Public Order – The legal regulation of the ideological instrument of coercion*, Yale University Press, 1968.

54 For a relevant discussion, see Peter Parker, *The Old Lie: The Great War and the Public School Ethos*, Constable, 1987.

55 Bengt Sundelius, 'The Nordic Model of Neighbourly Cooperation', in Sundelius (ed.), *Foreign Policies of Northern Europe*, Westview Press, 1982.

INDEX